THOMPSON WEBB

VOLUME 1
THE YEARS AT WEBB SCHOOL
1922-1975

Recollections of his Career and his Students
From Stories, Letters and Interviews

Assembled
with Introduction, Notes and Memories by
Thompson Webb, JR. and Thompson Webb III

Madison, Wisconsin, 1998
Seekonk, Massachussetts, 2005

Photo taken in 1951.

Contents

Preface

THIS book, begun at the suggestion of my son Thompson Webb III, is volume one of a memoir by my father, Thompson Webb, that my son and I have pieced together from documents that in his own words describe many of the events of his life and career. The book grew from an initial project in December, 1995, when Tom and I assembled one set of Dad's stories into a booklet for distribution to the family that we called "Stories from the Files of Thompson Webb," which were the contents of a file that Dad had labeled "Father's and Other Early Stories." A reading then of his other stories along with the transcription of the oral history tapes (made by James V. Mink of UCLA in August and September, 1969) revealed that enough material existed to attempt a reconstruction of his life and career from what was written. Besides the stories, we found three files with letters and a file with texts and notes for 13 speeches, many given at other schools during the 1950s and 1960s. (This material was all in file boxes retained by the family and was not included in the over 20,000 letters and documents stored in Thompson Webb's files at the Huntington Library in San Marino, California. With only a few exceptions, this volume comes from the family files and oral history.) Over the next two years, we had the documents keystroked into computer files and finally began assembling the scattered text into a book in late 1997.

His files contained many stories that he had begun writing or dictating in the late 1950s. Several stories bear the note: "First Draft, December, 1957," and therefore have been over 40 years in storage. These stories, mostly only a page or two in length, were in folders with such labels as "Old Boys," "Boys Not Accepted," "Celebrities," "Headmaster Experiences," and "Chapel Bells." Longer stories also existed—including "Shoestringing," his talk about starting the school; "Camping" about running summer camps in Tennessee; and "Conspiracy of Capital and Labor" about his work in the shipyards in San Pedro, California, in 1918. A fragment of a longer story that has been lost even hints at a plan to link these stories together because he refers the reader to the previous account of the events in "Shoestringing." He also had indices typed up with the titles of the individual stories arranged in groups, and he even had a list of stories "Yet to Write." Seeing the effort that he had made to record his stories inspired us. We could not write the stories that he left unwritten, but we could assemble what he had written and make their texts available. What pleased and amazed us was that we could organize his material into a manuscript that serves so well as the story of his career in this volume and the story of his growing up and family life in a second volume.

The key to our effort was working out a chronology of his life for Volume 2 and a division of his tasks at the school for Volume 1. We then arranged the stories into that order or those divisions. With the stories in place, we added excerpts from letters, oral history tapes, and speeches that told about his career and his family life. From this arranging of the documents came the current text and a picture of Dad's life that is even more complete than we imagined. We were fortunate also to find some documents written by other family members that added information or verified events. I have added a few of my memories when needed to fill out descriptions that Dad neglected like some of the early buildings and events at the school (see "The School in the First Years" in Chapter 2, for example).

The documents other than stories that are the substance of this book include letters and other texts contemporary with events and accounts from memory, Dad's and a few others', notably in the 1969 oral history transcript dictated late in his life. This use of many texts leads to a disjointed narrative with many gaps and some repetition, which we have tried to minimize. Some of the repetition, however, helps verify parts of the stories (such as "Shoestringing") by comparisons to records written during the events. Elsewhere excerpts from letters that describe different details relating to an important event or time in his life help fill out the narrative. The quilt that results from ordering and merging the many texts describes much of Dad's career, but a few notes are called for—explanations, expansions, and corrections (sparingly)—and Tom and I have attempted to provide what seems required as unobtrusively as possible. (For simplicity, notes in italics or brackets by me or others are initialed, but those by TWiii are not.)

What must be understood by readers is that many of the documents—most especially "Shoestringing," which is the initial story for this volume (see Chapter 2)—were told and written, not as history or as autobiography, but as stories for listening audiences. Dad was a storyteller, an entertaining raconteur. In his practice of the art, he made full use of its recognized license to employ embellishment, exaggeration, and selectivity in choice of details. A scholar who was in the upper ten percent of his class may be depicted in Dad's account as the valedictorian, if that sharpens the point of the story. The historian's purpose is to record events and facts, and to interpret them, as accurately as possible; the storyteller's purpose is to entertain, even when telling a "true story." For example, in "Shoestringing," when Dad says that the original school buildings in California had stood vacant for several years and all the windows had been broken out, he paints a vivid picture and heightens the interest of his listeners. As it happens, I am the only surviving member of the family party that in the summer of 1922 made the first visit by any Webb to the property that became Webb School. I was 5 years old, but I have clear recollections of that occasion. I do not believe that *all* the windows were broken, although there were enough to give my parents a sense of desolation and vandalism. Dad wanted to convey a strong sense of how that first sight of their new home impressed him and Mother. As raconteur he does it graphically and, in my opinion, "truly," even if the window count is inflated. Where Dad is author, the documents that follow are his stories. We have attached notes of explanation, including (for history) some facts that we found to be at odds with his, but I have not generally found Dad's recollections in any significant sense false.

Dad's stories are just as he talked. Almost all the passages in this book that are in Dad's words were dictated to stenographers or to the oral-history interrogator. There is evidence here and there in Dad's papers that he had read the results of some of his dictation. He marked a few errors for correction, but he seems not to have been consistent in this, or comprehensive.

Thus, most of Dad's words in this book are first draft. They reflect his conversational style and lack the polish that he would have expected to give them in anticipation of publication. A speaker can by emphasis clarify antecedents of pronouns in spoken sentences that, when written, are confusing. Pronoun and antecedent references occasionally become tangled. That is how Dad talked. With few exceptions, we have left them that way.

Transcribing dictation and oral history can raise many problems for the typist, among which are the punctuation difficulties of informal spontaneous conversation. In the excerpts from the oral history, informal punctuation has been altered only when necessary. In rare instances, where obviously a stenographer had stumbled over the dictation, we felt obliged to make changes to clarify the text, but those instances are rare and of minor significance.

Thompson Webb, JR.
January, 1998

Addendum:

A sabbatical semester from my teaching at Brown University has given me the time to prepare this set of nine chapters into the first volume describing my grandfather's career. The work returns me to the stories and words that my father and I labored over so lovingly while he underwent treatments for the cancer that eventually killed him in September 1998. This project sustained the two of us during the last year of his life. What a fitting gift from our namesake for this time in both of our lives. I handled the organization, acquisition, and keystroking of the stories, letters, and other documents; and Dad did the editing and worked on formatting and layout. These were familiar tasks for him because he had been a book publisher and editor in his career. We both laughed over the stories and kept being surprised at all the information that surfaced and fitted together so well into a reasonably coherent description of Thompson Webb's work at Webb School.

By presenting my grandfather's stories and writings, this book provides a key source for a biography of my grandfather and a history of the school.

Larry McMillin wrote a biography of William Robert "Sawney" Webb's life, *The Schoolmaker* (University of North Carolina, 1970), which my grandfather, Sawney's youngest child, encouraged and supported. At its core, it too had a rich set of stories that Sawney and others had told. I am hopeful that someone will take up the challenge for my grandfather and work to place his stories in a broader context, to sort out the facts and timing of events, and to turn his stories into history. The rich archive of over 20,000 documents in the Huntington Library can help with that task. So too can the ledgers in The Webb Schools' archive that list all the payments and income for the school. The scholarly detective in me sees data to compile and analyze and a whole raft of questions to pursue. But what fascinates me most is the discovery of the discrepancies between the stories and the facts. How and why did this master storyteller distort or mis-remember selected events? What truth or truths did he thus attain? He knew intuitively that an exact retelling of the facts could hide the broader psychological truth of what his experience was. How then did he accomplish his end whether it was consciously intended or not? As noted in my father's preceding comments, in some places, we have inserted in brackets factual information that conflicts with what my grandfather presented in his stories. But we have not researched all matters covered by his stories nor corrected all his exaggerations that were part of his storytelling style. I will welcome comments from readers whose memories of events differ from his.

For now I just love having this direct record of his stories and speeches in his own words. The printed stories may lack his kindly voice and rich Tennessee accent, but they remain a treat for those of us who sat spellbound at his feet when, with a tap of his fingers, he would lean forward and transport us with his words. His imagined reality became ours, and we could share his amazement and amusement at events. His sense of entertainment from life was infectious. We could rejoice with him in his rejoicing. As he aged, his stories fed him and all who listened. His was a rich life that he never tired of revisiting.

Thompson Webb III
May, 2003

Acknowledgments

INTERVIEWS of Thompson Webb conducted by the UCLA Oral History Program in 1969 contributed substantially to this book. The interviews appear in *Webb School in Claremont, California—Thompson Webb* (©1987 The Regents of the University of California. All rights Reserved. Used with Permission). We also reproduced with permission one letter from the Thompson Webb papers in the Huntington Library. We thank both the UCLA Oral History Program and the Western American collection at the Huntington Library for preserving valuable records from the past. We also thank the many people who have helped us including Susan Nelson, head of schools at The Webb Schools, for her interest and encouragement; Taylor Stockdale, assistant head of schools, for support; Pam McNeil, director of alumni relations, who supplied documents and photographs from the archives; Mary Hubbell, former director of alumni relations, who in 1998 supplied tapes, printed talks, and copies of the *Blue and Gold*; Paula Pitzer, former director of alumni relations, who interviewed me (TW, JR.) and my brothers in December, 1988, in the Jackson Library, and produced a memorable *Alumni Bulletin* in 1989 based on the interviews; Harrison Stephens for editing and advice; Tim Coates for scanning photographs; Vivian Pradetto for proofreading; Maryann Stubblefield for book design; Dick Dunham '61 for a tape of chapel talks; Dorothy Taylor for documents from the California Association of Independent Schools; Jon Frere, headmaster of the Webb School in Bell Buckle, for family letters from the school archives; Bob and Julie Webb for hosting TW III and driving him to Bell Buckle; Edward T. Price, JR. '33 for helpful comments and memories of the camp at Walling, Tennessee; John L. Webb for stories and copies of letters from the Thompson Webb papers in the Huntington Library; David Webb '53 for corrections; Emily da Silveira for sharing her memories; Arthur Thorning for information about Melvin Young '30; and Gerald Oppenheimer '40 for confirming a story.

1

Introduction

Introduction

THIS book, mostly in Dad's words, tells the story of his life as headmaster in the form of anecdotes and stories, some short and some long, that serve as snapshots and more extended descriptions of his career as a teacher, headmaster, camp director, builder, board member, husband, father, and grandfather. Ironically, Dad always said that the one thing that he didn't want to do was to be a teacher. He didn't want to have anything to do with schools. But when WWI came, the bottom dropped out of real estate in the Coachella Valley, and he sustained a devastating crop loss. He was left with debts that forced him, first, to teaching in Bell Buckle for his father, W. R. "Sawney" Webb, and then to Claremont in 1922, where he started his own school on the grounds of the former Claremont School for Boys. There he finally showed what he was really good at. He could run a school, manage it well, and be admired for it. He did not choose to be a schoolman; but once into administration, whether in summer camps or a school of his own, he found what he understood and did splendidly.

He began life in October, 1887 as the eighth and youngest child of Sawney and Emma Clary Webb, their only child born after the move from Culleoka to Bell Buckle, Tennessee. As the blonde baby of the family, he was both late leaving the family for college (at age 20 in 1907) and also late leaving in 1922 after returning during WWI when his father and brother had prevailed on him to help fill their teacher shortage in 1918. It was not until he could find his own place in Claremont at age 34 that his talents as a manager had a full opportunity for expression. Only with the founding of his own school could he show his ability to lead it to academic, financial, and personal success. This book traces that story and provides both a background for his famous "Shoestringing" story about the founding of the school and a description of his work building and running the school once it was on its feet.

Dad was always a gentle father. He had a great deal of patience and was comfortable to be with. (This is not to say that he spared the switch when he considered corporal punishment deserved.) When I was small, he was very busy and had little time to spend with me and my brothers, but I always liked to be with him. As I became a teenager, I found myself enjoying his company when I could sit down and be with him. I looked forward to those opportunities. Howell once noted that Dad thoroughly enjoyed us four boys and that was why it was such a pleasure to be with him. He loved being with us. For Bill, Dad was a patient, practical man in contrast to Mother. Mother taught him a lot of patience. Dad was always on time, and Mother was never on time. Dad was thoughtful and planned ahead. Mother was impulsive. That tension was at the core of their partnership. We four brothers grew up with his attention and love.

Others who have known Dad have described him as a gentle man. Acting as a gentleman was part of his Southern upbringing. His father had instructed him in the words of his [Sawney's] mother, "My son, if you are polite to the queen and rude to the servant that blacks your boots, you are not a gentleman. You are a fraud and a sham." His story of Charles Skouras '44 in Chapter 7 tells of the rewards of this upbringing just as the oral history text about his treatment by an English headmaster (see Chapter 5 in Vol. 2) shows his disgust with those who were not hospitable. But his sense of Southern hospitality does not begin to describe his gentle nature. He was a caring individual who showed this quality to his students, their parents, his faculty, staff, and family. In his gentleness, he differed markedly from his combative father, who championed causes, took on saloon keepers, and spoke out across the state of Tennessee and even the nation. By the end of his life, Old Sawney had mellowed a little as evidenced by his deathbed advice, "to have more fun," but Dad grew up hearing Sawney's chapel talks to the Tennessee school each morning. He was fully aware of his father's fame. In fact he was proud of his father's fame but feared the man and took his father's opinions on such practical matters as indebtedness too seriously. This was a burden to him that only his father's laughter in 1923 could begin to dispel. How then did he escape enough from some of his upbringing to develop his own way and style?

"Shoestringing" provides one answer to this question by showing the large personal gamble that he took in leaving Bell Buckle in 1922 to start his school, a gamble in part forced by his debts and the low pay provided by his father and brother. Shoestringing's main message, however, is about his personal success in business and does not describe where and how his gentle nature arose. This trait could have been genetic, resulted from birth order, or arisen because his father was 45 when Dad was born. Perhaps Dad's mother and sisters contributed to his gentle nature, for certainly Alla, Adeline, Susan, and Emma possessed such a nature, but we can only speculate because he never discusses this issue directly. The best evidence that we have is his letter to his sister Emma in 1916 (Chapter 3 of Vol. 2), his letter to his mother in 1919 when a young father (Chapter 4 of Vol. 2), and his tale of his romantic nature when using his first savings from 1907 to buy an engagement ring from Tiffany's in 1915 (Chapter 3 of Vol. 2). These snapshots of his personal nature only show it in practice but do not suggest its origin. They do demonstrate, however, that it was well in place by the time that he was in his late 20s. And almost 60 years later, it was still evident when he took Joanne Webb, one of his younger grandchildren, to dinner on her 20th birthday.

As headmaster of an independent school, Dad was sensitive to criticism of private education. This theme is evident in several places in the text (e.g., stories in Chapters 2, 7, and 8). He, of course, grew up in a private school and, though he went to the University of North Carolina, knew little else for his whole life. He had an economic interest in the well-being of private schools, and his work in forming the California Association of Independent Secondary Schools and later the National Association of Independent Schools (see Chapter 8) shows how he promoted this interest in a cooperative way. He also served on the boards of California Junior Republic, the Midland School, and Scripps College, where he could help other private educational institutions.

Dad was a storyteller. He regaled us all with his stories, in which his sense of humor shone through. He liked stories that had an ironic twist to them and brought a laugh. The oral history transcript is full of bracketed notes saying "laughter." In fact to read the oral history transcript is to enter his stories rather than to find a recitation of historical facts. Reading this transcript is also to discover that at 82 he was clear down to the details of long conversations within his stories but that facts outside of the stories (e.g. teachers' salaries) were forgotten and impossible to recall. Dad's father was a great storyteller as were Dad's sisters and brothers. Theirs was an age before electronic media when people entertained themselves, and personal stories recast to bring a laugh or to attract attention were the heart and soul of this entertainment. He was a master of this art, and fortunately he had the forethought to record many of his stories, which is a gift to us now and the core material of this book.

Thompson Webb, JR.
March, 1998

Thompson Webb III
March, 2003

2

Founding the School
1922-1926

Shoestringing

Thompson Webb founded the Webb School of California in Claremont in July, 1922. "Shoestringing" is the story that he told about his struggles to finance his school and his eventual triumph. It was a talk that he gave regularly at Kiwanis and Rotary Clubs in southern California, in part as publicity for the school. After retiring, he gave the talk annually for the seniors in his living room. The version that follows is from a talk that he gave to a gathering of bankers in Las Vegas, Nevada in the late 1950s. In it he sets the scene by telling how he first came to California in 1911 after graduating from the University of North Carolina. He joined his older brother John in farming and in selling real estate in the Coachella Valley, where he lived until 1918. That year the failure of an onion crop left him with a debt of $15,000 and the need for a new line of employment to support his wife, Vivian, and two young sons, Thompson, JR. (1 year old) and Howell (just born). After working briefly in San Pedro at a shipyard, he accepted an invitation to teach for his father, William R. "Sawney" Webb, and his oldest brother Will at the Webb School in Bell Buckle, Tennessee. By 1922, he was keen to find a higher paying job because his debts were causing him much concern.

Mr. Chairman, ladies and gentlemen, I am aware of the compliment you pay me in inviting me to speak before this distinguished group; men who handle large affairs, tremendous finances, and things of that kind. It seems as if my little story, which has been nicknamed "Wildcat Financing" or "Frenzied Finance," is almost peanuts compared with what you think about. But I was asked some time ago to tell something about the struggles of founding a boys' school; and after I told it, my friends nicknamed it "Wildcat Financing." . . . .

Father brought us up not to borrow money. He used to read us a note (he was all the time doing that), "I promise to pay at certain intervals of time so many dollars at such a rate of interest." And he'd say, "Son, that's a promise for three things, and time is just as important as the amount. I hate those scrubs you go to when a note is due who say, 'Oh, I'll pay you when

I'm good and ready.' That man has promised to pay on that day, and he is honor-bound to do it. I just don't sign notes, 'cause I'm afraid I can't pay them back on time; and I feel when I make a promise, I must keep it."

Well, having heard that all my life, I wasn't . . . telling Father I owed $15,000 and had nothing left but some equities that couldn't be sold. I just kept quiet and worked as hard as I could at teaching and helping him in every way I knew how. When the interest would come due in California, if I had it, I'd send it; and if I didn't have quite enough, I'd drop into the bank at Bell Buckle, borrow a little and add to it. And I kept that interest paid. I had gone there [in 1918] owing $15,000 and within four years I owed $20,000. Well, I had to do something else.

There had grown up in the South at that time some prosperity, and there were great mills and great factories and warehouses and banks and all sorts of industry—every one of them headed by Father's "boys," because that was the generation he taught when there was no other school. They had been successful men. So I wrote to each one of them asking for an important position with them, hoping to get a salary sufficient to support my family and pay off this indebtedness. And they all wrote me nice letters. They knew who I was, and they said they'd like to have me in their business, but I didn't know their operation. I'd have to start at the very bottom at a minimum salary and work my way up. And I didn't have time to work my way up.

I was in that predicament, when one day, I don't know why, Mr. Sherman Day Thacher, the owner and founder of the great Thacher School at Ojai, California, wrote me a letter out of a clear sky and told me that he was turning down hundreds of boys. He had known my father in the Headmasters Association, and I had met him out in California. It was known that Mr. Thacher had the highest-priced school in America; and I was teaching in the cheapest school, I suppose, in America.

He said there was a need for another school of his type on the Coast, and he would like very much to see me come out and start it. He thought he could send some of his overflow to me. Well, that was very exciting. I hadn't wanted to teach; but when I heard about the possibility of having a

Thompson Webb in 1922.

school that was high-priced like Mr. Thacher's, well, maybe I could repay the $20,000. I was terribly excited about it.

He went on to add that he had recently been to Pomona College, and one of the professors had driven him three miles out into the country to see a deserted school. He said that a preacher some five years before had come out from Chicago and had started this school. He had taken over 20 acres of sagebrush and put up three fairly good buildings, but he had failed financially and had to close the school and go back to Chicago. The people who had the mortgage had taken it over, and they had been trying desperately to sell this property, but they couldn't find a buyer. Nobody bought schools. He understood they would sell it at a mere fraction of its value, and he suggested that I write to Mr. I.W. Baughman in Claremont and check up on this matter.

It seemed silly for me to write to him, but I did inquire about it; and he replied by saying the property had cost a great deal, but they in desperation had come to the point where they were offering it at a mere fraction of its value. He said that I could have it for $40,000, half cash. Now, gentlemen, we didn't have $100 in the bank. My wife and I had what Uncle Remus called "the dry grins." There just didn't seem anything we could do about that. We didn't talk about it.

One day I got up and wrote Mr. Baughman the exact truth—that I didn't have any money, had been born and reared in a boys' school, had been teaching in one and thought I knew how to run one. I told him Mr. Thacher had offered to send me his overflow and, if there was any way I could get hold of that property on a 10-year contract, I thought I could charge enough and get the student body built up to the point where I could pay him back the principal and interest within the 10 years. I said, "Don't you put in that contract that I have to pay so much at any one time because I haven't any idea when I can pay it. I'll just pay you all I make." Well, of course, I knew a businessman wouldn't consider that, and I tried to dismiss it. In fact, it took Mr. Baughman about five weeks to work that one over. Finally, he wrote back and said there had been 19 people involved in that mortgage. He'd had to see every one of them personally; and, after a long talk with each one, they all came to the same conclusion: "You can't sell it anyhow; why don't you let that fellow try it?" He said, "We're ready to execute the contract." And we had bought a school in California and didn't have the money to get to it.

During that five-weeks' wait on Mr. Baughman, one of my old friends, Rayford Alley, came back from New York. He had grown up on a farm right there next to us, and we had played together all our lives and had been in the same class in Father's school. When I went to North Carolina, he went to Washington and Lee; and, when I came to California to farm, he went to New York and took a law course at Columbia. He was a brilliant student, beautifully trained; and when he got through, he was the top man in his class. One of the biggest firms in New York heard about his record, and they invited him to come and work for them and eventually made him a partner in the firm. We hadn't seen each other in these 15 years.

Here he was dressed up in his tailor-made clothes. Oh, he looked so natty when he came back and had that air of success about him. I was delighted to see Rayford. I invited him to our home, and he came three different nights and talked to me about his practice of law in New York. I kept mighty quiet about my farming in California. It was fascinating to hear him throwing the names of the Rockefellers and the Morgans and the Goulds and the Vanderbilts and Hetty Green—calling them all by first names. Apparently he was holding little legal affairs for every one of them, either for them or against them. He just knew them all. It was fascinating— these wonderful financial names I had read about in the papers all my life.

And the last night he said, "Thompson, we've been friends so long I don't think you would consider me immodest if I told you that I'm netting over $75,000 a year on my law practice in New York." And gentlemen, that sounded like $75,000,000 to me. That was a lot of money some 30-odd years ago. It would really be big today if it were coming my way. But that was big talk, and he confided that he was looking for good investments.

Well, that made an impression on me, too, but I said nothing about this fool letter I'd written Mr. Baughman, since I never expected to hear from him, and Rayford went back to New York. Then one day here came this letter, and we had landed our contract in California. So I said to my wife, "Now Rayford's my man; he's looking for good investments. I'm going to New York and talk him into this thing." "Oh," she said, "Tom, can't you write him? It costs so much money to go to New York." I said, "Oh, Sweetheart, this is one time I can't sell him in a letter, I must talk him into it." So I went to the bank in Bell Buckle and borrowed the money and went to New York.

It took me several days to convince Rayford that he wanted an investment like a school, far from home; but finally he said, "All right, Thompson, I'll back you for $30,000; $10,000 a year for three years." And he said, "At the end of three years if that school isn't on its feet, I'll be done." I said, "Yes, I will, too." He said he was coming to California on another man's expense account, and he'd take a look at that property. In July, 1922, he wired me from Claremont to come at once as he had closed the deal. Well, I didn't have the money to get there, and I didn't dare tell the bank in Bell Buckle that I was leaving town. So we sold our refrigerator [really an icebox—TW, JR.], stove, beds and things, and got enough cash together to get to Claremont with our three sons, with less than $100 left.

My wife had written to some friends, and they met us at the train. They knew where Mr. Baughman lived, and they took us around there. Mr. Baughman was glad to see me, and had the papers. Mr. Alley had signed them all, as my attorney. He asked if we knew where the school was. Yes, my friends knew. "Here are the keys, Mr. Webb; move in." I said, "Where's Mr. Alley?" He said, "Well, I don't know, he didn't give me any California address." "Well," I said, "did he leave a check for me?" "Oh no, he didn't leave any money; I haven't seen any money." "Well," I said, "he's supposed to finance me on this, and I need some help."

I went to Western Union and wired Mr. Alley in New York to send me the $10,000 at once, and then we drove out to see what we'd bought. It was 20 acres of sagebrush, and that first fellow had never cleaned the sagebrush off or planted anything. He'd put up some pretty good buildings on a contract, but vandals had been into them and broken all the windows and doors. I didn't need the keys; I could go in anywhere. And the place was thoroughly dirty. We couldn't go to the inn, so we had to camp there.

The neighbors were good to me. They lent me buckets and gave me water and lent me some brooms and shovels and things, and I worked just as hard as I could to clean up one apartment to make it fit for my wife and babies. It took me about two days to get that in shape, and then here came a telegram from Mr. Alley's office, saying that Mr. Alley hadn't gotten home and they didn't know where he was; so they had no authority to send me any money. Well, I could have gone on all summer cleaning those buildings, but I had to get some boys.

I had to arrange some financing so that I could get on the road to look for boys. So I walked three miles into Claremont and dropped into the First National Bank of Claremont and introduced myself to Mr. Belcher, the cashier. I had a nice talk with him and told him I would like to do my banking with him. He said he would be delighted to have my account. I explained to him about Mr. Alley and the $10,000, and that I was temporarily embarrassed, so would he lend me $500 for a few days.

Original buildings in 1922. Reservoir swimming pool, dining room, schoolhouse, dormitory with an apartment at the far right in which Thompson and Vivian Webb lived with Thompson, JR. (5), Howell (4), and Bill (1).

The "upper" dorm with Mr. and Mrs. Porter and an unknown man holding Bill Webb in 1923. The Webb family apartment was at the far end.

I took him so by surprise, that he poked the note out at me before he filled it in; and I signed it. Then he filled it in. "How long is this for?" he said. "Well, I don't think I need it over a week, but why don't you make it on or before September 15, when school opens?" So he filled that out, and I opened up a checking account on his money.

I hired a man and his wife to come and clean and repair the place. My wife directed that, and we ran some advertisements in the Los Angeles paper. At once here came an inquiry from Long Beach. A man wanted a catalog. I didn't have any catalog and had no time to write one. The only thing I could do was go over there. So I walked the three miles into Claremont and got a Red Car into Los Angeles and another one down to Long Beach. I walked out to the house, and nobody was home. The neighbors didn't think they had gone far; so I sat down and waited two hours on the porch until that family got home.

I think of that as probably the low ebb of all my experience, the two hours sitting there with uncertainty, waiting for those people to come. But they finally arrived, a nice family, a nice boy, and I thought they were going to enroll him. I pulled out a contract I had typed, proposing to charge $500 in September and $500 after Christmas, a total of $1,000 for the year. The father wouldn't sign it, and said he wanted to think about it.

I came home, and my wife was jumping up and down. She had a letter from a lady over in Van Nuys wanting a catalog. So I was up before daybreak and took the rides and the walks and so on, and got to Van Nuys about 11 in the morning, the hottest spot I ever saw in my life—that happened to be a hot spell. And when I inquired, I found the lady lived on a ranch, five miles in the country. Well, I couldn't afford a taxi, so I walked out there in the heat of the day, and it was terrible. When I got there, I was graciously received by a charming mother, and she introduced to me her five beautiful daughters! She was looking for a girls' school. Well, she was embarrassed about it, and I was terribly upset. She gave me some nice cold water to drink and drove me back to the car. And so for a few days it went like that. Then my wife's father, the good minister, got back to his Los Angeles church, and he drove out to see what we were doing. When he heard the story, he said, "Well, Tom, you need a little automobile. You come in tomorrow, and I'll endorse your note at the Security Bank for $500, and we'll get an automobile." So we carried that out.

By that time the advertisements were bringing in lots of inquiries, and I would get in that little car and go into Los Angeles and Pasadena. If the parents weren't at home, I went to the next, and next, and next, and came back to the original; and I had a nice talk with a lot of people. I found many people who wanted their boys to work their way through, because they had no money. And that's a great thing—to work your way through— but right then I was hunting for cash customers.

By the first of September, I found, after visiting several hundred people, that there were 20 that were very likely customers, but nobody had signed up. I quit going to see new people, and I went to my most likely man and said, "Now I want you to sign my contract." He said, "How many boys have you?" So I said, "I haven't any yet, but I expect to have 20." "Well, when you get the 19, come back."

I went all the way down the line, and everyone of them said the same thing. I couldn't get a signature. I decided I had to have some boys, and I booked up seven of them for nothing and took them, making out a contract that they were to wash dishes, do yard work, or janitor work, or something

in return. Then I went back to my first man. "How many boys have you?"
"I have seven." "That's not enough for a ball team. When you get the rest,
come back." I went all down the line; and every one of them said, "How
many boys have you?" and no one signed up.

When I got home the first week of September, having been turned
down again by all these people, there was a letter from Mr. Alley. I opened
it with great glee, but there was no check in it. He said he had been hunting
for several weeks in the mountains of Mexico, not knowing what was going
on at home. When he got home, he found his wife had filed divorce
proceedings against him, and her attorney had attached everything he had
in the world. He was sorry [that] he couldn't back me.

Now, gentlemen, it never occurred to me that I didn't have financial
backing. That just hadn't occurred to me. I wasn't expecting the rug to be
jerked out from under me like that. I thought I had been honest. I had
borrowed this money and promised to pay it on the 15th of September,
and here we were caught like that. I was all in a tremble when I went into
the house to look for my wife. She was in the bedroom dressing the babies,
and I read her that letter. We took stock. We owed our $20,000 in
Tennessee; we owed $40,000 for the place; we owed three notes, and in the
meantime I had borrowed another $500, making $1,500 that was due next
week. We had seven boys for nothing and nobody for anything.

She looked at me with the funniest little expression. She said, "Tom,
this looks like a crisis." She said, "Don't you think we ought to pray?" I said,
"Oh, sister, what have you been doing all summer? I've been praying all
summer, haven't you?" She said, "Yes, but I think we ought to pray
together." We knelt down beside the bed together, and I want to tell you it
wasn't ordinary praying that time. We reasoned with the Lord. "How do you
get out of this thing?" We thought we were honest. "How do you get out of
it?" There was just one conviction that came to us: Wait until the 15th of
September and see what happens.

Sure enough, on the 15th of September here came 14 boys, seven of
them for nothing, and seven paid down their $500 apiece. So with $3,500

in the bank I paid those three notes that day, as agreed. Then we paid the little interest things that were coming up and divided out the work. I taught eight classes a day and my wife taught five as she had to look after the babies. We had to have a cook in the kitchen. For help with the curriculum I had to hire a young man who was the son of the president of Pomona College.

We started out and were running the school very nicely until we came up to the first of October, and the grocery bills and things of that kind came in with some interest bills. I paid everything right on time, but it took the last cent I had. Then I began to lie awake at night. I'd used these boys' money, and I had to carry them, but I didn't have the money to do it. Where was I going to get it?

I went to every source I could think of looking for money. I couldn't find it; and when the first of November came, here came bills for over $900 just for groceries, books and supplies. They were merchants' bills and had to be paid by the 10th, I thought. I made up my mind I'd pay them by the 10th, so I went back to see Mr. Belcher at the First National Bank of Claremont. He said, "Mr. Webb, I'm sorry but my directors have forbidden me to lend any more money on a school." I said, "But you got the money back, didn't you?" "Yes, but they said not to do it anymore."

So I got into my car and drove down to Pomona, and drove up and down the streets of that town looking over the banks to see if there was one big enough to handle me. The First National seemed most likely, and I went to the door on which was printed "Charles Stone, President." I looked up Mr. Stone, and found a delightful gentleman. I told him I wanted to borrow a thousand dollars and would he please look up the banks I had done business with and see if he couldn't let me have it as I had no security. "Very well, Mr. Webb, but first tell me what is your gross income?" I said, "$7,000." "What are your estimated expenses?" I said, "$15,000." He said, "Mr. Webb, that's not bankable; you should see your personal friends."

I went back, and my wife and I made a list of them. We started with those that were supposed to be wealthy, and I went to see the wealthy friends. Like that man in the Bible who either married a wife or bought a yoke of oxen, they were the poorest lot of people I ever saw. I couldn't get a penny out of any of them, and never did. That was terribly discouraging.

Finally we came up to the 10th of the month when I felt those bills had to be paid. We had no money to pay them. I moved my classes into the front classroom. I could watch the driveway hoping that some car would come in with two or three new boys who could pay down some money. None had entered since the beginning of school.

Nothing happened all day until the last class was over, and in came the worst-looking old Model-T Ford snorting up the driveway. The top was all blown out—the old canvas top was gone. It was a terrible-looking, shabby old thing. The man was dressed in work clothes, and he hadn't shaved. I went out to see what he wanted; and when he got close to me, he said, "Hello, Thompson." When he spoke, I recognized him. It was old Bill Bates, who had 40 acres next to mine in the farming days down in the valley.

He said he was on his way to Los Angeles to get a plow, and he just thought he'd stop in and see what I was doing. Bill always looked like that. He lived in a one-room shack, cooked for himself, did his own farming, and never seemed to have anything but that old rattletrap Ford. I was very glad to see Bill. He was a good neighbor, and I invited him to come in to supper. No, he wouldn't come into anybody's house looking like that; so he got out and cranked up his old car.

I could just see it humping itself as it went around the circle of our flagpole. He came back by me, threw on his squeaky brakes, and leaned out, saying, "Thompson, you know anybody who wants to borrow $1,000?" I said, "What are you talking about, Bill?" "Well," he said, "I have some left from the farm this year, and I want to put it out at interest. Do you know anybody who'd like to have it?" I said, "Oh, Bill, I'd love to have it, but I'm running a losing business, and the banks have turned me down. I don't think you ought to let me have it." "Oh," he said, "you can have it."

He went down in his overalls and brought up a dog-eared old checkbook, went down on the other side and got a 2-inch pencil and began to write. I said, "Let me get you a note." "Oh, I don't want any note," he said, "I'll tell you when I want my money back; you just send the interest when it's due." With that he pressed it in my hand and was gone. I went in and filled out all the deposit stubs and checks and got them in the envelopes and mailed them before 6 o'clock that night. I'd met the deadline. That night I slept.

Before that, some nights I was so sure I was going bankrupt that I'd get wrought up; I'd just cry like a baby in bed. But that night I slept. The next morning I woke up, and my emotions were gone, my head was clear, and I felt we were going to make this thing. Then all of a sudden it came to me. "What are you going to do the first of December?" And out of bed I came.

I kept hunting for another $1,000 I was going to need the first of December. I went to see all of my poor friends this time, but I didn't find any with money. We came up to the first of December, and the bills came in again, amounting to nearly $1,000. During that first week a letter came from Mr. Alley. I opened it, and inside was a check for $1,000. He said his wife's attorney had overlooked one good account, and he had been able to collect $2,000, which he was dividing with me. He said, "I'll let you know when I want it back; don't ask me for any more. That's all I can do." And that was all he ever did! When he asked for the money, he got it back. [from oral history: Couple of years later he wanted it back; I sent him a thousand dollars with interest; he returned the interest, thanked me for the thousand dollars. When the Depression of '29 came a few years later, he wrote me to know if I could lend him a thousand dollars and I did, which he subsequently paid back with interest and I returned the interest. And those [were] our transactions.]

That saved Webb School. After Christmas when the boys came back and paid down their $3,500, we ran nicely until April. When April came we needed another $1,000. During the Christmas vacation I had met a lot of my neighbors and was talking to them. They were all talking about this man Baughman, who had given me the keys. They said he was the wealthiest man in our valley, a trader in citrus properties, that he prided himself in driving bargains, and that he was the shrewdest man you ever saw in your life.

They said he could drive the price to the bottom penny when he was buying and to the top penny when he was selling. They said there just never was anyone like him, and he took such pride in doing it. They said, "He's the biggest philanthropist in this valley: He gives to all the good causes like the YMCA, the Boy Scouts, the churches, the Chest, and every worthy cause. He gives more than anyone else and does it with a smile; he's not stingy, but he prides himself on his trading."

That was an interesting picture of a man, and I decided to go see him. I went to his home and introduced myself to him. He hadn't seen me since he gave me the keys to the school. We talked for a while, and I came to the point. I said, "Mr. Baughman, I need $1,000 to finish the year, and I want you to lend it to me." "Oh, no indeed," he said, "I put thousands of dollars into the first plant there that the preacher started, and I lost everything. No, sir; I'll have nothing to do with this."

Well, gentlemen, I knew it was my last chance. We either won or lost on that deal. I stayed with that man nearly three hours before I could convince him he ought to help me. He said then, kind of disgusted with himself, "I know I ought not to do it, but get in the car and I'll endorse your note at the bank." I didn't know where we were going, but he drove me up to the First National Bank of Pomona. Then he took me in and introduced me to Mr. Stone. Mr. Stone lowered his glasses and said, "Yes, I know Mr. Webb." Mr. Baughman said, "Mr. Stone, Mr. Webb wants to borrow $1,000." "Yes, Mr. Baughman, I know." Then he said, "Well, Mr. Stone, I'll endorse his note for $1,000." Mr. Stone smiled, "Why certainly, Mr. Baughman. Certainly, Mr. Webb. What a pleasure it is to let you have it." It's amazing what the right name does on a note. That saved us.

I was still teaching in the front classroom, and I'd look out every day and see Mr. Baughman going around the campus. He had never been there before. At first, I didn't pay much attention to it; but when it became daily and I could see him looking in every direction, it dawned on me that the old gentleman was worried. He thinks I'm going to skip out of here tonight. He's just coming up here to check up. If he had given me that money, he wouldn't have worried about it. But he had made a sort of business deal, against his best judgment, and was mad at himself. I could see him losing weight and developing lines under his eyes; and you know, it worried me, because I wanted to go back to see him in May. I didn't see how I could ever talk him into another $1,000.

The first of May came and the bills came, and I was wondering how to approach him this time, when up drove a taxi and out stepped my dear old Father and Mother from Tennessee. They were over 80 years of age. There was nobody in the world I would rather have seen. They hadn't told us they were coming. I was delighted to see them, but the first thought that popped into my mind was—I hope Father doesn't ask me anything about finances. I had never told him about borrowing a penny. He was pretty polite for a couple of days, and then he got me in the corner and said, "Son, how are you doing financially?" "Well," I said, "Father, I have broken your rule. I have borrowed some money, but I've always been able to meet every payment the day it was due, just like you brought me up."

"Son, that sounds fine, but how are you doing it?" he said. "This outfit won't pay it." I tried to change the subject and get on to something else;

Family photo when Sawney and Emma Clary Webb visited in April, 1923. Loulie and Robert Howell holding grandson Bill Webb, Thompson and Vivian Webb with Howell in front, Thompson, JR., Emma Clary Webb, and William R. "Sawney" Webb sitting on the steps to the apartment in the dormitory where the Webb family was living.

but, no sir, he was determined to know, and he was going to have the answer. I wasn't willing to lie to him; so I told him the story I have told you. I knew he was going to be humiliated and embarrassed that a son of his would do a thing like that. I thought he would be thoroughly angry (I knew he could get angry); but, you know, it hit him differently. I suppose age had mellowed him. He began to laugh. I never saw Father laugh so in my life. "That's the funniest thing I ever heard of," he said, "I didn't know anyone could get in a predicament like that."

After wiping tears from his eyes, he said, "Son, how much money would it take to finish the year?" I replied, "I think I can do it on a $1,000." He said, "Well, your mother's got a little money. I'll lend it to you. It might take more than you figure. Just make a note to your mother for $1,500 at six percent since you won't have to pay any interest while I live. When I'm gone, I know you'll take care of your mother. Son, make that $2,500. Take $1,000 down to that bank and pay the note that has Mr. Baughman's name on it, and make them stamp it 'Paid.' Take it around to the old gentleman. Hand it to him and let him get some sleep." So we finished that year.

I worked in summer camp all summer [Camp Robin Hood at Lake Arrowhead, see Chapter 6 in Volume 2] and had a time just making food for my family. When I came back in September, we didn't have a boy enrolled. It looked so desperate and I was so tired I didn't know what I'd do; but that first morning, before I had breakfast, in came a lady and a boy, and she enrolled him. Then came a man and a boy, and we enrolled that boy. The telephone was ringing, and my wife made appointments to see people that afternoon; and, you know, within 10 days we'd reached our capacity of 28 boys and had three on a waiting list. They just came from here, there, and yonder. I don't know where they heard about us. I asked no questions. I needed boys, and I was taking them.

Then I called a teacher's agency and said, "I must have two teachers," because our only teacher had gotten a better job. The agency said, "Public schools have picked over the list, and only two are left. They just came in lately, and we don't know anything about them." I said, "Well, I must have

*Students and faculty with Thompson Webb at the far right
ca. 1924 in front of the schoolhouse.*

them; so send them out." We opened school the second year with 28 boys
and two teachers.

We hadn't been running 24 hours before I discovered that out of the
28 boys, I had 12 of the meanest boys I ever saw, and I learned my lesson.
You want to find out who the boys are you're taking before you take them.
It was a wonderful lesson. These were terrible boys, and the two teachers
were just as bad. They took the bad boys' side, and we had a continuous
row going on there. We couldn't get the school started at all. Then the
decent people began talking about taking their boys out of school, and my
back was to the wall. This thing couldn't go on as it was. We had to make
our decision.

So my wife and I did some more praying. Then I went up to school,
and I sent 12 boys home and dismissed the two teachers. I refunded the
students' tuition, and I gave the teachers some unearned salary. I thought I
could quiet it down that way, but it didn't suit anyone. Those parents didn't
want their boys back any more than I wanted them, and we had an awful
time. There was a great head of steam on a little teapot, fussing and rearing
there for about a week. Finally, all quieted down.

The agency called me and said they had two new teachers, men with
distinguished records in great schools of the East, who had arrived in

California late and would consent to teach. Those two wonderful men stayed with me for years. Then came new people with boys. "And where did you hear about us?" I asked. "Oh, we heard about those toughs you sent home," they said. "We've been looking for a school that had standards of behavior and the courage to live up to them."

I admitted the standards, but I knew I didn't have the courage; my back was to the wall, and I had acted because there was nothing else to do. It was a great lesson in learning to use courage, but, anyhow, the school was filled. We had one of the happiest years you can imagine.

[from oral history: At commencement President Blaisdell made us a sweet little talk, and we had a benediction. When it was over, I looked around and there wasn't a dry eye in our little auditorium. Everybody realized we'd been through a great experience and it was just emotional. Never seen such a thing before or since.]

At commencement, Mr. Leo Chandler, who was then trust officer of the California Bank of Los Angeles, thanked me for what I had done for his son, and said he wanted to bring his friends out and get them interested in the school. He said, "First, won't you let me lend you some money to paint these buildings?" I said, "Mr. Chandler, no bank would lend me money." He said, I'm not talking about the bank, I'm talking about a personal loan between you and me. I hope you can pay it back, but if you never do, it's for a good cause." I said, "Mr. Chandler, I have never met a banker like you before." He said, "Come in and have lunch with me at the University Club tomorrow, and we'll talk this over."

The next man to come up was a Colonel Sutphen, just back from overseas. He had his big old belt on and a couple of eagles on the shoulder of his uniform. He shook my hand and in his big old rough sort of voice said, "Webb, I'm delighted with what you've done for my son Joe. I never could get him to read, and now you've got his nose in a book all the time. It's wonderful what you've done for Joe. I want to bring my friends out here and get them interested in this school, but this place looks like hell. Let me lend you some money to fix it up." I told him, "Mr. Chandler said he would do something like that."

He went off looking for Chandler, and when I went in for lunch the next day, there were those two men. They had been talking since breakfast about their plans. They told me to eat lunch quickly and get home and get started. They wanted those buildings painted inside and out. They wanted gardeners to knock down the sagebrush and plant trees and grass, and they wanted me to add 12 rooms to the dormitory.

Then they thought I'd better have a little infirmary in case of illness. Finally, the Colonel said, "You build yourself a cottage and get your brats out of that dormitory." He was talking about my little boys. I said, "Well, gentlemen, how are we paying for this?" "Oh, send us the bills," they said. "We'll pay them as they come in; and when we get them all together, we'll give you a note." Believe me, I was awfully busy that summer directing the workmen, selecting the 40 boys and another teacher. You see they had given us 12 more rooms on the dormitory. That housed 40 boys. We opened up so happily that third year.

The infirmary, which was behind the dining room.

Shortly after we'd been going a while, parents of three boys called on me. They told me the parents of all the boys had had a meeting in Los Angeles, unknown to me, the night before. They purposely didn't tell me. They said they wanted to be free to discuss the situation, and they'd been appointed as a committee to call on me to tell me they were kicking at the price. "Well, gentlemen," I said, "if you knew how much money I owed, you'd know I can't do it for less than this."

"Webb, we've unanimously agreed on a price, and you'll have to accept it, whether you like it or not." They looked so glum. My heart sank. I said, "What's the verdict?" One of them said, "You tell him." Then another one said, "You tell him." Finally they began to laugh, and one of them said, "Your price is $1,300." I said, "What do you mean? You've gone up?" They just howled. "Yes, we've gone up $300, and we've made it retroactive. Here are 40 checks for $300 each. We've all thrown in the pot. Now Webb, that's not for you. That's to be spent on the boys. We know you're doing all you can with what you have. We want a better school. We want you to give those boys all the milk and good food they can consume. We want you to get a physical-education man to direct their athletics and to drag the brush off that hillside over there so they'll have a place to play. We want a nurse in that infirmary."

Swimming pool and the infirmary in the foreground and the lower dorm, upper dorm, schoolhouse, dining room, and corner of the garage in the middle 1920s after the buildings were painted white.

They went on enumerating. "You just spend this money for these things to make a better school," they said. And we were certainly busy accommodating them. In the spring some of them came out and said, "Now we're going to lend you the money to put 20 more rooms onto your dormitory." So we added the 20 rooms. "Do you think we can get 20 more boys at this big price?" I asked. "Leave it to us; we'll get them." And they did.

During that year, unknown to me, the parents had another meeting, and they raised the price to $1,600. Then they said, "This is not for you. We want some sanitation around here, some sewer lines and septic tanks." They buried thousands of dollars under the ground that no one will ever see. "And we want that hillside graded into a level field and put into grass, and we want this and we want that. You've got to have some teachers' cottages. Just go ahead and make this a better school."

So with the 60 boys we were able to do that. They lent me more money to build more dormitories. Our kitchen was too small; so we had that torn out and enlarged. My wife and I went in to the hotel supply company to pick out some new equipment amounting to about $1,500. I knew my friends would pay that and stick it on the note, and I'd be paying interest. I didn't see why the merchant couldn't carry that, so I said to him, "Could you send the goods out now and let me pay for it in about 60 days, when school opens?" He said, "You'll have to see the credit manager."

I had never heard of a credit manager. That was a new one to me, but the clerk introduced me to a young man, and the young man said, "What are your assets?" "Well," I said, "I haven't got my books with me; I don't know what they are." "Well," he said, "estimate them." I began to count up everything I could think of that would be an asset, and I said, "Well, I think our assets are $100,000." Then he said, "What are your liabilities?" "Well," I said, "I don't know about the current accounts, 30-day accounts in the neighborhood, but believe me I know about the notes. I'm watching them all the time." I counted them up and said, "On notes I owe $120,000." He said, "You mean your liabilities are greater than your assets?" I said, "Oh, yes!" He said, "That beats me. If people will lend you $120,000, I'll take a $1,500 chance on you. I'll send the goods out."

Coming home I got to thinking about that. There wasn't anything in my books about liabilities and assets. I didn't know how to do that kind of bookkeeping. I kept an accurate account with each individual. That was all I knew. But I thought I ought to know more about that, and made up my mind to get an auditor. About three days later I found just the right man, and he's been trying to keep me out of trouble ever since.

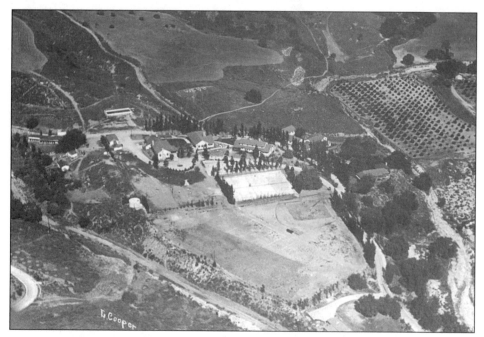

The Webb campus in the late 1920s before the gymnasium was built in 1931. The stables, garage, and swimming pool are at the back left; dining room, schoolhouse, upper dorm, and lower dorm are behind the tennis courts; and the Webb family home is among the trees to the right of the tennis courts. The Price family home is in the foreground below the ball field.

When I got home, Mr. Chandler and Colonel Sutphen were there, and they had a big roll of blueprints. They decided the school needed a library, and they were going to lend me a big sum of money to put up a beautiful building. I listened to them awhile, and then I said, "Gentlemen, quit lending me money. I know the value of a library, but I can get books down at the college. They'll lend them to me temporarily. I just want to get my liabilities and assets in shape. Please quit, please quit!"

It took a lot of persuading to make them quit. They let me alone then, and we ran along through the depression of 1929. The school kept full. Occasionally, they lent me some money to add a few rooms to the dormitory, because those rooms would produce. When 1930 came, I paid off the last of that indebtedness.

I wish Father could have lived until then. He was gone, but I would have loved to look him in the face and say, "Father, I've met every obligation on the day it was due or before, just like you brought me up." I could truthfully have said it. I know Father would have said, "Well, Son, how'd you do it?" I'd have said, "Father, you told me to watch time on a note as such an important thing, and when this one was coming due I went over there and borrowed the money to pay it. I kept up my credit because I always met the obligations when they were due."

My creditors probably never found out how badly off I was. I believe I was paying out 10 to 12 thousand dollars a year in interest at one time; but when I began to pay off something on principal, the next year the interest was less, and I could pay more on principal. It was a wonderful thing to see this great balloon coming down to nothing.

You might think I would have had enough sense to stay out of debt, but by that time I had established credit with Mr. Stone down at First National, and I didn't have to go back to my friends. I'd tell him I wanted to build a new building, and he'd say, "All right, how much is it going to cost?" I'd tell him, and he'd let me have it. One day I said, "Mr. Stone, how far can I go on this credit?" He said, "Not over $50,000." It never occurred to me I'd borrow that much money from Mr. Stone.

I put up my building and then taught school until I got it paid for. Then I went back and borrowed some more and bought some more land. I paid it off, and went back and borrowed some more and built another building. It went on like that until the recent war [WWII] was over. By that time we had built up a school for 165 boys and 17 full-time teachers. They and their families lived in houses we provided on the campus, all dining together in the big dining room. It was really quite a collection of people. It took me a long time to pay off a little bit of a debt the last two or three years.

We had come to the point of inflation. We could make only $500 or $600 a year. Before that we'd been making money to pay debts, but here I was up against it, and knew that I couldn't build another building. I wouldn't dare borrow money when I couldn't earn it back. We couldn't improve what we had. It was a terrible quandary to be in.

Subdividers had come along in every direction and were building on four sides of us. One of their men came up to me one day and said that they would like my land, but they would knock down the buildings. By this time we had 68 acres of land. We had started with three buildings, and we had 33 little buildings at the time. He said, "We don't want the school, we just want the land." I said, "What'll you give me for it?" They said, "$500,000." Well, that was something to think about. For land I had paid $250 an acre, they were talking about paying $7,500 an acre.

I called in my four sons, who are all teachers now and have their own families. I said, "You're my natural heirs, shall we sell out? We wouldn't owe any increased increment on this. I know it's worth more than $500,000, but you can't sell a school. We can sell the land, and they'll knock the school down. What do you want me to do, boys? I'm not going to be running this thing much longer." They all said, "Why, Dad, we don't want the school destroyed. We want it to go on forever. Let's incorporate it like Caltech and Pomona and Stanford and the rest of them and make an eleemosynary institution with a self-perpetuating board of trustees, a non-profit institution that can seek gifts. Let's perpetuate it forever."

Nothing could have made my wife and me happier than that. We called in, after much consideration, 15 friends and asked them if they would serve on this board of trustees. They agreed to do so. The attorney formed a corporate entity, and we deeded the whole works to them. We had 165 boys then with deposits of over $40,000 for the next year. We turned it all over to them, including all the property and the contracts for teachers and students. There was no indebtedness.

I wanted to know just what we'd given them. I didn't know. I knew what the land was worth, but I didn't know what the buildings were worth. I called in a real-estate appraiser. "What are these buildings worth?" He said, "Mr. Webb, you can't appraise them. We appraise on the basis of what the buildings will bring on the market, and no one buys a school. You can't appraise that." Then I looked in my books to see what they cost. You know I couldn't tell a thing. That old high-powered auditor had been depreciating everything. Here we were teaching in buildings that were no longer there.

But when the new board wanted to insure the property for fire insurance, they called in the fire-insurance company, and those people made their own appraisal on the basis of what it would cost to put those buildings and equipment back. They did a lot of measuring and stewing around there for three or four days. They came up with a value on the buildings and equipment of $1,200,000.

Now, to me, that's the value, plus the value of the land. We didn't make that; no, inflation made it. The rooms I built for $300 a room were appraised at $1,500 a room. The land I bought for $250 an acre was appraised at $7,500 an acre. It was inflation that made the value. I haven't flattered myself to think I had made any million dollars. It has been hard work. I lived at just the right time when a young man could put back everything he earned year after year and build it up until he had built a great factory, a great mill, a great department store, or a great school, if you please. It all went back. I don't know what our young people are going to do. It can't be done again like that. That day is gone.

It's my hope that the trustees will not enlarge the school too much, but that they will build it into one of the great academies of America, such as one finds in the East for instance; and I dream and think of what they will accomplish.

It's been lots of fun; but before I sit down, I would just like to inquire if any of you have any idle funds you want to put out at interest. If you do, please don't tempt me!

First Public Telling of Shoestringing
Howell Webb, from the interview with the four Webb brothers, December, 1988

Dad was a member of the local Kiwanis Club, and one day sometime before 1947, a speaker at the club canceled on short notice. Dad got a frantic call to ask whether he could come down and pinch hit. Dad said that he would be glad to, but what did they want him to talk about? They said that he should tell them the story of how he started his school. He went down and gave his Shoestringing talk for the first time off the cuff, and it made a great hit with Kiwanians. Soon other clubs asked him to speak. Later he gave his talk to the National Association of Independent Schools. It was accepted as enthusiastically there as it had been at the local Kiwanis Club.

Documents

Shoestringing was Thompson Webb's centerpiece story about his career and school. He loved telling it. As a mixture of history and good story telling, it deserves analysis and verification. This section with its letters from 1922 to 1925 gives contemporary accounts of many of the events that he told from memory in Shoestringing. They record some of his early dealings for the school; some of the help provided by Rayford Alley, his mixture of appreciation and disappointment in what Alley provided, and his trials in recruiting and disciplining early students.

Letters Concerning Purchase of Webb School, 1922
Draft copy of a letter to Dr. W. C. Garrison (Divinity School, University of Chicago) written sometime between May 23 and June 8, 1922. { }'s set off words that were struck out in the draft letter.

Dear Sir,

Several weeks ago I received a letter from Mr. S. D. Thacher of Ojai, California, telling me that the Claremont School for Boys was for sale as he thought that I might be interested. Since then I have had some correspondence with Mrs. Carvin, giving me the price and terms.

She quoted me $38,000, $8,000 cash and balance on time. As it stands the price seems beyond my grasp. {If this is the only possibility offered then} I have some property but no cash. It so happens that my property is in California too, being undeveloped land. It is high-class property but not liquid. Seemingly this deal requires immediate action for the success of the coming year.

I wondered if you would consider a proposition on a contract basis without a definite amount of cash but on a percentage of the income of the school, if I could win your faith in my ability to make a success of it. If you would consider this as a possibility without binding yourself in case a better offer were made you, I would be glad to come to Chicago and talk the matter over with you fully. I believe I can make a great success of the school if I can float it for a year or two but I do not consider it good business to start out with too big a millstone about my neck. If you are in a position to help me at the beginning, I think I can make you a better deal, in the long run, in return.

I have been reared in a boarding school that has made a pre-eminent success, judged by the men it has turned out. After taking my A.B. degree at the University of North Carolina with an average in scholarship of 90 1/2, I followed the advice of my physician and lived an outdoor life in California for several years. My trouble was with my stomach and not my lungs. There I built myself into perfect health. In the war, I was called back here owing to a shortage of teachers and have been a teacher and bookkeeper in this school for four years. I am called the bookkeeper but I am more than that as I collect the money, issue the checks paying all bills and taking care of practically all {detail} finances, except the profits.

The school had a small number of boys left on their hands each summer who had no homes or else had to make up failures to hold their classes. These were sent off with an instructor and some tents to the mountains. They were an unavoidable nuisance. When I arrived the camp consisted of 12 boys and an instructor and cook. I was told to take charge of them for the following summer. Since it had to be done I made up my mind to make a success of it. I looked over the credits of the boys in the school and where I could help a boy's course by a summer's work I talked with him about it. The result was I had over 50 boys the first summer and had to employ two other instructors. The following year the school gave me efficient and sanitary equipment of screened cabins and let me pick the camp site. With the backing of the school we brought the number the second summer to 95 boys. This was done without any advertising. I believe it is a question of only a few years when the number in camp will be limited as in our regular school. In this camp I have had full charge {as any acting headmaster, I have had to see to all the business} and feel that I have had quite a bit of experience in building up and running a boarding school.

I want to say {about myself} that I consider myself more of a businessman than a scholar. My experience since I left college has been more along that line. I was given the business end here when I first came, together with . . . teaching in the Beginning sections. There are 270 students in the school which made a great deal of bookkeeping. I have asked for less business with some advanced work to teach but as my brother will not entrust the business to someone else, I refused the higher work for lack of time to prepare it. For this reason, I recognize the handicap on the scholastic side, and plan to join with me in this enterprise a man of unusual scholarship who has had 15 years experience in preparatory work.* I believe together we will make a forceful team.

I would like to refer you to Mr. J.M. Westerfield president of the First National Bank of Banning, California, for reference as to my business character. I dealt continually with his bank while in California as my property is near there. I would also refer you to Mr. C. S. Albro of the Security National Bank of Los Angeles.

I want to refer you to two men in Chicago who are old Webb School boys. The first is Josiah Sibley, pastor of the Second Presbyterian Church, who is my brother-in-law. The other is Frederick Shannon pastor of . . . . I was just a little fellow when he was in school and haven't seen him since, but I had his son in my camp last summer.

* This was a teacher named Starr Cooper, who taught at the Peddie School in New Jersey. At this time in early June, 1922, Rayford Alley had proposed to Cooper and TW that they might be partners in the new school, but on June 9, 1922, Cooper decided against moving to California.

Interesting to see that he chooses two men who are pastors to recommend him when he is writing to a divinity school teacher. Interesting overall to see how TW sells himself at this critical time in the negotiation for Webb School. He notes his experience in the business end of the work and in recruiting boys for the camp. He also plans to hire someone else to be the scholar at his school. This practice follows the tradition of his father who had John Webb, a brother, as the scholar at the school in Bell Buckle.

Draft of letter to George S. Sumner at Pomona College in Spring/Summer, 1922. (Not clear that it was ever sent.) { }'s set off words that were struck out in the draft letter.

Dear Mr. Sumner,

This long distance trading is very unsatisfactory at least. I wish I could talk with you, for I think we could soon come to some very decided understanding, either to trade or not to trade. I feel that we might make a deal if we could get together, but as it looks tonight I do not see how we can.

What little property I have is tied up in non-income real estate with some indebtedness against it, which has been a good thing in some ways as {the land is good and has a great future}. Indebtedness is an incentive to make a young man save. But, of course, too much indebtedness is out of the question on any enterprise that may not be self-supporting at the beginning.

{Realizing that I might get in a tight place and need financial backing} When your letter came stating that you personally thought we might get together on a nominal rent for a short term of years with option to buy at $30,000, suggesting a rental that would cover only interest to building and loan and several small loans, I guessed that the building and loan would amount to about $10,000 and the rent would be quite reasonable. I then wired for definite figures and bought my ticket to New York. I did not get your answer until my second day in New York [Just before May 20, 1922]. I went there to see Mr. Rayford Alley, one of my closest life-long friends, who has made a most remarkable success as an attorney in New York. He has made a great deal of money and was at one time associated with Mr. Satterly, a brother-in-law of Mr. Morgan. He gave me his full time while I was there and went into the proposition thoroughly. It so happens that he backed a similar enterprise for girls last year in New York, and the young lady teachers failed to get a single student, which has left him owning the property. He was willing to go in with me and go to Claremont to try to close the deal with one provision, that you and your associates would guarantee us 10 full boy students the first year. He regarded the first ten boys as the fight and felt that you and your friends were in influential

positions and could doubtless get them if you would put your energy
and enthusiasm behind it. With 10 boys as a nucleus, I would have a far
better chance to get the next 22 than I would to get the first 10. He advised
me by all means to let it alone unless you would do that much and said that
he did not care to put any money into it on any other terms but was willing
to go out there to see you if you would meet him that far, that is guarantee
the 10 boys.

He regards a failing school as the poorest investment I could make and
said that he had far rather help me build a new one entire than take over a
failure unless you could overcome the failure yourselves to some extent by
getting me 10 boys. He is going to San Antonio on Friday the 26th of this
month [May, 1922]. If he is going to California at all it will have to be at
that time. Unless I receive a wire from you before that date accepting this
provision, of course Mr. Alley will not go to California.

Should you and Mr. Alley get together and close the deal, I would take
it over with the consciousness of a big power behind me. It would then be
"up to me" to make a full success of it to its present capacity. Should I do
that I am sure he would back me with any reasonable developments I
should need to make in order to increase the capacity of the school.

While of course I would want the option to call for very reasonable
payments to extend over a long term of years, it would be my very earnest
endeavor to pay it off at as early a date as possible. In fact I would put
my real estate on the market with that in view. I had much rather put
non-income property to work by saving me the interest on the deferred
payment. {As we now stand I would not trade the real estate for the school
until I knew.}

But I would not be willing to buy the property until I had tried out the
school and satisfied myself that it can be made to pay. When I had proven
that to myself I don't think I would be long in exercising the options and
clearing up the property.

If this were my only opportunity {in life}, I might {be forced to} take
greater chances. I have a wife and three babies and I don't feel that I should

take chances. I am offered the principalship of a private school, in a nearby city, with an enrollment of 150 pupils and property valued at $75,000. I am offered half the profits with a guarantee of a minimum of $4,000. . . . This has to be accepted or rejected within a short time.

The Webb School is a partnership to be perpetuated at the death of one partner by the appointment of another by the surviving partner. The property has recently been endowed and new buildings are now under construction. This is leased in the articles of incorporation perpetually to the partnership known as Webb School without charge. My father and brother are the present partners and my brother has offered to make me my father's successor if I will remain with the school. I ask that this be kept strictly confidential. I only speak of it in order that you may understand my motives. Financially I would make a mistake to leave it but for my personal development I should leave at least for a period of years. I will always be the kid brother and have a very small voice in the larger questions that come. I realize that I should begin to stand alone and develop the qualities that I believe to be mine. For that reason I expect to leave here. I would prefer to live in California if I could do so to advantage. At the same time I cannot afford to turn down the principalship of a very successful school with a definite minimum salary and plunge into a large indebtedness and a failing school in California unless I am given an opportunity to prove that I can put it on its feet. It will be necessary that the directors take some of the gamble with me if I come there. {If you are willing to do so you will have to indicate it at once.} Of course I expect you to accept the best bid you can get and realize that you would be foolish to consider me if you have cash bidders.

Letter dated May 22, 1922, on Claremont School for Boys stationery

Dear Mr. Webb,

I am sending this line to ask how you feel about taking the school over by this time. I have stopped mailing catalogs and if you are not going to take the school over, I shall turn the inquiries I have to another school. I should like to see you take it and build up a fine big school here. Judging from the literature you sent me I believe you can. Let me hear from you.

Sincerely, Frances M. Carvin

This letter from Frances Carvin provides a date for the negotiations, and the draft of the letter to Sumner reveals some of what TW and Rayford Alley agreed to during the May meeting in New York.

New York Trip and Arrival in California

from interview with the four Webb brothers at The Webb Schools, December, 1988

TW, JR.: I remember when Dad came back from New York [in May, 1922] bringing mechanical toys for Howell and me. I did not know the purpose of that trip. That is a moment in the prehistory of Webb School.

Q: What about moving here?

TW, JR.: We moved here in [mid-July] 1922. My mother's father was a Methodist minister in Long Beach. We were met at the train by my grandparents in a Model-T Ford sedan and drove down to Long Beach to their house. We stayed with them. I remember that there were times when my father was gone for longish periods—a day or two or something like that. That summer was a very active one for Dad. He had to find boys. That was his job that summer, to seek out students to come to the school. Howell, Bill, and I with Mother spent that summer mostly in Long Beach with my grandparents.

I remember when with my grandparents and my parents, I guess with all three of us [boys], came up here for the first time to see the school. This was the first time that my parents came to this property. The school buildings had been closed for years. This was the middle of summer. They had a key to the door to the old dormitory where the new library now is.

That building had two access doors, one toward the school building and the one toward the Alf Museum. We went in by that second door. I remember the odor of the building. This was a wooden building that had been closed. This was the middle of summer. The odor was that of the oil that was used in the sawdust that janitors use. They pour this oiled sawdust on the floor and sweep it up. This odor just overwhelmed me.

In his Shoestringing story, Dad says that all the windows were knocked out, that the building was in very bad repair. I don't remember it that way. There were some broken windows. I do remember going through that building and my parents inspecting it for the first time. This was the place where we were going to be living. In Shoestringing, Dad says that we camped here that night, and he pursued the business of dealing with the people in Claremont. But I think that we did not camp here. We went back to Long Beach to my grandparents' home.

New School
from letter to Emma Clary Webb, July 22, 1922

Mother, we become more and more in love with our place. It is a perfectly splendid establishment. I do not see how we could plan a place any nicer except as to size. It is a small school but I can easily room 40 boys in the dormitory. There are 24 rooms in it but all rooms are small but all have two closets. The scenery and location could not be improved upon. The swimming tank is large and deep and serves as a reservoir in a way. It is high above the buildings and the old water is used for irrigating the grounds whenever the water is changed. Beside that there is a concrete tank, a large one, up high above everything where the domestic water is kept. They have had a well and pumping plant to fill it but have agreed to make connection with the city water for us very soon as it will be less care to us.

I am running day and night to see people about their boys. I feel reasonably certain of three boys to date and have good chances of getting six more or even eight more. I have written to a large number from whom I have not heard as yet. I still have a large number of addresses to see and can keep busy this week at that. Of course, I cannot hope to fill the school this year, but I have no reason to be discouraged as yet as I am getting acquainted very fast.

I know Father will help me to get a name for the place very fast when he comes out. I am in hopes that you and he can come very soon. I have a nice room for you just across the hall from us. It is as large as any in the house, has two nice closets and a toilet room with a toilet and washbowl. We have the only private bath, in connection with our rooms just across the hall from you. There are baths for the boys on both floors.

The place is way up high where we can see all over the valley. Orange groves are on three sides and the mountain on the other. The roads are paved from our place in three ways. There was an old car [that] came with the place which I traded off for a new Durant, the finest car I ever drove. If Sugg brings the Chevrolet to me we will have two cars. You and Father can have the Durant. It operates like a Buick in all its levers.

Recruiting Boys
from letter to Rayford Alley, July 27, 1922

Your letter has entirely rejuvenated my spirits and enabled me yesterday to get two more boys for the coming year. I feel that I have secured these boys though no one seems to care to sign up and deposit in the first conversation with me, which I think is quite natural and proper. In both cases, I felt that we made friends with the parents and that they showed a marked interest in the school. Both of them are coming out to see us at the school within the next few days, and one mother told me that she felt sure that I could count on her boy for next year if I cared to have him. She went so far as to say that she felt that my call was the answer to her continued prayer for the proper place for her boy. I felt very much touched by the spirit she showed, and I was very much impressed with the manly little boy that she offers to entrust to us.

In the other case I have some misgivings in regard to the boy. I think I have learned to judge most boys on short acquaintance. I know from the appearances of this boy that he is bordering on the ragged edge of "toughdom." We would surely clash in the first day or two of school. Should I win, it might be the making of a man in him, but if he has gone too far to be conquered by reasonable methods, of course, we would have to ask his withdrawal. In this case I feel that, when the parents come to the school, I must make a frank statement to them and let them fully realize that, if they enter him, they are doing so at their own risk and experiment, and not at mine. I am willing to undertake to conquer the boy if they give me the opportunity with their eyes open. I suspect, however, that this is a case that needs a house of correction where corporal punishment can be used most liberally.

I have had my car one week today and in all that time have driven 800 miles and interviewed a large number of parents. Out of this number, I feel that I have from 12 to 15 excellent prospects. I don't know why people seem to be so slow in making a deposit, but as yet I have not secured any money on the boys though I have been assured of their intentions to enter them. I am told by Mrs. Carvin that some years there are no actual engagements to the school until within a week of its opening. This is a condition that I intend shall be changed next year. I firmly believe that there will be no trouble in filling our school to overflowing next fall, and we must convince our patrons that an early enrollment is necessary in order to get in. I still have plenty of people to visit. My wife and I have so many friends scattered all through this state, and all of them whom we have seen have shown such a marked interest in our new work and have given us so many suggestions about people who are looking for the proper place for their boys that I feel that we can keep continually busy in our search for them and that we have a splendid chance of filling our school by fall. Of course, I may be overoptimistic, but I had rather feel that way than otherwise. We are meeting a most delightful class of people and making many friends whom I feel will be of value to us in the future.

Mr. Thacher sent me a list of names whom he had declined. From this list there were two in Los Angeles. I went in day before yesterday to look these up, little realizing that I should know one of them whose name occurred on the list. When I located him, I found him to be a vice president of the Los Angeles Trust and Savings Bank and a very special friend of my wife's people. He had determined to keep his boy at home for another year after being refused by Mr. Thacher. His office was so crowded and time so short that I had no opportunity to convince him to change his mind, but he asked me for one of my catalogs and told me that he had the placing of six or eight boys in school this year who were wards of his trust department. He said that if he had only known about our plans he would have been very glad to have given us those boys but doubtless in the future he would have other opportunities and that we might count on him to "nail some shingles in our roof."

With this cue, I went to see Mr. Ed Elliott and other high officials in the Security Trust and Savings Bank and had a splendid introduction to their trust officer, who took my catalog and said that he would keep us in mind. I think that we are laying a good foundation through these channels.

I fear in some ways that we were a little bit extravagant to purchase a car at this time, but living so far from the car line, it seemed impractical to get about without one. In the past week, we have accomplished 10 or 20 times as much as we did in the week before. John and Brother Howell [his brother and father-in-law] declined to give up their cars, and we were unable to reach the people who were inquiring about the school. In so many cases, when we get to an address, we find that the people have moved down to some beach on a vacation or back into some mountain resort. We secure their new addresses from the neighbors and, consolidating them with addresses in their neighborhood, go out the next day and round them up. There are a large number so far that I have been unable to locate at all. You may readily see that the work is tremendous and can understand that I have been going continually day and night.

Should we get the 20 boys or more this year, I feel that we will be able to take care of the payments of which you spoke in a short note of yesterday.

You may rest assured that we will not get interested in any other investments out here until our school is an assured success. I greatly hoped that you could be able to work out some plan by which my land might be cashed in and enable me to pay off the indebtedness on it and to have working capital to put into our school enterprise. As I told you in a previous letter, I shall be glad to turn it over to you to handle in any way that you see best. I feel that this has handicapped me too long already.

You will never know how much you have done for me already and how bright you have made my work here.

Fall 1922 Report to Father

from letter to W.R. Webb, September 30, 1922

Dear Father,

Your very helpful and encouraging letter came today. I cannot thank you enough, for I need plenty of encouragement. Two engagements did not show up at the opening, which was not a surprise but was a big disappointment. I didn't know who would fail, but I expected someone to do it. Since then I have taken in one boy, which gives me 15 in all. Two are working their way, two are day pupils at $350 tuition for the nine months, including their dinner with us. Sawney is one, and on two more I made cuts to get them. My present gross income is about $9,000 with the possibility of it going $1,000 more. One of the present boys is trying us for a short time. If his health holds up, he will enroll. He had the mastoid operation several months ago and his parents were anxious about him. My present income is not sufficient to cover my entire expenses for the nine months as I figure it now. I think I will be forced to borrow a little money to get through, possibly $2,000. My expenses are heavy here. However, if I could get a half dozen more boys, the expense would not increase much. I think that would turn the tide to profit instead of loss. I have figured on the basics of the school's expenses and not on my drawing one cent out of it. I have made up my mind to let my taxes slide until better days unless John can help me, which I cannot hope for. I have written him today begging him for me. I fear he can't as land is not selling at all, so far as I can learn. As long as things are in that condition he will not be able to pay me anything he owes me either.

I never would have come out here except that Rayford Alley was going in with me on this. He wouldn't go in unless the owners would guarantee to get us 10 boys. They agreed to do that or take the loss on the property in proportion to their shortage. Rayford came out and wired me he had made the deal [and] to come at once. When I got here he was gone. He had made a good trade for the property, at about half its value in 10 annual payments. That was in the form of an option for two years. In the meantime, I am to pay a rental of $1,500 per year, which is less than interest. But he had released them from the obligation to get the 10 boys. We didn't have a prospect on July 10th. Then Rayford wrote me that he did not want to claim any share in the profits and such help he gave me would be in the way of a loan. I sent for $1,000 at once. He sent me a note for $1,000 with his endorsement on it and told me to raise the money on that. Of course, the banks didn't know him. I may get some help from Rayford yet, but I saw where I stood then and set in to cover my troubles with enough boys to pull me out. Father, it is wonderful what I have done to get up as much of a school as I have. I really think I may add enough boys along to make the thing pull through. I keep getting inquiries. The people here before me told me they always got a few tourists' sons along in the fall. They also got a few new boys at Christmas. A few additions like this will make me come out. I feel that if I can keep things going nicely this year I can have plenty of boys next year. My boys and patrons are boosters so far. I will be here in the spring and early summer to work up my group for next year. I am going to put on a summer camp too in charge of some young man. I think there is a big opening for it. I can get 25 boys now for that from the people I visited this summer. There is nothing of its kind here and I believe I can make it go right off with very little equipment.

I have been in about as deep blues as any man ever staggered under; after I got here and found no boys guaranteed and I was signed up to a two-year lease on this place. I took that all right until Rayford acted as he did. That took the bottom out of my plans. I didn't see any way out. The opening day all servants quit and walked out. It was the next day before we could get a cook. Mother Howell came over and helped Vivian cook for the crowd.

Father, I have a nice set of boys, considering. They have been pleasant, and some of them are studious. One is feebleminded, I feel sure. His father told me he had been injured on the head when a child but the doctors all assured him the boy would outgrow his trouble, and he said he was outgrowing it but was backward by three or four years. I took him as he is a full-pay boy. When he came, I found he is quite slow to think, but he swims, plays tennis, rides horses, reads papers, etc. He gives no trouble at all. I fear the effect on our reputation, but I don't know what to do but to keep him.

I have told you the whole thing like it is. I don't want you to worry about me, and I don't want you to say anything about Rayford. He may help me yet if I need it. I will certainly call on him if the pinch comes.

The Role of Rayford Alley in Founding the School
TW III

Rayford Alley was a classmate of my grandfather at the Webb School in Bell Buckle. In his capacity as a lawyer and negotiator, Alley helped my grandfather obtain the best possible contract for renting and later buying the Claremont School for Boys in 1922. He also provided free legal advice to him during the first two years of the school. For this help and his general encouragement, my grandfather was most appreciative. But my grandfather was also disappointed and depressed that Alley never joined him in business or helped finance the new school to the tune of $10,000 or more. As explained in the above letter, my grandfather came to California thinking that Alley would be in with him as a partner in the school. Some discussion of such an arrangement had gone on between them, but then Alley pulled back from becoming a partner and later had to remind my grandfather more than once that he was not his partner. A series of letters that Alley wrote to my grandfather in 1922 are on file in the Huntington Library and show that Alley never committed to making a big loan. He and his wife divorced later that year, and he had large expenses and anxiety because of an operation on his daughter. Alley only provided a loan of $1,000, which was repaid, and then much later, my grandfather loaned Alley $1,000, which he repaid [see p. 12 in Shoestringing]. So despite my grandfather's disappointment in 1922, they remained friends.

Why then the distortion of facts in Shoestringing about his dealings with Alley? The answer lies in hopeful thinking, the vagaries of memory, and the art of good storytelling. For me, Shoestringing is in large part an elaborate humorous telling of how my grandfather ultimately gained his father's approval after growing up fearing the man. Within that story with mythological overtones, Alley becomes the fall guy who adds to the hero's struggle. That my grandfather came to believe his version of the story is no surprise, and that his version differs from some of the facts is also no surprise. Psychological truths in stories often emerge from rearrangement and exaggeration of events, and an exact history of the events would not have captured his audiences' attention. What remains amazing is how much of Shoestringing follows the facts as these documents demonstrate; and, by comparing the story to what these documents tell, each reader can discover some of my grandfather's mastery of the art of good storytelling.

After Parents' Visit, 1923
from letter to W.R. Webb, May 15, 1923

A few days ago I received a letter from Mr. Thacher in which he said, "I start east tomorrow for my class meeting and for the inspection of a number of schools and colleges before the terms close, but I want to thank you for persuading your father to stop and see us, and to tell you what delight we took in him. It was the very keenest possible pleasure to meet him and hear him talk. I should like to have heard him for a week continuously, but he and your mother hurried on the same afternoon. What a wonderful keenness of mind and speech he possesses. You can see at once the source of his peculiar success. I hope that you are going to achieve a similar one." I have written him asking him to include Bell Buckle in his inspection of schools. I felt that you would enjoy having him, and I know that he would find a great deal to interest him there. I do not know his address but am sending the letter to Ojai asking them to forward [it].

The day I received this letter I had a phone call from Mr. William Thacher asking you to make their commencement address on the 15th of June. He was very much disappointed to find that you had gone back to Tennessee.

I am getting some interesting letters about the camp [Camp Robin Hood, see Chapter 6 in Vol. 2] but as yet have only one deposit. It looks as if Boynton has about 60 teachers working for groups. They have sent out about 25,000 folders and half that many letters to prospective parents. Of those who are interested the teachers supply them with the catalogs.

One man is coming out to see me about putting his boy in school for next year. A Frenchman who speaks Spanish called on this man. He is a Mexican of great wealth and lives in a palace in the best part of Los Angeles. His name is General Pelaez. I talked to a young Mexican in Pomona College. He told me that General was well-known and very wealthy, that he was considered to be a bandit in his country, that he made raids on the oil fields until the oil men hired him and his army to guard the fields. This seems interesting at any rate.

Fall 1923 Report to Father
from letter to W.R. Webb, October 21, 1923

I appreciate so much your letters. I have wanted to write you for some time. I know that you are exactly right about the debts. I have known so for a good many years. I was pinched badly enough on valley lands to realize what bonds debt puts on a man. It was in desperate protest at these bonds that made me determine to fight my way out, either to lose the whole thing or get on my feet and out of debt. I was going in the hole worse each year at home. All I could earn wouldn't catch up with my expenses.

It has been marvelous how I have been blessed here, but I cannot consider myself safe or a success here until I get out of debt. According to my contract, I had to make a payment on this place this year, which I have done. I had to meet my obligations on the camp, which I have done. This has taken the most of my cash. I am watching every corner I can, and I believe I am managing the school much better than I did last year. I have tried in every way to scheme some way to build a very simple cottage for my family. I have felt that it was necessary and in accordance with your advice last winter. You told me to get my children out of the dormitory, and I have seen the great need of it. I know no other way to do it as I have no other place to live. Last spring I discovered a boy teaching Thompsie and Howell obscene practices. He had also stolen articles. I expelled him right out and spent a great deal of time with my children. We have been on our guard continually, and we feel that no permanent injury was done but it was a very narrow escape. I cannot afford to have that happen again, and I cannot watch the children every minute. The children have been away from the boys ever since, but they are coming home soon.

I have tried desperately hard to sell the land in the valley, both mine and yours and also Brother Howell's. I went to Mr. Morgan Adams, my friend of the Arrowhead Lake Co. [see Chapter 6 in Vol. 2], who is one of the big financiers of Los Angeles, for advice about the sale of the land. He sent me to one of his friends who is a big operator in desert lands. This man told me he knew Coachella Valley and that good land there had a big future, but that farm land was not selling anywhere and could not as long as there was so much difference between the farm dollar and the manufacturing dollar, that he thought they could see the faint gleams of a brighter day ahead but how long he could not tell. He said that we had enough of that good land to make it an attractive proposition to an operator when there was an opening and that he was glad to know about it and would remember it. He told me that the real estate commissioner and federal officials were having a meeting in Los Angeles shortly to see if they could better the conditions and that he had been asked to meet with them, that he also had an engagement with a man who was on his way from England in search of farm lands for a large colonization enterprise that involved some

$12,000,000 to be put in farmlands. He felt that all this in time would sell but how soon he could not tell.

This oil well up here has created an excitement. Some of the directors of the Claremont School became sorry of this deal with me and schemed to put me out. They took my contract to an attorney and thought they had a technicality by which they could do so. They called a meeting of the directors and showed their plan. Dr. George Sumner of Pomona College, Joe's friend [Joe is likely Josiah Sibley, his sister Adeline's husband, who had gone to Pomona College], was on the board and refused to go with them and stood my ground for me. He told me afterwards that I had better get my deed as soon as I could. The papers are now being made. They give me a deed; I assume a first mortgage of $9,000 and give them a second mortgage for the balance. In the second mortgage there will be an agreement permitting me to negotiate a new first mortgage to the amount of $15,000 or less in case I want to pay off the present one of $9,000 and keep the rest for improvements or running expenses. This does give me some borrowing power if I should need to exercise it.

I went over Friday to see Vivian. She seemed well and Thompsie and Billy were well. Howell had been quite sick, an infection of the inner ear, which had caused high fever and an earache. The doctor had pierced the eardrum and relieved the situation but he said the tonsils were to blame for it all and had to come out soon. Mr. Howell [Vivian's father, who had heart disease] improved for a while but went back to preaching and has not done so well. We persuaded them to give up the idea of taking a church this year and come stay with us. I am very much afraid he will never be well again.

I have a much better set of boys this year, but I had one tough piece of discipline with two large boys. When I was in Long Beach about three weeks ago, they were profane. Ernest Powell heard them and told them to get off their horses and do something. They said they would not and rode off. That afternoon when they returned, they defied another teacher. I got home Sunday morning before church and heard the whole thing. I at once phoned their mothers and asked for permission to whip them which was granted in both cases. One mother, a Chattanooga woman and friend of the Oliver Andrews, told me to do anything to conquer her son except break his bones. I took the other one first and gave him a mighty hard thrashing, and he more than agreed to do all Ernest had told him to do, which was manual labor. Then I took the Chattanooga boy and did him likewise, but, when I was through, he said he was going home. I told him that that suited me exactly, but he would have to get his mother to come after him as she had brought him here, and until she did come, would have to meet all appointments, and to go to his room and get ready for church. He said he wouldn't go to church. I told him I had an idea he would. He went to his room and began packing. I called to the boys to get in the cars for church, and he didn't come. I went to his room and told him to come on. He told me I couldn't make him. I went over and took him by the arm. He jerked back and turned around and bent over to pack a suitcase that was on the floor, exposing exactly the surface I would most rather have. I swung with all the power in me and gave it to him with the flat of my hand, which turned him up on his head in the suitcase. He came up crying and asked me why I didn't knock him down. I said I am getting ready to do that next and jumped for him. He yelled in a panic that he would go and believe me he went. He sat through a long, dry sermon, and when we got back he came in to tell me that he was over his anger and didn't want to go.

Both mothers phoned to know how we came out, and both drove out a few days later to thank me for the way I handled them. They have been different boys since, though one of them lost his head today over a horse and was impudent to Ernest when he reproved him. I soaked him to 15 hours of heavy manual labor, to take up all his playtime for the next week. He is from one of the wealthiest families in Los Angeles. I would like very much to make good on this boy, but I fear I may have to send him home yet. I don't think the Chattanooga boy will ever lose his head again.

One of the boys who was working his way was disgruntled over his work and quit studying. I told him he had to work or get out. He didn't do any better so I moved him on tonight. I think it is going to have a good effect and I haven't lost anything. Two full-pay boys took up his work at $5 per week between them. It was costing me $10 to keep him.

Loan Payment to Parents, May, 1925
from letter to W.R. Webb, May 14, 1925

Enclosed you will find my note for $2,840, signed as requested. I thank you more than I can tell you for this very handsome gift which you have made us, in the reduction of the note. I feel that we could tide over our finances here successfully, and would much prefer to have you keep the money and spend it on a trip to California, as I have hopes of being able to retire some of this indebtedness before a great while in a way that would net some cash.

Mother Howell got home day before yesterday and has kept us all tremendously interested in her many graphic stories about the family and home. I do wish so much that we could see you all.

Our little family is well at present, and we are hoping that they were not exposed to scarlet fever; but we now have four cases of scarlet fever in the school. We had, fortunately, just finished our new dormitory and were able to put these boys there with some nurses. The hospitals would not receive them and they were all boys from a distance. Two parents are now on their way, crossing the continent to join their boys. But all of the cases were light and the danger point has been passed. The only question is the fear of more breaking out.

We have had a most wonderfully happy year at the school, with no questions of serious discipline until stealing broke out about 10 days ago. A number of boys lost all the money they had, and yesterday I had enough evidence collected to force two boys to admit they had done it. One mother arrived last night and took her boy home. We are now expecting the other father any minute.

You may be interested to know that we have enrolled the 9-year old son of Zane Grey for our Camp [Robin Hood]. The enrollments for the camp are coming along very nicely and I think we will have 50 or more boys.

Note: Six percent on $2,500 is $150, six percent on $2,650 is $159 for a total owed after two years of $2,809, and he paid $2,840, which is close, given that original loan dated from March 30, 1923.

The School in the First Years

Stealing Water

In July, 1922, I arrived in Claremont to start my school, the Webb School of California, in the deserted plant of the Claremont School for Boys near Claremont, California. I had a contract with the executors of the defunct school to purchase the plant. When we moved in, there were no public utilities connected. Shortly we had gas, electricity and telephone connected, but no water. The executors had agreed to bring water to the school from the Southern California Water Company. I found that they had to lay a pipeline to the company plant more than a mile away as there was no connection nearer. I asked what the old school did for water. It seems that they had bought water from a neighbor rancher by the name of Elder and were connected by a pipeline to his source, but he had cut this off. I called him, requesting that the water be turned on. He refused, as he had furnished the old school for nearly five years on a temporary basis until they could lay this pipeline to their supply. He explained that the law of California would require him to continue furnishing water forever if he had furnished it for five years. He had warned them that he would cut it off before the five years were completed and had done so. He explained that he was sorry, but he could not take a chance of being forced to furnish water forever and would not turn it on.

I went to the executors from whom I was buying the place, demanding water. They claimed they had let a contract for the pipeline to be laid and I would have to wait for it to be built. This would require two months to complete and might not be ready by the time my school was to open.

My family was camping on the campus without water. We were trying to clean and mop up without water. My neighbor, a quarter of a mile away, was giving us water which I had to carry by hand in buckets. At the time, I did not have an automobile. This was very bad. I telephoned Mr. Elder, but he was positive. He would not turn it on. Day after day I carried water many times.

After several weeks I decided to make one more effort. On a Sunday morning I called on Mr. Elder at his home and found him sitting on the porch with three men, his neighbors. I made a great appeal, picturing my tribulations and need and the fact that my line was now under construction and begged him to let me have water until my connection was made. He turned to his neighbors and asked them to be witnesses to his statement that under no conditions would he furnish me water. Then he said that if I stole water, unknown to him, he would not feel hard toward me. He asked me if I knew where the cutoff was. I used his water for about three or four weeks until my line was connected. Some two years later, I received a bill for that water, which I paid with thanks. Mr. Elder had a kind heart.

Original Buildings and Campus
interview with the four Webb brothers, December, 1988, and memories of TW, JR.

Bill: The dining hall in those early days of the small school only occupied the back of the dining hall building. The front part was a recreational room [called the Club Room]. On the porch just outside was my father's office. The whole school was composed of the schoolhouse with a pergola that led to the dining hall building with my dad's office on the right, the recreation room ahead, and the dining room behind it. The only other building was the old dormitory and the stables. That was pretty much the whole school.

Dining room and schoolhouse ca. 1922.
Note the concrete steps to the dining room porch and the pergola.

TW, JR.: The original dining room was oriented north-south with the porch at the southeast corner toward the east. The porch had concrete steps to the south, and at the back (north) end of the porch was Dad's office, that was enclosed. The porch led on to the pergola to the east, which was circular and paved in concrete. It was an open space with columns of river stones around it that held up wooden beams on which vines grew. There were benches and a fireplace in it. I remember Mother bringing marshmallows on a few occasions and our cooking them over the fire in that fireplace. Later in the 1930s, Howell, Emily [Price da Silveira], the Whitneys [George '31 and Brad '35], I and other friends had parties there with dancing.

The pergola then connected to a porch on the dining-room side of the old schoolhouse, which had smooth concrete all the way around to the north side of the schoolhouse. At first, the porch also went west-to-east through the schoolhouse as a hallway that cut off the three rooms on the north end from the rest of the schoolhouse. We used to skate out of the recreation room in the dining room and go across the pergola and all the way through the schoolhouse on smooth concrete. It was lots of fun.

Pergola in the 1930s.

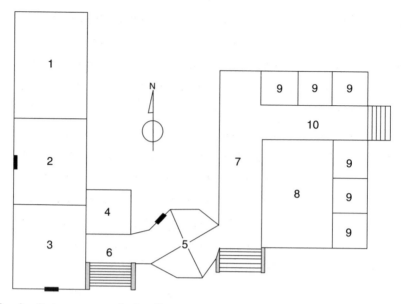

Plan for the dining room and schoolhouse in 1922 as drawn from memory by TW, JR. in March, 1998. 1. Kitchen, storage rooms, and sleeping rooms for help. 2. Dining space. 3. The "Club Room," which later became an extension of the dining space. 4. Headmaster's office. 5. Pergola. 6. Covered porch. 7. Uncovered porch. 8. Study hall. 9. Classrooms. 10. Covered walkway. The concrete floor was smooth across 5, 6, 7, and 10. Drawing is not to scale.

Q: The palm trees that are here now. Were they along the driveway?

TW, JR.: Yes, and there were many more than now exist. The driveway went between the Alf Museum and what was called the upper dorm and was lined by those palm trees. The dirt road and driveway into Webb was so ill marked in places, however, that the milk truck ran over my tricycle that I had left near the dorm where we were living. Mother asked Dad to go out to speak to the man about it the next day and Dad talked to him about it, but I cannot remember what happened next or whether the tricycle was ever repaired.

I remember my parents planting Lippia grass that would grow in the dry cleared soil and not need much care or water. They had to dig down to put in its roots. It had one disadvantage over ordinary grass and lawns because the blossoms attracted bees that stung my bare feet.

Jack: My life started in the upper dorm when I was two weeks old, though I have no direct memories of life there. The family was living in the dorm when I was born in November, 1923. The sounds in the dormitory apparently carried very easily from one room to the next. The inside walls were really more like partitions without insulation. I feel a certain responsibility for prompting the building of the family home.

TW, JR.: When we moved here, the old [upper] dorm had been built in the teens of this century when it was considered very healthful to sleep on a sleeping porch. The rooms in the old dorm were arranged that way. There was a sleeping porch on the outside and then there was a little study room for each pair of boys on the main floor of that building. The upper floor had single rooms. Our family occupied a family suite—two rooms and a bath—on the ground floor for the first three years of the school until the family home was completed in 1925.

Apartment in the upper dorm where the Webb family lived from 1922 to 1925. Note the screened-in sleeping porch.

The upper dorm had a dark basement in which wonderful things were stored. It was inside the stone foundation which stood as high as 8 feet on the side across from where the Jackson Library was built. (Before the library was built, a house for the Vedders was built on its site. This house was moved up toward the smoke shack area to make way for the library.) The dorm was at grade level at the other end. There were little windows (6 x 12 inches) at the top of the foundation wall. Howell and I discovered a ladder on the outside and placed it where we could climb 6 or so feet up and then wiggled through one of the windows. Once inside, we found old furniture stored there. We just crawled around inside and explored. No one was watching us.

The new dorm had two basement rooms with windows facing north. It was built on a bluff and was at road level by the road but its basement was above ground level just a short distance east of the road. Deuel's glider was built in the basement room nearest the street in 1928 (see stories in "Student Life at Webb School" in Chapter 6), and this room later became the biology room where Ray Alf first stored his fossils. Science equipment was in the other basement room.

Board-and-batten construction was used for both the upper dorm and the new dorm. Two-inch battens covered the vertical cracks between the siding boards that were 1 inch thick and 12 inches wide.

Commencement Sites on Campus
TW, JR., as told to TW III in January, 1998

The first commencement in 1923 was small enough to be held in the dining room with the speakers standing at the north end. The next two or so were held in the Club Room with speakers standing at the south end with their backs to the fireplace. The way into the dining room was opened up for extra seating. After that, the commencement was moved to the green area to the north of the pergola and Dad's office between the dining room and the schoolhouse. From there, commencement moved to Mother's garden with diplomas handed out on the porch by the family dining room. That is where the speakers sat with the faculty that included Uncle Ed [Price], Glenn Vedder, and others. Howell and I graduated in this setting in 1935. In 1943, commencement was held in the chapel, but when Gordy graduated in 1965, commencement was in the grounds of the Alamo, where it had been for some time.

Students riding horses. This photo was used as a publicity photo for the school.

Horses at Webb

TW, JR., from the interview with the four Webb brothers, December, 1988

This school was patterned on the Thacher School as closely as my parents with their own tradition in Bell Buckle could do it. At the Thacher School in those days every boy had a horse. Horse activities, gymkhanas and camping trips were very much part of that school program, and that was a part of this school in its initial stages. There was a stable down [and behind] what is the Price Dining Hall now. A number of years later, there was a new stable out where the swimming pool is here today. In those days, many of the boys had horses. To a small youngster growing up that was very fascinating, and I spent as much of my time looking at horses, talking about horses, watching blacksmiths, and that sort of thing.

Old Stable and Garage at Webb

TW, JR., as told to TW III in March, 1998

The original stable was along the back drive into the school from Webb Canyon. This drive intersected the main drive by the old garage that stood where the Price Dining Hall is now. Between the stables and the garage was a large oak tree under which there was a hitching rack, a long metal rod that was held up by some 4 by 4 posts and horses could be hitched to it. This was where the blacksmiths came and worked. A blacksmith would drive up in an old used truck with the forge and other gear in back. He would then set up shop under the tree and work down a line of horses putting on shoes. He would have a fire going, and the fan to make it hotter was operated by a crank. I remember getting asked to turn this crank at times. As a small boy, I liked hanging around when the blacksmith came. He often had no one there to talk to while shoeing the horses but a small boy like me. It was fun to watch him work.

The first stall in the stable had a tack room attached to it. The Chevy [see Chapter 6 of Vol. 2] was parked in either this stall or the tack room. Boxes were stacked up behind the garage. They had contained cans and food for the dining room. Howell and I would play there and line the boxes up to make a ship.

Milk and Ice on Campus

Bill Webb, from the interview with the four Webb brothers, December, 1988

Mother and Dad felt that it would be economically feasible for Webb School to have some milk cows and have its own dairy. A small dairy was built across the driveway, just north of the office building, where the Price Dining Hall is now. There were some cows that were there. Ron Johnson '27 has a plaque in the Jackson Library with a milk bottle on it because he was a local boy who was hired to milk cows at that time in exchange for tuition. That has been memorialized with his milk bottle.

In those days, we did not have refrigeration. In the summertime when the school kitchen was closed, the ice trucks would come up. The iceman would bring in chunks of ice for our refrigerator, our icebox, down at the home. During the regular school year, there was an ice plant that was part of the kitchen, and it would make these huge blocks of ice that then went into iceboxes.

The Milk Cow Story

The first year of our school, my father and mother came to see me, and they wanted to see how we were getting along. Dr. Blaisdell, president of Pomona College, had called a meeting of teachers on a Saturday morning at Bridges Hall of Music, and he heard that Father was here and invited me to bring him to this meeting. There must have been two or three hundred teachers there. They would discuss problems in education and asked a man to speak for five minutes, and then they would discuss it from the floor for a little while and someone else would speak. One of the speakers made a plea for manual training—the importance of teaching young people skills with their hands and being proud of honest work. He made a fine address, but he closed it in a way that upset Father. The closing remark was that he would rather his son could milk a cow than to read Latin and Greek.

Well, in Father's school, he always required some Latin and Greek and greatly approved of it, but his school was on a farm, and many boys worked their way through. When that remark was made, I could see Father brace right up. He didn't like that and he was called on next. He paid the gentleman a compliment on his appeal for manual training and how important he thought it was that everyone had skills with their hands and would be proud of honest labor, but Father wound up saying, "That boy of mine (pointing at me) has milked cows many years on our farm. I'd be very much ashamed of him if he couldn't do that. But I'd be very mortified if he couldn't do some things that a calf doesn't do better!"

That story got into the *Readers Digest*, sent in by Dr. Remson Bird, who was many years president of Occidental College. It went all over the United States and I heard it dozens and dozens of times on my travels. It was quoted in *Time* magazine, which gave credit for the remark to Mr. Horace Taft, brother of the president and administrator of the Taft School. The following week among the letters at the beginning of the magazine was a letter from Mr. Horace Taft stating that the remark had been made by Sawney Webb.

The smoke house.

The Smoke House

TW III and TW, JR.

To cope with his inability to prohibit smoking among students at Webb, my grandfather established and then built a small stone house as the one place where students were allowed to smoke. The habits of his students forced him to make a practical exception to the rule against smoking cigarettes that he had inherited from his father's school. (See discussion in Chapter 2 of Vol. 2 of this problem in his letter to his father on July 4, 1907, from his first summer running a summer camp. Earlier that summer, he also had concerns when the boys did schoolwork on Sunday.) — *TW III*

Dad always called the stone hut where smoking was allowed the smoke house. His term came from rural Tennessee, where wooden huts were used for smoking or curing hams. I did not understand this distinction until I visited Tennessee in the 1960s, where I was introduced to the buildings and the term in its native setting. In using smoke house, Dad had picked a term that was familiar to him, but he never corrected anyone else who called it the shack or smoke shack. His term was simply the smoke house. — *TW, JR.*

Telling Father about the Smoke House and Lighting a Lady's Cigarette

Father was violently opposed to cigarette smoking. He smoked a pipe or cigar, but he didn't tolerate cigarettes under any conditions; and when boys applied to come to his school, he sent them a questionnaire to be filled out, about many things, and one question was, "Do you smoke, and if so, what do you smoke?" If it came back that he smoked a cigarette, he didn't take him. If he smoked a pipe or cigar, it didn't make any difference.

He told his four sons that he had no right to ask us not to use tobacco, since he did, but he didn't ever want to see us smoking a cigarette. He had an idea that it was doped with opium or something.

Well toward the end of Father's life [1926], we knew he wasn't going to live very long, and I went back and stayed a few weeks, frequently sitting by his bed and chatting with him. I finally ran out of things to talk about, and I finally got my courage to tell him about a situation that I'd had where I'd found I couldn't stop smoking on the part of the older boys and I'd built a smoke house on the campus where they could go to smoke with my permission and [each boy's] parents would be notified that he was doing it. They were not to smoke around the grounds or in their rooms, where they would be apt to influence younger boys to begin. Father seemed interested in my way of handling it, and we talked a bit. Then I told him that two ladies from Mexico came to see me about entering a son of one of them. She was the wife of the treasurer of the Mexican government and brought this other lady with her to translate and talk to me, as she didn't speak English. We had a nice talk in my living room, and then they wanted to see the school, so we wandered about the campus and saw the various facilities, and they asked me about a little rock house, and I explained that was the smoke house and how we allowed the boys to use it. We came back and sat down in our living room, and she said she wanted to put her boy in and how much would we charge? She wanted to give me a check. I think at that time I only charged $1,000 a year and expected to be paid $500 at the beginning of each semester. She wanted her son to have a horse, and a good many of our boys did have horses. She asked what a horse would cost, and I told her

I thought we could get a nice one for $50. She wanted a good one, so she said she would give me $100, and I thought we could get a saddle for $50, and she said she would make that $100. She wanted a nice one. She wanted to deposit enough money in case her boy got sick or needed anything, and she totaled it up and gave me a check for $2,000.

Then the interpreter said Mrs. Ochoa would like to know if she might smoke there or did she have to go to the Smoke House? I said, "Father, I looked down and she had a cigarette in her fingers and a lighter in her hand; and, of course, I told her she could smoke in my living room, and I lit the cigarette for her. I know you hate cigarettes, but what would you have done? Would you have lighted her cigarette?" He said, "Son, did you say she gave you $2,000?" I said, "Yes." He said, "Son, I'd have lighted it for $200!"

Her son Y.O. Frederico E. Ochoa is listed in the class of 1928, but only attended Webb from October to December, 1925, when illness prevented him from returning. He later became a clown, and his picture is on p. 38 of the Webb School of California Alumni Bulletin, 1974-76.

The Siren
TW, JR., from the interview with the four Webb brothers, December, 1988

In the earliest years, the only signal for calling boys to the dining room for meals was a metal triangle in the back of the old kitchen. In the '20s, my father acquired a siren. I think that there was a story about it, but I can't remember it now. It was a large siren, the size that would be on a firehouse. He had it installed on the gable roof of the classroom building with the siren directed to the north. That became the official signaling instrument of the school. It sounded at 6:30 for boys theoretically to get up. Then it sounded a five-minute bell before breakfast, and that's when they did get up. And then it made another blast at 7 to indicate that anybody who was not in by that time was late for breakfast. It also sounded the schedule of the school's activities.

When the siren was first installed up there, it was loud enough that it not only woke the school but it woke neighbors. My father heard about this.

There was considerable indignation at first, but the neighbors became used to it, and the protests diminished until Thanksgiving vacation came along. Then all the neighbors were late to their offices on the Friday after Thanksgiving. There had been no siren as the boys were at home. [laughter]

Teachers and Courses at Webb School the First Year

summary by TW III from p. 53-54 in the oral history

In the first year of the school, four teachers taught all the classes. My grandfather taught math (most likely); my grandmother taught English; John Sugg, who had helped my grandfather with his summer camp in Tennessee and had driven out from there in the Chevrolet [see also The Mayflower Motor in Chapter 6 of Vol. 2], taught science; and Brooks Blaisdell, the son of President James A. Blaisdell of Pomona College, taught math and some Spanish. History and Latin were also taught, but in 1969 my grandfather could not remember who had taught them.

Mrs. Tyndall and Joe

About the third year of our school the enrollment had reached 40 boys, and I had to have help in my office. I ran an advertisement in the *Pomona Progress* which produced Mrs. Tyndall. She was a widow with a boy about 4 years old by the name of Joe. She had to have accommodations for herself and Joe, which seemed to create complications. However, we had our son, Bill, about the age of Joe. We agreed to give it a try.

That proved to be the luckiest thing that could have happened to us at the time, for she was one of the most remarkable secretaries a man ever had. . . . Mrs. Tyndall had a perfect memory. After the first day of school each year (she was with us for 19 years), she knew instantly the home address and telephone number of every parent, with no reference to the book. By the time of her last year, our enrollment was about a hundred boys. It was a sad day for us all when she died.

Students and Student Issues

Eugene Hirsch '26

The first year of my school, September 19, 1922, we had 14 boys. Eugene Hirsch was one of them, a boy of 14 or 15 years of age. His father paid the stated first payment including $100 deposit for incidentals such as pocket money and any unusual expenses, haircuts, etc.

When his father left him with me, he handed me a one-hundred-dollar bill saying he wanted Eugene to have anything he wanted. I told him I had an ample deposit and this was not needed. He insisted I keep it and give Eugene all the money he asked for, and there was plenty more where it came from.

I felt that boys should be budgeted and trained to be careful with money. This attitude came as a great shock to me, the first year I opened the school. I could not understand anyone so reckless about money. I had never known anyone with so much money except an old miser who never let a dime get loose.

The first night at 9 o'clock, I told my 14 boys to go to bed. In a half hour there was a knock on my door. I opened it and there was Eugene. He said he would like to go to bed. I agreed that I wanted him to go to bed. Why didn't he do it? He then said, "Who is going to lay out my pajamas?" The next morning at 6 there was a knock at my door. Eugene wanted to know if he could get up. I agreed.

When Saturday came around, I told all the boys to come to my office for their spending money. All showed up but Eugene. I sent for him and asked if he would like his spending money. He said, "Not yet." Each Saturday I would tell them to line up for spending money. All would draw it but Eugene.

In about a month, Eugene did come in and handed me a quarter and asked me to keep it for him. I inquired where did he get it. He told me that he sold his dessert at the table. Every little while he came in with a dime or quarter for me to keep all year long. Never did he draw a penny until his father came for him the day school closed. Then he asked for his spending money, and I had to give him $106.45.

In a long life in boarding school, I have run into many odd quirks, but I have never seen another like Eugene. I could understand his father telling me to give Eugene all he wanted after that.

Paul Cook Sent Home

This is about a boy named Paul who entered our school the very first year. Paul was one of the biggest boys I ever saw. He must have stood 6 feet 4 and weighed 250 pounds or more. Paul was a spoiled boy. He had been in the habit of having his way about everything, and I had lots of difficulty with him. He was clashing with me about everything and yet there was nothing that was fundamentally immoral. He was just willful and determined to have his way. At that time I had teaching for me a Mr. Brooks Blaisdell, who was about 5 feet 4, a little stocky man. Trouble had been going on between Paul and Blaisdell and between Paul and me, always clashes about everything. I had been fed up to the point where I didn't see how I could keep him any longer unless we could get him to be cooperative. I talked to him over and over again, and would get promises from him, but the minute he was crossed, he would lose his temper.

Finally, the day came when Blaisdell came into my office in the middle of the school morning and said he refused to teach Paul any more. He had put him up to the board in the Spanish class to write a sentence in which he had missed a word and was told that was wrong. He said Paul flew around and smashed him in the face with the eraser he had in his hand. Blaisdell said, "That's just too much. I can't keep him anymore." I said, "Well, it is too much for any of us." I sent for Paul and told him to pack his things, that I was advising his parents to come and get him at once. In a reasonable time here came his father and mother. At first they were very courteous and considerate and listened to my story. Then I told them they would have to take Paul home. They begged me to forgive him this time, and he would be a good boy. They begged and pleaded and wheedled.

I stood my ground. I had made up my mind. After they could get nowhere with pleading, they began to get angry and to talk very ugly, but that didn't get them anywhere. They became more and more angry until they were absolutely insulting, and I had to tell them to leave my office. I wouldn't let anybody talk to me like that, to get their boy out of school now.

So they took Paul and left. It was a matter of great disappointment to me. I was interested in Paul and needed him, but I couldn't have that kind of conduct going on in school. There was nothing else that I could do. In the old days when Father was a boy, the teachers would use a switch and correct a boy. They would usually get decent conduct out of them in that way, but I couldn't use corporal punishment. That day had passed, and all I had left was to send him home.

It must have been some 25 years later when one day the secretary brought to my office an elderly couple who came in and introduced themselves. I did not think of the name nor recognize them. They were seated and the gentleman said to me, "You don't seem to recognize us." I said, "No, I am sorry." Then he said that they were the parents of Paul whom I sent home the first year. Then I did remember them. They told me that they went home and got to thinking about what Paul had done and what I had done, and how badly they had talked to me, and ever since then they had been ashamed of themselves and had wanted to come and apologize, but it was hard to get up the nerve to do so. At last they were here to say they were sorry for the way they had talked to me. They said they realized that I was right and they were wrong. I thanked them, of course. I was happy to have an old scar like that cleaned up. Then the gentleman said to me, "We owe a great deal to you, though you don't know it. When Paul first came home, he was quite morose; he wouldn't even talk, just grunt when we would speak to him. He wouldn't go to school. He would take his gun and wander out in the woods all day, or go down to the beach by himself, and for a couple of weeks he would have nothing to do with anybody. He was just simply in a brown study. We tried to get him to go to the local school, but he wouldn't go. Finally he told us one day he was never going back to school; he was through, and that he wanted a gas station." "So," he said, "when I was convinced that's what he wanted, I went down to our town and bought the best gas station in town and turned it over to him. At once Paul cheered up. He got a lot of pleasure out of it. He was greeting all of his friends and greeting us when we came by and working hard pumping gas and washing windshields, and he made his station a very popular place. In the course of months one day when I went down, Paul said that he had bought the station across the street. I asked him how did he get the money for that. He said, "I made it on this one." And so, from time to time, he was buying stations in other towns. Now, Mr. Webb, he has a string of about 50 stations and is getting a far greater income than I ever had. Paul married some years ago and has some children, and now he has become president of the Rotary Club of our city. He has been president of the Chamber of Commerce. He is senior warden in the Episcopal Church. He is head of the Boy Scout movement. He takes an active part in the campaign for the Community Chest fund. In fact, Mr. Webb, he is the leading citizen in our town. I think anybody would agree with me on that. He stands out for everything worthwhile, and we are so proud of him we don't know what to do.

"At Thanksgiving we had him and his family around to eat turkey with us." And he said, "After we had had our meal and pushed our chairs back, I turned to him and said that we were so proud of him we didn't know what to do, that he had made a great success of his life, he was doing just exactly what we would like to see him do, that there had been days long ago when we were discouraged about him, but he had certainly made good now." He said that the tears ran down Paul's face and after he got control of his voice, he said, "Dad, do you know what did it? Do you remember when old man Webb (I was 34 years old at that time) expelled me from that school?" "Yes." "Well, Dad, I had been able to get around every teacher I ever saw up to that time. I could talk them out or bluff them out of punishing me. I would get around it, and none of them had ever made me obey, but," he said, "when I came up against him, it was a stone wall, and I couldn't get out of it." He said, "It made me awfully mad, but I got to thinking about it, and after a while I said, 'I'm going to show him what I can do,' and I've been trying to show him ever since." He said, "You see Mr. Webb, we are greatly indebted to you for some big things you did far greater than you ever realized. You were right, and we were wrong."

Sawney's Explosives

Father's nickname was Sawney. My brother John produced his first grandson and named him for Father's nickname and put in the name, Ben, for his other grandfather; so the boy is Sawney Ben Webb [b. July 25, 1910].

The swimming pool in use in the early 1920s before the infirmary was built.

When young Sawney was about 13 years old, he was put in my school at Claremont as a boarder. At the time, the school was just beginning. I think I had only 14 boys that first year.

On one Saturday morning as I sat in my office, I kept hearing a big bang that shook the windows. I was busy and did not go out for some minutes, though the big bangs came frequently. When I did go, I saw the students all around the old reservoir that we sometimes filled with water for a swimming pool. There was no water in it at the time. Young Sawney was standing on top of one side. I saw him drop a large rock inside and jump back just as the big bang came, and a shower of small rocks went into the sky and the boys all dodged as they came down. I ran up to see.

Sawney had a glass quart jar of yellow powder about half full. He would pour a few thimbles full on the concrete floor, get up above and drop a big rock onto it to detonate it. Obviously, it was powerful stuff. I asked him where he got it. He said that he had made it by a recipe he found in a science magazine. I took the jar away from him and told him that the half jar he had been holding would blow him to kingdom come if he dropped it. I started off wondering what to do with it and turned and asked him if he had any more. He said he had a gallon of it in his desk in the school room.

I have often thought that the new school might have ended in the sky at that time. Our driveway on the campus circles around the perimeter of the grounds at least a half mile in length. We put guards along the way and poured a little line of the powder on the road nearly its full length. When all were alerted, we touched a match at one end. Before we could catch our breath it flashed to the other end.

William R. "Sawney" Webb, Thompson Webb, JR., Emma Clary Webb, Sawney Ben Webb, Richard Webb, and Thompson Webb, April, 1923.

Jim Wiggs '25

Jim was one of the boys about the second or third year of the school. His mother, a very charming lady from the South, came to me and said she wanted me to take her son Jim. Then she told me that when Jim was a baby, her husband died, and that she had loved him more than anything in all the world, and that she was so torn to pieces that she just never could discipline

Jim as a little baby, and that when she'd say no, and he'd lie down on the floor and kick and scream, she'd always give way to him, she'd never been able to say no to him, and that he'd always had his way about everything. If he couldn't get it one way, he'd get it the other; and that she knew she'd just about ruined him, and she wanted him under a man that could control him and would make him obey, and asked me if I would do it. I told Mrs. Wiggs that I'd be glad to undertake to do it on one condition, and that was that I might use corporal punishment if I saw fit to do so. She said, "By all means. Do anything in the world you see fit except break his bones." And so with those instructions, we took over Jim.

Jim was a great big strapping boy, and was 15 years of age, large for his age, bright and cheerful and pleasant. Everything was wonderful with Jim and we all liked him very much up till one point one Sunday; I think he had been there a month before we had any difficulty at all. But this partic-ular Sunday, Jim got mad about something and refused to obey me and I told him that he had to obey me, and I would not let him do what he proposed to do. He made a great scene about it, said all right, he was going home, he wouldn't stay in any such school. And I said, "No, Jim. You're going to church with me just like the other boys do." In those days, we all went down to Claremont to church. No, he wasn't going to church, he was going home. I said, "No, Jim. Your mother brought you here and she'll have to come and get you. You're not going in that way. You can phone her and have her come and get you, but I'm not going to let you go until she does take you." No, he was going down to his room and pack his things and go right on home, and out he went.

Well, I got out my car and went down to the dormitories to take my load of boys to church, and the other teachers were loading up with their loads. Jim was to ride with me and he didn't come out, so I went to his room and there he was, packing his suitcase which he had down on the floor. And I said, "Jim, come on. Go to church." "I'm not going." I grabbed him by the arm, and I said, "You are going." He gave a great surge away from me and said, "I'm not going." With that he picked up a shirt and leaned over his suitcase to put it inside, with his back towards me. Well, I swung the hardest blow I could think of with the flat of my hand right on the place where babies should be spanked, and turned Jim over in a somersault. His head went into the suitcase, he went right on over, because I had hit him awfully hard. I knew I couldn't hurt him there, couldn't injure him there. And then I was right on top of him and had him by the throat and raised my hand up again and I asked him how many licks like that would it take to take him to church. He said, "I'll go, sir, I'll go." And he got up, sobbing all over, and came on out and got in the car and went to church. He sat down in the pew by me and all during the sermon, sniffling, sniffling, sniffling the whole time. When church was over and we came home and we were getting out of the car, I said, "Now, Jim, go call your mother and tell her to come and get you." He said, "No, sir. I don't want to go home. I'll stay."

Jim did stay. I never had another case of discipline with him. He was a wonderful boy. Everything was all right. He'd found out that there was one time he wasn't going to have his way and he never questioned it again.

At that time a number of boys had horses at the school, which they owned and kept there and rode, and I knew they'd go off nearly every day on these trips together, up into the hills and around the canyons. I never knew exactly what all they did on those trips, but it came out later that one of the things they liked to do on Sunday afternoons was to go up into Live Oak Canyon, which was full of underbrush and lots of blackberry brambles and things of that kind. They had discovered that a number of young couples would come up there on Sunday afternoons and spoon. And these couples would get off by themselves in among the blackberry brambles, where they couldn't be seen very well, and be sitting in there, and our boys would come along on their horses, six or eight of them, and kind of scout along on the edge, spotting various ones wherever they could see them. And then they'd get way up at the head of canyon, and one of them would yell, "Yonder he goes." And with that, all these horses would strike out in a gallop and the boys would beat their hands against the chaps and make all the noise and holler, "Yonder he goes. Catch him, catch him. Yonder he goes," a-cloppety-cloppety with these horses, down through the brush, and scared the daylights out of these spooning couples and make them run in every direction. They'd done this a number of times when finally some fellows who had evidently had experience with them before suddenly pulled out a pistol and began to shoot, bang-bang, at them. And that turned the tables around, and our boys turned tail and ran off on their horses as fast as they could come.

I never knew anything about it until after the shooting and then the news came out. That ended the troubles in the canyon as far as our horsemen were concerned.

Bob Law '29

During the second year of the school, we had a full quota of 28 boys and two teachers, but very shortly we had to let 12 of these boys and the two teachers go home. The teachers were no good and wouldn't cooperate with me in the least, and those 12 boys were bad ones. Gradually other boys percolated in and we filled it again. In the meantime, the Boynton's Teachers' Agency sent me two teachers who [had] arrived in California after school had started, but these were men who had splendid records. One of them was Mr. Hirsbrunner, who had been a principal of a high school in Indiana, I think it was, for a long time. He was a marvelously fine man and remained with me for many years. The other was a Major Bennett, who had a doctor's degree from Yale, but had recently been serving as a major in the English army, having entered the war against Germany before our country got into it.

At that time we had at school a boy named Bob Law '29 who was only in the 8th grade but I think he was 16 years old. He was a stocky, heavy, short boy, and he had given us a great deal of difficulty in the matter of discipline. There wasn't anything fundamentally wicked about the boy at all, but he just liked to bedevil teachers and to disturb study hall, and nobody was going to make him behave himself, and he had really made it very difficult for the young teacher I had before that. So I explained to Major Bennett, when he came out, about Bob Law and that he was the seat of all our trouble in study hall. The major assured me he could handle it. And so the first morning he went in and called study hall to order, took his seat behind the table in the front, and began to read his book. Things were quiet for about five minutes, and then Bob Law brayed like a donkey. The major never looked up from his book. He just said, "Shut that up, Bob and don't do it again." Well, that kind of surprised people, that he didn't do more about it, but he didn't. In about five minutes Bob did it again. The major slowly, deliberately put his book down on the table, stepped upon the table, and jumped over two boys and landed on Bob Law, knocking him out of his desk and onto the floor. Then he took Bob and he just bumped his head up and down on the floor like a woodpecker. Then he picked him up and held him up in the air, slammed him down in his seat, went back behind the desk, and he took his book and went on reading. He never said one word, and no word was necessary. Bob Law was a good boy from then on, and so were all the rest.

One day during that year, I had arranged with the Indians in the Coachella Valley to put on a fire-eating ceremony. I had seen them eat fire down there before. And so I paid for this one, and they were to have a fire-eating ceremony for us, and I took the entire school down to spend the night and camp out. Well, the Indians sat in a kind of a ring and had a mesquite fire going in the middle of it, and the men and women and children were all sitting around the fire in the ring and they were singing an Indian chant. It was a monotone thing, but they sang it together, and they rocked back and forth in rhythm. And finally, when there were plenty of very red coals burned down, Ambrosia Castilla, the fire eater, got up. He was bare-footed and had rolled his trousers up to his knee. He stuck his foot into the fire and raked out some coals. He got one about as big as the first joint of your thumb, picked it up in his hand rather deliberately, and threw it into his mouth. By that time it was good and dark and you could just see the thing shining through his cheeks. And he'd come up and blow steam in everybody's face. When that one went out, he went over and picked up another one and threw it into his mouth, and then he'd go the rounds blowing steam in everybody's face. I don't know how in the world he did it or how he could stand it, but I'd seen him do it before, and the boys were amazed. After we got home, they were talking about it a good deal and Bob Law said he could do that. So they built him a fire, and he threw a coal into his mouth. And that boy couldn't eat for three weeks, he burnt his mouth so badly.

But that wasn't enough. After that, we began to find a great many of our glass tumblers from the table were broken, a chunk out of the side of it. One or two, we weren't surprised, but it got to be more than that. So some of the boys told us Bob Law was eating glass. When we investigated, we found that he would bite a side out of a glass and chew it up in his mouth and spit it out. But he ruined a good many glasses that way.

I used to let the boys practice shooting with their rifles. We, in fact, had two or three .22 rifles belonging to the school, which we would let them use. Well, one day Bob Law went up there with a rifle of his own. It was a .22 short, and never had been made to shoot .22 longs. Bob tried to put a long into it and it didn't seem to go, so he put the point down on his shoe, put the long in behind, and hit it with something to drive it in. Well, the bullet went off, went through his toe, and the brass cartridge went up by his nose and went through his hat; and it was quite a few days before Bob could walk on that foot again.

Mrs. Hilton's Views of Private Schools

In July of 1922 I arrived in Claremont, California, with my wife and three small sons, having contracted to purchase a deserted boarding school property in which to start the Webb School of California. The first day, I called at the office of Dr. Blaisdell, president of Pomona College. I was received by his secretary, Dr. Robert Bernard, and taken in to see Dr. Blaisdell. We had a pleasant talk, and he invited me to bring my wife to a reception he was giving to his faculty and the new faculty members that night. When we arrived he introduced us to his wife, and she in turn introduced us to Dr. and Mrs. Hilton. Dr. Hilton was the biology teacher. Mrs. Hilton asked me what department I would teach in. I told her that I was not teaching at Pomona College but starting a new private school in Claremont. She came back at once with the statement that she did not believe in private schools. I asked her if her husband was not teaching in Pomona College, a private college. I said we propose to teach grade 9 to 12, and her husband was teaching grade 13 to 17 in a private school.

Her remark gave me a great setback. I had never heard it before. In Tennessee, where I came from, I never had heard of anyone who did not believe in private schools. There were no public high schools except in the large cities, Nashville, Memphis, Chattanooga and Knoxville. Tennessee had not recovered from the Civil War, and people were too poor to carry much of a school tax before 1922.

People out here thought a private school was for delinquents or morons. Many people told me they did not believe in private schools. It took a long time to convince them that we proposed to conduct a school for first-class boys and to give them the best preparation for college. In time we overcame this and almost never hear it now. Some years ago we began receiving many more applications than we could take.

Introducing Himself at Stanford, 1925
from a letter to W.R. Webb, August 1, 1925

I have two boys who want to enter Stanford University next year. Stanford is rather particular in their choice of students as they cannot take more than about half that apply. I wrote them on behalf of these boys but received no encouragement. As they did not know me and had no past correspondence or acquaintance with me, I felt the best plan was for me to go to see them. [He and Vivian included a stop at Stanford in their 11-day tour of California scenic sites. See Letters to Parents, 1925, in Chapter 5 of Vol. 2.] At Palo Alto we had a nice bath and then went out and visited

Stanford University. This was Sunday afternoon and we took things quietly and looked over the entire plant. The next morning I had a nice interview with the registrar and his assistant in regard to our two boys.

Headmaster Review of the Past Year (1925-26)
from the Commencement number of the Blue and Gold, *June 11, 1926*

To review the progress of the school during the past year is an exceedingly difficult task for the distinct reason that we are not satisfied with its results, while at the same time we are pleased with its results. There are two distinct ways in which to view it. From one viewpoint, we see such improvements that might have been made. From the other viewpoint, we go back and review the past four years of the school, and in comparison the fourth year stands out so brilliant[ly].

The Honor Committee the past year has been a very energetic body. They have worked hard and faithfully and have done a great deal toward making life pleasanter in the school. I am confident that through their effort to maintain high standards of conduct on the part of the students, they have greatly improved the behavior of many of their fellow students. I am confident that by their principles and effort they have influenced students to choose a path of rectitude when they were wavering in the balance of uncertainty.

When we review that matter of the conduct of the student body during the past years, we see so little that was grossly wrong. We see much that could have been improved, and for that reason we are not satisfied, but we feel so thankful that, out of the 50 boys enrolled during the past year, we have had so little of major consequence. As headmaster, I feel that I owe a great debt of appreciation to this little group known as the Honor Committee for their splendid cooperation in fighting to maintain the fundamental virtues, and I thank them from the bottom of my heart.

In an athletic way, we felt very much pleased with the football team [It won its first game ever and ended with a record of 2-3 under Coach Glenn Vedder]. They worked very earnestly, and on the whole the results were very gratifying. There was a good spirit of sportsmanship shown throughout, an earnest effort to win on clean, fair play, but when defeat came it was borne bravely and in genuine spirit of sportsmanship.

We felt particularly proud of our gymkhana team, the first one we have ever sent away from the school to compete with another institution. We felt that this team covered themselves with glory in the fine way in which they fought and the fine spirit which they showed on the entire course. We felt that it was a distinct honor to the school to have met the Thacher School in competitive sport. The Thacher School was so gracious in their entertainment of our boys, and their praises and compliments for our team were a source of great satisfaction for me.

On the spring term, of course, we have been dreadfully torn up by the construction work that has been going forward on our athletic field. This has greatly hampered the athletics for the term, but it is such a big thing for the future. We shall have one of the finest athletic fields in the country when the complete plan is finished. We owe a great deal of appreciation to the men and women who have so generously made this field possible. This without a doubt will greatly advance athletics in this institution.

I remember that leveling of the athletic field across from my parents' home. A man came with horses that hauled a fresno, which is a large bucket scoop that the horses dragged to scoop up dirt and move it from high places to low places. — TW, JR.

3

Building the School
1926-1968

New Buildings at Webb

A.W. Brandt and Spanish Architecture

from "Webbs Remember Webb" by Paula Pitzer in The Webb Schools Alumni Bulletin, *1988-89, p. 14*

[Besides the family home,] three other buildings went up in the first decade: the Price house [in the fall and winter of 1927-28], the original gym (now the Hooper Student Center), and the office. All were designed by the same architect, or rather, by the same mining engineer, A.W. Brandt . . .Those three buildings, with their red tile roofs, establish a colonial note which carries through most of the school's architecture today.

Bill: Brandt was not an architect by training but had been a mining engineer who had spent most of his life in Mexico. He had a wonderful flair for Mexican type of architecture.

Jack: As I heard it, in finding an architect, Mother and Dad looked around at other buildings that had the character that they wanted in the office building, and it was while driving on Huntington Drive in San Marino that Mother looked over at a residence and said, "That's it. That's what we want. Stop the car, Tom." They went over and knocked on the door and a lady answered. Mother asked her, "Who is the architect of your house?" She said, "My husband is." They had stopped at the Brandts' residence. That is how he happened to become the architect of the school office and other buildings on campus.

from interview with Bill Webb at The Webb Schools in December, 1988

In talking to Dad some years after the office was built, he was smiling about it when recalling the deliberations over the plans. He needed an office to replace the one on the porch of the old dining hall that was no longer adequate. He and Mother planned continuously for the new structure. They sat down with Mr. Brandt. Dad said that he came to a stalemate with Mother, and he realized that the office would never be built if she continued to work with him on it. He finally was able to get a truce with her, and he alone did the final planning. She said, "All right, Thompson, go ahead anything you want." So he did it or as he said, "We would still be planning that office today."

Loan for New Gymnasium
from oral history, p. 72-75

TW: . . .Right away, with this larger group and this larger price [in 1925], I began to reduce my indebtedness pretty rapidly. Each year there was less interest and more principal to be paid. We got up to 1929; the Great Depression came and I didn't know how in the world we would get through. Nobody enrolled a boy until about two weeks before school opened; then they all came in and filled me up. And the next year [1930], they filled me up, and I went down to the bank, and I paid off the last of the indebtedness, everything I owed, principal and interest. I wish Father could have lived until

The newly built office building, early 1930s.

The front desk and reception area of the office.

Headmaster's office in the late 1930s.

then. I would have loved to have looked him in the eye and said, "Father, I paid every debt the day it was due, just like you brought me up."

I know that he would have said, "Son, how did you do it?"

Well, I would have said, "Father, you taught me to watch the time on the notes and I was always watching them, and when this one was coming due, I went over here and borrowed it and paid it when it was due, and then when this one was coming due, I went back and reversed it, and I did tightrope-walking for 19 years by watching the date. It's built me a credit."

Q: Could you tell me at the time when all the debts were paid off, how many people were you then enrolling in the school?

TW: I think about 60. Somewhere between 60 to 75. We did occasionally grow a little. Well, I wish I'd had enough sense to have stopped right there when I had it all, but the boys needled me for a gymnasium and they wanted me to build a gymnasium. They got out and begged their parents, and they got about $6,000 subscribed. They came and said they had this much and could they have a gymnasium. Talking with my builder, I knew he couldn't build a gymnasium for that. I thought, well, I'll try to do the best I can; the boys raised $6,000; I'll see how much I can raise.

So I went down to see Mr. Stone. I told Mr. Stone I wanted to build a gymnasium and I'd have to borrow money to do it, and I said, "Do you think you could finance me on it?"

"Well, how much money do you want, Mr. Webb?"

I said, "The size of that gymnasium depends on how much you can lend me." [laughter] I had hoped he'd maybe lend me $10,000.

Q: That would be, what, around 1931, '32?

The original gymnasium built in 1931.

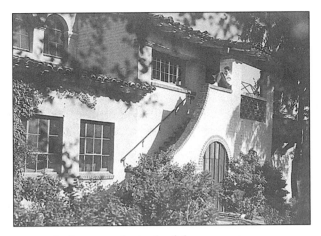

Stairway at the back of the gymnasium.

TW: I expect.

Q: You could build a sizable building for $10,000 in that period.

TW: He said, "Mr. Webb, you may have anything you want up to $50,000. Don't ask me for more than that."

I'd never given him security; he knew I had no security to give him. Well, you could have knocked me over with a feather; I just couldn't believe my ears. But that's what I'd accomplished, I'd built credit. [For contrast, see episode in "Shoestringing" when Stone would not lend him $1,000.] I knew years when he lent me up to $70,000 without security. When that dear old gentleman died, a man named Raymond Smith came in as president, and he used to let me have what I wanted. He insisted on me buying stock in that bank, and I said, "Raymond, you're lending me lots of money while I'm building these dormitories and buying land; I haven't any money to invest like that."

He said, "Here's some stock you can have for $1,800 and I want you to buy it, right here."

I said, "You know I don't have the money to do it."

"Here's a note, sign it, for $1,800."

He sort of just made me do it.

Well, I took it and the bank would pay its dividend, about enough to pay the interest on the note for a few years. Raymond Smith died and then

The campus in the mid-1930s. The gymnasium is the center of the photo with the three original buildings now partially hidden by trees above it and the office is to the left. Above the office is the garage and swimming pool and to the right are the Alamo, which is partially complete, and the stables, which had been moved from the left of the garage.

The campus in the late 1940s once the chapel was built, the Alamo was completed, and Quonset hut was placed next to the stables.

they sold the bank to the Bank of California and various shares [inaudible]. I think they gave me nine and then the Bank of California sold it out to the Western Bank Corporation. They gave me a lot more shares; out of that I got 1,330 shares in Western Bank Corporation. They pay me my $1,800 every year in dividends; that's what my banker did. Helps me to live now that I'm not on salary.

Jackson Library, 1937

Jackson Library
from oral history, p. 100-102

Q: Meanwhile, you had the library, your father-in-law's library [of ministerial books from 1923], but I wonder if you could tell me about the acquisition of that perfectly splendid library that you have. It's such a beautiful building.

TW: We had a boy named Tom Jackson ['30] here in school from Martha's Vineyard, Massachusetts. He was a delicate boy and had trouble with pneumonia in the wintertime. The doctors advised the parents to bring him west. So he came to us for four years, one of the sweetest, finest boys I ever knew and a great student. He went to Caltech. Before Christmas that first year, he dropped dead. [He had been out running a mile or so for a physical education class and dropped dead of a heart attack in the locker room.—JLW] It was a terrible upset to us and to his parents; he was an only child. His body was shipped back East and seven years had passed, no correspondence between me and his parents. Then one day, Mr. Jackson called me up from Pasadena, said, "We have come out to Pasadena and we are staying at the Vista del Arroyo Hotel. Will you and Mrs. Webb come and have lunch with us tomorrow?" We would. At that luncheon, he said, "Dr. Millikan brought us out here; he's begging us to put up a building in the name of Tom here at Caltech." He said, "We've listened to him and talked about it, but Tom didn't love Caltech, he loved Webb School where he was for four years." He said, "He hadn't been at Caltech long enough to love it. We've decided we'd rather give the building to Webb School than to Caltech." Dr. Millikan backed off.

We were delighted, but I told him that this school belongs to me; it isn't an institution. You don't get any tax reduction on it. He said, "I understand that, but we want to do the thing Tom would like. We think he'd like a library, and he would like it at Webb School, if you'll accept it. And we hope you would like our architect; we'd like to have Myron Hunt."

We said, "Well, he was the one we'd like to have; he built our home." And that was fine. So he called in Myron Hunt and we all had conferences about this library.

Dedication Ceremony for the Jackson Library
from the Blue and Gold, *1937, Vol. XII, No. 4 by a student reporter*

The Thomas Jackson Library was dedicated last Sunday with the most impressive program in the history of the school. Three speakers who were chosen because of their association with Thomas Jackson, in addition to Mr. Willard Jackson, Mr. Webb and Student Body President Harry Kirkpatrick '38, delivered brief but appropriate speeches to an audience of some 500 students, parents, and their guests.

Speaking for the Ojai Valley School, which Tom Jackson attended before coming to Webb, was Mr. Edward Yeomans. As one of Tom's classmates at Webb, Mr. [Hall] Martin ['30] spoke. Finally as a representative from the California Institute of Technology, where Tom went after graduating from Webb, was Dr. Robert A. Millikan.

Originally scheduled to take place on the grounds outside, the service was transferred to the library itself because of rain. The main floor was covered by at least 200 chairs, all filled, and the balcony overflowed with

The Thomas Jackson Library.

more people. The students, unable to find places elsewhere, sat in the aisles on the main floor, and even crowded onto the speaker's dais.

The program began at 3:45 when Mr. Webb made brief introductory remarks in which he expressed his sincere appreciation for the gift,

Interior of the Thomas Jackson Library shortly after its completion.

and gave a history of the library collection both here at Webb and at the Webb School in Tennessee.

Mr. Willard Jackson next presented the library to the school in the name of Mrs. Jackson and himself in memory of their son, Thomas Jackson. He said in the presentation that it was his desire to do something for the school which did so much for his son. The building was accepted by Student Body President Kirkpatrick, who expressed the appreciation of the students, present and future.

Mr. Yeomans gave the next speech. He told how the Ojai Valley School never had to use the ordinary educational methods with Tom. Thomas Jackson, he said, was an eager student, the kind any school could be proud of, the kind that never needed any urging.

In one of the most sincere and effective, as well as humorous speeches of the day, Mr. Martin, classmate of Tom and now a master at Webb, described Tom while he was here. Mr. Martin related several amusing and pointed anecdotes and told especially how Tom loved Webb and had faith in its growth.

The last speaker of the day was Dr. Millikan. He spoke impressively, emphasizing the importance of the written work throughout the ages, from the first time thought was recorded to our present time, then mentioning the greatness of such a gift as the Jackson Library.

Mr. and Mrs. Jackson next lighted for the first time the log in the fireplace. Then, as the Glee Club after singing Sibelius' *Dear Land of Home* stood in rank, and the entire assemblage stood up, Dr. John Darr gave the benediction. His prayer inspired reverence in everyone, and at its conclusion —with the burning log casting wavering shadows on the books—there was one respectful moment of silence.

Dedication Speech for The Jackson Library
from the Blue and Gold, *1937, Vol. XII, No. 4*

It was good of you to gather with us on this rainy day. It has been said, "Rejoice with those who rejoice." In that spirit I know you have come, and in gratitude to Mr. and Mrs. Jackson, and in loving memory of Thomas Jackson.

This is an occasion of joy and thanksgiving and dedication. To those of us on this campus this building is the realization of a dream of many years, going back 68 years. I shall give a little of the history and background of the library.

In my father's school is a great library. We boys were taught to use it and revere it. So often I have heard my father say that the greatest invention of all mankind was the 26 letters of the alphabet. He contended that they were of greater consequence to man than either fire or the wheel. He often told us that by the use of the alphabet we could associate with the greatest minds that lived—as it enabled us to reach out beyond our locality into every nook and corner of our world, and beyond our time, into the dim distance of history.

He said no invention was comparable to that. His library was the great center of his school. In 1870 when he founded his school in Tennessee, there were no buildings. He started it in a one-room basement under the church, but there he began to accumulate books. Later, the town raised a fund for the building of the school and turned it over to Father—a great sum in those days and in that location: $13,000. Not enough to provide adequate buildings and library but all the town of Bell Buckle, Tennessee, had to give. Father put $3,000 into the buildings and $10,000 into the books. Through the years thousands more went into books, and finally the school received a fireproof building in which to house them.

When we came here in 1922, there were three buildings. We desired at once a library and began to collect books. The first great gift to the school was that of books, over a thousand of them, the library of the Rev. Robert P. Howell, my wife's father. Mr. Howell was a great soul and a lover of books. He had a splendidly selected collection which he loved more than any other worldly possession. These books he gladly gave, and started this library. Since then we have continually added from our own funds and by gifts from a large number of friends. Some of these were large gifts. Our books grew beyond our space. Their surroundings were not entirely comfortable or conducive to reading, but the books circulated through the private rooms of the boys.

And then Mr. and Mrs. Willard Jackson came, and have brought us this building, in which to house our books. They selected a great architect to build it: Mr. Myron Hunt.

It adequately provides for our present and future needs. You will see that there is much room for a growing library. Downstairs you will find a large room that is intended to be used for a stack room. It will hold 30,000 volumes when the stacks are installed. We shall need much of that some day if our dreams continue to come true.

We intend that this shall be a great library and that our boys shall know how to use it and to love it, and by so doing we shall keep faith with Mr. and Mrs. Jackson.

This is a beautiful building and beautifully furnished. In fact, I did not see any library in my recent trip to famous American and English schools that could approach it in beauty and perfection nor one so adequate for the purpose for which it was built. I saw some larger buildings and many greater collections of books, such as the famous Eton Library in England, but I saw no building that pleased me so much as this.

I hope you will not feel that I am boasting. It is not in that spirit that I say these things, but most sincerely I am expressing my estimate of this library, and by so doing to express my thanks to Mr. and Mrs. Jackson and my respects to Mr. Hunt, the artist and architect, and to the Messrs. Stover, the contractors, and to all those workmen who have added their skills to complete so splendid a building.

I am so grateful to have it bear the name of Thomas Jackson. Tom stands in the minds of his teachers at Webb as representing the finest in boyhood, a splendid scholar and workman who never shunned a duty or obligation. He had a perfect sense of justice, a charming sense of humor, and the finest of sportsmanship. May I give you an illustration? He was a skillful horseman. In his last gymkhana he tied with another boy for first place. The tie was decided by a race between the two, in which Tom lost. He took it in fine cheer and not one of his companions—not even his parents—heard him say that the winner had a better horse.

This building on its opening day is not full of books but it is full of tradition, and love, and sacrifice, "good measure, pressed down, shaken together, running over." There could be no more appropriate tradition on this campus than the life of Thomas Jackson.

This is an occasion of joy and thanksgiving and dedication. This building is dedicated to the awakening of ambition, to the quickening of intellect, to the growth of wisdom, to association with the greatest minds of all history—in the name of one who lived abundantly.

We are grateful today to Mr. and Mrs. Jackson.

Book Storage on Campus
TW, JR.

Up until the Jackson Library building was built, Webb School had no official library. The R.P. Howell or Pop's library was placed on the shelf on a wall in Dad's original office on the porch of the dining room. As a small boy, I remember looking up at some of the six-inch thick books, which had statistics in them. Nobody ever took them down. They were just there for the book count needed for accreditation. There was also a bookcase at some later time in the recreation room of the dining room that had books in it. It was just a shelf full of old textbooks and other such that no one had thrown away. Books may also have been on a shelf or shelves in classroom number two in the schoolhouse. It was the least-used room for classes in the schoolhouse. Howell mentioned this place as the room originally used for storing books.

Uncle Ed [Price] became responsible for the library once the Jackson Library was built. He did work there and began to organize the books. The shelves were in the mezzanine and gradually these filled up. As I remember it, the library was always open. The school had no official librarian. Uncle Ed was the one to give it some organization.

A different view of the development and migration of the library comes from the December, 1988 interview of the four Webb brothers. Howell claimed that classroom number two in the old schoolhouse was the first location of the library. Later book storage was mainly either in the former office on the porch or in the Club Room. From there, the book collection was moved to the Jackson Library in 1937. Whatever the history of the library at Webb may be, TW did not make the book collection the center-piece of his school the way that his father had done in Bell Buckle in 1886.

Miss Pease (Mrs. Myron Hunt)

When I started out from Tennessee to come to California and build a school, a friend of mine told me that Mrs. Myron Hunt, who was one of the most distinguished educators in California and stood in the very top of society, could be a great help to me if I got acquainted with her. I came out and delivered a letter of introduction.

As a young woman, Mrs. Hunt, who at that time was Miss Pease, had started the Polytechnic Elementary School in Pasadena and made a great success of it. Mr. Myron Hunt, the great architect, lost his first wife, who left him three little sons. Mr. Hunt put them in Miss Pease's school, and in the course of time he married her.

Mrs. Hunt was a member of the board of the California Junior Republic with me, and her husband planned our home and our library here at the school. That way we had many connections.

Landscaping

The First Agave Plant at Webb
TW, JR., as told to TW III, December, 1997

In the summer of 1935 after school had closed for the academic year, Mother found out that a lot in Claremont south of the Pacific Electric and the Santa Fe tracks had been standing undeveloped until then. Some agave plants were growing there, and Mother had been told that anyone who cared to dig one up could have it. Mother suggested that Howell and I find some assistants, hitch a trailer to the car, and go down there to dig up the root of an agave. She wanted us to bring it up and plant it on the school

The original agave plant about to be moved up to the Webb campus in 1935 by Thompson Webb, JR., Vivian Webb, Bill Webb, Jack Webb, Howell Webb, and Josiah Sibley, JR., a first cousin.

property. We followed her instructions. We recruited several helpers. I think we had both Bill and Jack as well as Josiah Sibley, JR. '37. All of us went down with picks and shovels, and we dug around that century plant. It was a fully developed plant, but it hadn't put up its flower stalk or made any seeds. We dug and we dug and we dug. We had a deep trench all around the century plant, but it looked as though the tap root probably went down as far as China. There was just no digging it up.

After we had dug for a long time, exhausted ourselves, and blistered our hands in the effort, we had found no end to the root which just kept going on down into the center of the earth. I then hit upon the idea of using a length of cable that was in the car for towing purposes. We attached one end of the cable to the frame of the car behind one rear wheel and carried it around under the century plant and then back to the frame of the car under the other rear wheel. I then got in the car and put it in low gear and drove away, thus cutting the taproot and freeing up the bowl of that agave plant. We didn't know whether this would kill the plant or not, but we knew that we weren't going to get to the bottom of the tap root, and so we decided just to try it out. We put the plant into the trailer, and I drove it up to the school. In a spot along the road that parallels what is now the dormitory called the Alamo—it didn't exist at that time—we dug a pit for the agave under mother's direction. Then we put it in that pit and shoveled dirt in around it and gave it plenty of water.

It didn't die from the mistreatment. In fact, it apparently put down a new tap root, and several years later it put up a flower stalk and created agave seeds that fell on the ground near it. As time went on, other agave plants grew up in that community and later on they apparently were picked up and replanted around the chapel. There are now hundreds of agave plants around the Webb School campus. All of them are offspring of that original plant that I helped excavate in that vacant lot in Claremont.

Price Dining Hall, 1961

Our Motto: "Plain living and high thinking"

In 1961 Thomas Moore Price and his beloved wife, Alice, gave to our school a new dining room and kitchen. It is one of the finest dining rooms for its purpose I have ever seen. The kitchen is without doubt the best I have ever seen. There are many as beautiful and even more expensively equipped, but this one is so perfectly planned for the convenient maneuvering of each chef, baker, salad maker, garbage collector, delivery man and in rooms for storage and freezing that one can easily see that Tom was one of the world's great engineers. Alan Syple was the chief architect, but he and Tom knew when to get assistance for unusual technical items for which they brought in specialists.

The dedication of the Price Hall was a great occasion. A number of top officials of the Kaiser Company were here in honor of Tom. Many of the friends of our school and parents of the students were here. We seated and fed over 500 at one time.

Bob Reynolds, president of the Board of Trustees, presided. Tom made a beautiful presentation speech, one that touched me very deeply and brought tears to my eyes as he spoke of our long friendship at college and for 50 years since.

It fell to me to reply. I told Tom about our beginning, having a temporary arrangement to purchase this old deserted school property. The buildings were dilapidated and looked terrible in a field of desert brush, and I had no money to improve them until boys enrolled and we could earn the money. We started with only 14 boys.

I told him I remembered some of the lines of poetry our English Prof., Dr. Edwin Mims, at Carolina made us memorize. I knew he remembered them, too. One line by Wordsworth stuck out, "Plain living and high thinking." As I surveyed our dilapidated houses, I knew we were in for plain living. Therefore, when I put out my first catalog, I used "Plain living and high thinking" as a motto, and it has been in every catalog since. Then I turned to Tom and told him he had blown off the first half of our motto. All we had left was "high thinking."

The secretary who was taking notes later brought in her minutes. At that point she said, "All we had left was high living."

After the group broke up, Mrs. Willard Jackson, who had given the school our beautiful library, came to me and said she had enjoyed my reply to Tom, but she said she got a chuckle when I said Wordsworth wrote the line about plain living and high thinking, for that came from Emerson. I told her I had such a poor memory that I had been worried about that and had taken the precaution to go that morning to the Thomas Jackson Library, given by her to our school, and checked it. I was right, though Emerson may have used it, too.

Dedication of the Price Dining Hall in 1961: Alice and Tom Price,
Fred Hooper, Vivian Webb, Grace Hooper, and Thompson Webb.

Remarks of Tom Price at the Dedication, October 28, 1961
from the 1962 Webb School of California Alumni Bulletin, *p. 11*

Back in North Carolina, when I went away to the state university, my father gave me $100 and that was it. That was the most he could do. Now when you've got $100 to go to school on, things are pretty hard. My first

Students eating in the original dining room.

two years were very meager years. I didn't have many friends. But there was always one fellow who was always friendly and cordial to me, and that was Thompson Webb.

I want it to be known that my wife and I gave this building out of love for Thompson Webb. He is my real reason. I can't honestly say I did it for the students, for I don't know many of them. I didn't do it to save taxes, for honestly I don't make that much money. . . .

I think any boy who has come to this school is to be congratulated for having the opportunity to come under his influence and the example of his ideals.

Comments about Tom Price and The Dining Room
from letter to Mr. and Mrs. Walter Stokes, a board member of the Webb School at Bell Buckle and a former classmate, December 21, 1961

I expect Walter would remember Tom Price at Chapel Hill. He was in the class of 1912 and was about the poorest boy in the whole college. He became a civil engineer, and from the beginning of the Kaiser Company he was the head engineer of the great institution. He has had a wonderful record. I have seen a good deal of Tom in recent years, as they have a

$500,000,000 steel mill within about 20 miles of us. He has no sons, but he does have a lovely daughter. To our great surprise he came forward and stated, unsolicited, that he wanted to build our school a new dining room and kitchen. It came about one day when he dropped in and I invited him to lunch and had to ask a student to give him a place. He said, "You mean you haven't a single place in this dining room for a guest?" I told him that we were seating over 200 in there, and feeding them from a kitchen that was built to feed 50 and that there were some who couldn't get in. In a few days he called me and said that he and Alice were sending $250,000 for a new building. I enclosed some pictures I have taken of that building, which we have been using now for this past fall term. It will seat and serve over 400 people at a time, which gives us some elbow room for you and gives us ample room for expansion when dormitories are built to accommodate the boys. We could only take 152 boarders this year and had something over four or five hundred trying to get in above the quota we have set. Some of that group turned away were excellent students and interesting people.

Tom Price was a student at Chapel Hill when Dad was there. We did not know him or hear of him during the years when I was growing up in Claremont, but he appeared in the late 1930s when Kaiser set up a big plant in Fontana, California, within 20 miles of Claremont. According to the 1962 Webb School of California Alumni Bulletin, *p. 6, Tom Price "was vice president of the Kaiser Company, of Kaiser Engineers International, and of several Kaiser subsidiaries. One of the earliest associates of Henry J. Kaiser, he was the second oldest employee in length of service, and had major responsibilities for such projects as the Hoover Dam and a section of the Panama Canal locks project." Thomas M. Price served as a Webb School trustee and "died unexpectedly on Sept. 12, [1962] in his office at Kaiser Center, Oakland."—TW, JR.*

Tom Price
from interview with the four Webb brothers at The Webb Schools, December, 1988

Bill: Tom Price was a close friend of my father's at the University of North Carolina. He was the eldest of eight children. They were strapped financially. When Tom was at the University of North Carolina, he washed dishes to work his way through college and to send a little money home to help the family. He never had time for recreation. After finishing in engineering, he headed out west to Spokane, Washington, to look for employment. In the window of a photographic studio there, he saw a sign saying, "Engineer Wanted," and he went in to talk to the photographer, who was not an engineer. He said that there was a bridge that needed to be built, and he thought that he would bid on it if he could find an engineer. Tom joined him, and the photographer turned out to be Henry J. Kaiser. Tom was his first engineer, and he grew with the company and became a very wealthy man because of it.

When I was assistant headmaster here in the late '50s and early '60s, Tom was in our old dining hall visiting Dad, and it was very crowded. Some of the boys were seated at the headmaster's table. Tom mentioned to Dad that it seemed awfully crowded. Dad said, yes, he wished that he could build a dining hall, but they did not have the funds. A short time later, Tom Price called Dad and said that he wanted to build a new dining hall and kitchen for the school. As this lovely building was being designed by Alan Syple, we all worked very hard with Alan to make sure that it was going to accomplish the needs of the school now and possibly a larger school in the future.

Because I had worked in public relations before joining the Webb School faculty, I was gung-ho to get a lot of PR out of Tom Price's gift to the school. I talked to him hoping that he was going to say that his belief in the Webb School and his belief in independent secondary education and so forth had led to him to make his gift of $250,000 for this dining hall. Tom just looked me square in the eye and said, "That is not what I was doing." He said, "When I was a poor boy at the University of North Carolina, your father was the only person who took the time to be my friend. And that's the reason."

Jack: The dining hall was not Tom Price's only gift to this school. When Tom Price came to California, it was to help Kaiser build the Fontana steel mill. When that was dedicated [in the late 1930s], he invited our family to attend the dedication. I drove the car for Dad. While attending this event, I heard Henry Kaiser saying in the microphone, "Westward the course of empire." Of course, he not only established his empire as far west as Fontana but later went farther west across the sea to Hawaii. This was in advance of World War II and the great need that the country developed for landing craft and aircraft carriers. Tom Price was the host of the family at that occasion.

He and Dad saw each other occasionally, and he became aware of a need on the campus when he was here once. Down between [the Jackson Library] and the Chandler soccer field, there had been a deep crevice that had been Thompson Creek. The field, then recently acquired as part of the campus, had been leveled for use as a ball field. A bridge was needed to cross the creek and Tom Price thought that he could contribute the bridge. It is a flat steel bridge about as wide as this table is wide. It is now on the far eastern side of Chandler Field, [where the Thompson Creek has been diverted. It is still used, though rarely because it goes to a gate which is usually shut]. At the time that he donated it, it was on the west side, almost under where the Vivian Webb Dormitory is now. Once in place, it served as the way of getting to the Chandler Field then. Tom Price had already begun donating things to the school when he saw a need. The later dining hall gift was a major step up, however.

Bill: The bridge arrived on a big truck and trailer. Tom Price also hired a moveable crane because it was quite a heavy item. It had to be lifted in place by a large crane.

In a eulogy to Tom Price in 1962, Fred Hooper noted gratitude "for the following substantial gifts: the surfacing of the quarter-mile track and 220-yard straightaway; the bridge to the eastern athletic field; a large contribution to the building fund for Dormitory E, a contribution, in fact, which made possible the building of the dormitory; and, of course, the magnificent Price Dining Hall and kitchen." 1962 Webb School of California Alumni Bulletin, *p. 6.*

Vivian Webb at the entrance to the original dining room with the list of former Webb students who had been elected to Phi Beta Kappa in college.

The Old Dining Room and Pergola, 1961-1965
Gordon Webb '65

My first year at Webb in 1961 was the first year of the Price Dining Room and the last year that my grandfather was headmaster. I remember the old dining room as the assembly hall. We met there after breakfast on Wednesdays and Saturdays. On the other days we met in the chapel. We would have breakfast at 7, chapel or assembly at 8, and classes started about 8:30. Supposedly we were to clean our rooms before 8, but no one did this. For the days, when we were in the chapel, we sang hymns and had a Bible reading. Students would give talks two days each week, a master would talk one day, and the headmaster talked on the other day. When we met in the assembly hall, we would have announcements and a short talk (if so, it was not inspirational in tone as those in the chapel) or a discussion. The faculty sat in front and the students were in the audience. There were 200 students or so in the school then. The pergola was used by faculty members for meetings of clubs or meetings with groups of students.

*Vivian and Thompson Webb on the steps of the
original dining room in the 1960s.*

Replacing the Original "Upper" Dorm, 1959

Headmaster's Letter: Review of 1959
from the 1959 Webb School of California Alumni Bulletin, *p. 2*

As I look back over the last year, I think that I can say, with confidence and satisfaction, that it marked another stride toward our constant goal of first-class work done by first-class boys. Disciplinary problems were at a minimum, and interest and effort in all aspects of the school program at a maximum. To next year, I look ahead with mingled feelings: some trepidation at the magnitude of the problems to be met, and a certain exhilaration at progress being made to meet them.

As many of you already know, our major problems arose out of the fact that last spring the County Fire Department condemned 21 dormitory rooms, which left us with 143 firm enrollees for next year and 114 spaces in which to put them. A description of our plans for coping with this emergency will be found elsewhere in this *Bulletin*.

I wish to emphasize to you, however, that these plans were *not* hastily hatched to meet the crisis. They are plans which have been discussed and matured by the trustees over a period of four years, and are designed to put Webb on a permanent footing of new excellence. We are merely

Student studying in his dorm room in either the upper or lower dorm.

putting them into effect somewhat sooner and perhaps more vigorously than we had anticipated.

It is my hope and dream that Webb may be the pioneer in arousing those who contribute large sums to promote higher education to a realization of the fact that an unprepared student cannot profit by the finest university facilities. It seems absurd to me to allow a clever boy to dawdle through 12 years of school and then expect him to exert himself to the full upon entering college. And even if he does so exert himself, it will take him a year or more to overcome the handicap of deficient preparation, as any college administrator will confirm. Colleges and universities on the Pacific Coast receive annually tens, if not hundreds, of millions of dollars in grants and donations for buildings, for scholarships, for research, for faculty salaries, while I very much doubt if private secondary education in the same area averages as much as half a million a year.

The private schools on the Coast are all small and all are, comparatively speaking, young schools. They have no large body of alumni, and the great majority of their alumni are young men in no position to make large donations to their schools, much as they might like to do so. Inflation has made it impossible for the schools to furnish their own capital funds. Their only hope of obtaining these funds is to convince those who are able to furnish them that there is no point in erecting a top-heavy structure of higher education upon a weak and inadequate foundation of secondary—yes, and primary—preparation.

If you share my conviction that the private schools on the Pacific Coast are rendering a valuable service to the cause of true education and to the nation as a whole, and that that service has up to now received totally inadequate recognition, I ask you to do what you can to propagate that conviction among those who are in a position to do something about it.

Alan Syple and Frank Jameson '41
Bill Webb, from interview with the four Webb brothers, December, 1988

Frank Gard Jameson was in Jack's class of 1941. He had been very successful in business after World War II. He gave the first Alf-mobiles to the school for Peccary trips. He then wanted to give a dormitory, and it was completed in the early '60s. Frank made the gift after he heard that the fire department had condemned the upper dormitory and that students could no longer reside in that building. He also heard that the school did not have the funds to build the replacement. That is when he came through with his gift when it was a crisis. The old upper dorm was then used for study rooms for day students during the daytime.

The new dorm was designed by Alan Syple, who built the headmaster's home at the top of the campus. Dad and Mother had asked me to find an architect not only to design these new buildings but also to create a master plan for the campus. Doe and I investigated, and we had settled on two architects: George Vernon Russell of Pasadena, who had recently completed the master plan for the University of California at Riverside, and Alan Syple, who was an architect in Beverly Hills. He was just a superb architect. He designed our home, the headmaster's house; the Jameson Dormitory; and the Price Dining Hall.

Ray Alf, Paleontology, and
the Raymond M. Alf Museum

Paleontology at Webb
from oral history, p. 151-158

TW: Malcolm McKenna '48 got so interested in paleontology here on these trips with Mr. [Raymond M.] Alf; of course we don't teach paleontology, we just play it and go on trips. But he specialized in the field, got a Ph.D. degree, and became a professor at Berkeley. He then was called to be the head of the Department of Paleontology at the American Museum of Natural History in New York where he is now.

*Ray Alf (far right) in the fossil storage room of the Jackson Library with
(from left to right) Bob Warford '63, Steve Grauer '64, Steve Boyer '64,
Bruce Parks '63 (plaid shirt in the back), John Boyer '63, Peter Treadway '63 (in back),
Bob Mixon '63, Dave Procter '63, Jan Jansen '63, Bill Aanstad '63,
Craig MacClean '63, and Bill Schulze '63.*

Q: While we're talking about paleontology, I wonder if you would say some more about Mr. Alf. I believe the other day you told me that when he came to teach biology at Webb—and I understood that's what he first taught—

TW: That's what I hired him for.

Q:—he didn't know anything about geology or paleontology.

TW: That's right. [Alf was new to teaching when he joined the faculty in 1929 at the age of 24. His background was in mathematics and astronomy, but he was hired to teach biology.]

Q: Could you tell me something about how this interest developed and what it's meant to the school?

TW: Well, I had the habit of taking my boys on camping trips, especially my children at that time. [See "Camping on Weekends" in Chapter 5 on Running the School. TW seems to have confounded events here.] I promised my son Bill to take him on a certain weekend when the boys would be home, out on the desert, camping. Something important came up and I couldn't leave, and I had to tell Bill I couldn't go. Then he asked me if one of the teachers would take him, could he go. And I said he certainly could. So we asked Mr. Alf, and Alf was glad to take him. When they got out there on the desert, Bill was sliding down a mud bank and tore the seat out of his pants, and he got around to see what had snagged him and there was a tooth sticking out. He called Mr. Alf and they looked at that thing, and they got a chisel and something out of the car and chiseled out a head; they didn't know what they had. They brought it home, and Mr. Alf was curious enough, he took it over to Caltech to Dr. Stock, who was professor of paleontology. Dr. Stock told him it was the head of a peccary, the ancestor of the pigs, and that it was from the upper Miocene period. He said paleontologists had been hunting for 50 years for a peccary from the upper Miocene and never had one, one missing link. They had peccaries before and after and they never found one in California. This one's in California and is the missing link. Says this fossil's worth $10,000 and that excited Bill and Mr. Alf.

Mr. Alf began to read paleontology and got more and more excited and finally, when he'd been here about seven years, he took a year off and he went to the University of Colorado and stayed two summers and one whole year and got a master's degree in geology and paleontology. Since then, he's taken many trips to many universities for courses but never put them together to get his doctor's degree out of it. But he's become a famous paleontologist and he writes for the technical journals until everybody knows him in the technical field. [Alf actually was on leave for a year at Colorado starting in 1938. The first summer trip across the West to search for fossils was with Bill Webb and Art Clokey '39 in 1939. Later Alf was a Research Fellow in Vertebrate Paleontology at Harvard University in 1961-62. I tried (TWIII) to visit him there in January, 1962, but he was in the field with Malcolm McKenna.]

Ray Alf and seniors moving a slab of rock with tracks on it during the spring trip in 1961.

Q: I know that when I was chatting with Benedict Rich last Saturday night, he paid Mr. Alf a very high compliment. He said, "He's an amazing man." I wonder if you could tell me something about the trips, and about the museum which we looked at and which certainly impressed me. I've never seen anything like that. And his work, particularly in the

Grand Canyon, and his interest in tracks. I see that animal tracks seem to be the one thing that he's most interested in. Could you speak about that for a while?

TW: Well, when you said track, I thought you meant track meet.

Q: I mean animal tracks.

TW: This came from being on an Olympic team as the fastest 220 runner in America [laughter] and that's the way I got him. He was in the Los Angeles Athletic Club and I heard about him; he had to have a job. I went in and employed him. He was about 20, just graduated from Doane College. [Actually Alf was 24 and, though a championship sprinter who competed with and beat some Olympians, he never competed in the Olympic Games.]

Q: From where?

TW: Doane. It's up in [Crete,] Nebraska.

He came to teach this one thing he said he could teach, biology. Well, he had an amazing amount of curiosity and he never gives up, he [was] just hunting, hunting, hunting. He's taken the boys down into the Grand Canyon. I asked him the other day, "How many times have you been to the bottom of the Grand Canyon." And he said, "Probably eight times." And he wasn't a jackrabbit. [laughter] Well, he taught them geology according to the textbooks of the different geologic periods as you went down. It told him that according to the textbooks the bottom of the canyon was the oldest stone man had ever seen and was laid down a billion years before there was life. Every time he'd go down he'd peck around in it and see what he could find and he began to find some funny little circular things in the stone that was supposed to have been made by dripping water on mud. He got curious about them and he took them out and then took them to Berkeley and sawed them into fine sheets so that he could see through it. There were the organs of the jellyfish, revealing there'd been life in this world a billion years before the scientists knew it; and actually were mistaken about the age of that rock on the bottom of the canyon. He's upset the textbooks and they've got to settle that, just what it is.

Q: He has been, as I could see, interested in animal tracks, and I gather that he's traveled all over the western United States.

TW: They're going all the time all summer; he has six of these wagons, station wagons, four-wheel traction, great big things, you know, take about eight or nine boys each. He has a teacher drive them, the boys in there and he takes about 30 of them, older boys and they

Ray Alf in front of museum display.

camp for five weeks. They go through Utah and Colorado and South Dakota and Nebraska, Wyoming, wherever they can find fossils. They camp out, dig these things, bring them back, clean them and put them on display.

He's very much interested in tracks, got interested in the dinosaur tracks. He began to find these three-toed things in the mud where the animal had stepped and then occasionally he'd find one that looked, that was like the animal had left his foot. It was positive, it wasn't negative. He wondered if nature made casts, although at Seligman, Arizona, they had flagstones, mines, or quarries, whatever you call them. He went over there. He began to split these things, and here he'd find the negatives where a lizard or something had run through the mud. Then on the other side would be the positive print; just identical with this. That first layer of mud after it got the tracks in it hardened into stone, subsequently a new layer of mud ran over it and filled those little holes and made the positive print. He looks along now, he finds rows of negatives and positives showing that nature has through the years made casts of the tracks in the mud.

Q: Wonder if you could tell me a little of the background of how the new museum was built, where the wherewithal came for the science complex, too. I was most impressed by that area.

TW: Well, I had stated back some 12 or 15 years ago that we were going to turn the school over to a board, a nonprofit institution which could receive gifts, and we had gone into the organization of it. The attorneys were drawing up the papers for the incorporation, and Mr. Dwight Taylor, whose son had been the first, the Westinghouse [Prize winner in 1949; *see "Dwight Taylor" story in Chapter 6*], came out to see me and he said, "I'm very eager to contribute towards a museum for Ray Alf and I want it named for him. And I want to give you $10,000."

Q: I suppose it's because Mr. Alf had a great influence on his son.

TW: He had. He said, "In appreciation for what Mr. Alf has done for my son, I want to put up $10,000 and start a fund to build the Alf Museum and name it Alf Museum."

And I said, "Well, I'm hoping to be incorporated very shortly; better hold the check back until we're incorporated so you can get your reduction." So he did. So when we got it all in shape he sent the $10,000 and we put it in a building and loan, and I announced it and began to ask for money and I just didn't get responses. Occasionally somebody would give me $1,000, occasionally $5,000; and over a period of some years this built up to be about $75,000 and the trustees said, "Well, why don't we put up a Quonset hut and get the museum started."

Well, that didn't suit Alf and it didn't suit me; we wanted a good building. So we held back. Then this boy from Louisiana came out and gave us $50,000.

Q: How did that happen?

TW: He knew Alf well. He'd gone on all these camping trips with Alf when he was here in school; he'd go to every one they'd let him on on weekends and then he'd go every summer. He went the summer after his first year and after he'd graduated for that summer he went. So he gave us $50,000 and then George Getty '42 said, "Well, gee, we're getting enough

Raymond M. Alf Museum.

to do something now; I'll give you $100,000." Then others piled in and Millard Sheets said, "Well, I'll make the plans for the building as my gift, draw you the blueprints and everything, about $12,000 worth of work."

Q: Did Millard Sheets send his sons to Webb?

TW: Three of them. When we got through, the thing had cost nearly $400,000; we were short about $6,000 paying the last bill. George Getty said, "Well, my horse came in yesterday. I'll pay that." So it was paid up. And did I tell you about how we got the equipment?

Q: I wish you would.

TW: Well, George suggested that we send a list of equipment that each teacher wanted and he said to the teachers, "Now you put down everything you can think of that you want in your laboratory; don't leave out anything. Curtains and carpets and benches and chairs and microscopes and everything you want. Put it down and put a price list behind each item, and somebody will come along and say, 'I can give you this one,' and somebody'll come along, 'I'll give you that one.'" Well, Mr. Alf's list when tabulated ran over $45,000 with all the expensive microscopes he wanted and that kind of thing. Physics and chemistry each ran over $25,000. We sent them out and in the course of a very few weeks it had all been subscribed. Mr. Taylor, who gave the first $10,000, brought a check of $50,000 to Mr. Alf and told him he wanted him to have everything he could get, everything he wanted. Mr. [Charles B.] Thornton, known as Tex Thornton, contributed $25,000 for the physics laboratory, saying that unquestionably Webb had prepared his boy for Harvard and [he] had graduated the top of his class. Mr. McKenna gave $25,000 for chemistry and that's the way we got this handsome establishment. [The building opened for use in 1968.]

Q: That certainly is a fine building.

TW: Beautiful job.

Q: Beautiful job.

Prayer at Dedication Ceremony, November 3, 1968

from the 1968 Webb School of California Alumni Bulletin, *p. 16*

Our Father, we lift our hearts in joyous thanks to thee this day. We thank thee for the good people who shared their blessings to make this building possible, men and women who have given of their means, their arts, and their skills that the generation of students to come may grow in knowledge and understanding.

We thank thee for the dedicated teachers whose excellence through the years has inspired the gift of this great science center. May this school and its teachers, in the years ahead, hold close to their hearts the sacred obligation to grasp the opportunity that this affords to advance science and truth and the understanding of thy laws, that all mankind may advance towards the goal of the good life. Put the arms of thy love about us and bless us, everyone, on our way. Amen.

John Iversen, Ray Alf, and Bill Webb examining a fossil in the basement of the Jackson Library in about 1960.

Bill's Peccary Find

from The Webb Schools Alumni Bulletin, *1988-89, p. 30 (written by Paula Pitzer from a story told by Bill Webb in December, 1988)*

Bill Webb is the one responsible for the discovery of the peccary.

The peccary was discovered on the biology class fossil hunting trip in 1937 [actually November, 1936*], at the Barstow Syncline. After hours of hunting and digging, Bill became bored and started sliding down a gravelly hillside. His pants caught and ripped on something sharp, and upon investigating he found part of a jaw with tiny teeth. He dug and uncovered most of a small skull. Inside was what appeared to be a mold of a brain.

[Ray] Alf also became very excited, since this seemed unique. They brought the skull home and showed it to Dr. Chester Stock of Caltech, a world famous paleontologist. Stock confirmed that they indeed had a special find. However, it was not the mold of the brain that was important; it was the fact that this particular skull was a "type specimen." That is, it was the only one of its kind ever found, and it filled a gap in the train of evolution. Dr. Stock wrote a scientific paper on the skull and named it after his friend Dr. Childs Frick, *Deseohyus fricki*. Frick had been searching unsuccessfully for such a link for some time. What was it? An ancient peccary, ancestor of modern swine.

The discovery triggered Alf's desire to earn an M.A. in geology, with an emphasis in paleontology, which he accomplished the following year, and inspired the Summer Peccary Trips. The enormous collection of fossils which resulted from these trips led to the building of the Raymond M. Alf Museum.

According to the Progress Bulletin, *Pomona, California, June 19, 1937.*

4

Building the Chapel
1938-1955

Building the Chapel

Wish for a Chapel
from oral history, p. 78-79

Q: One other thing that I noticed when we visited the chapel, you talked about her [Vivian]—I think this was a joint effort—the study of the California missions and how all this preceded, really, the finishing of the chapel and how it had a big influence on its style and construction.

TW: Yes, we were very eager to have a chapel. We always required a little prayer service at the beginning of the day as my father did in his school and we required them all to go to church on Sunday, all students. In the beginning we had those services, first year at the Claremont Church. There was only one church; we could take them in our cars. After that the school was too big, and we would invite ministers here on Sunday and have it in our living room. Then later when the library was built, it was larger, we held it there. But we wanted a chapel very much. She and I had visited all of the missions of California and loved them; we thought that it would be a nice idea to have something of a mission. We knew that we would never have enough money to hire something to be built that would be as nice as

The Vivian Webb Chapel and Kimberly Tower.

we wanted, [and] concluded the only thing that we could do was to build it ourselves. We had a very artistic builder doing work for us around who helped us with the designs, taking this idea from that mission and another one here, there and yonder and putting it into blueprints. My wife was very much interested in that design. I built the chapel myself. With the help of some Mexicans, we made the adobe brick.

Chapel Measurements
Jack Webb, from the interview with the four Webb brothers, December, 1988

I was 15 or 16 when Dad began building the chapel. I had just gotten a permit to learn to drive and still needed adult supervision when driving. Dad wanted to go to San Juan Capistrano to measure the old adobe mission chapel there [called Father Junipero Serra's private chapel] and firm up the plans for his chapel. He got a tape measure, and I drove him. Once there, we walked over not to the newer chapel that had collapsed in an earthquake but to the old adobe. We paced off the length and tape-measured the width of the walls. Dad had me hold the tape measure at one end and he pulled it out to see how long a distance between the arches. Then he asked me how high those arches were. We guessed between us what to write down. Dad wrote out the measurements on paper to take to an architect who would sketch the first drawing for the chapel. That was in 1938, I think.

Building the Chapel 1
from an interview of TW made by two Webb students in January, 1972

I thought it would be fun to build a chapel. I heard of a way of making adobe with waterproofing. The old-fashioned buildings made with adobe were not waterproof, and water could melt them down. So they plastered most of them with waterproof plaster, but I didn't think I could deal with plaster. Somebody told me that Standard Oil had perfected a method of putting a little oil into the mix with the mud, and the adobe then would reject water. So I took it up with them by mail, and they invited me to come into Los Angeles to see some of the things they were doing. I visited

Thompson Webb turning the drying bricks on edge.

a house that had been in a flood. It was in a river bed where there had been a big flood that rose over the roof and ceilings of this one room house, but the adobe stood up. They said that they had made that out of the bricks with their oil. I saw two of the houses that they had made in that valley, and it was working. So then we decided to use it. One day Standard Oil sent a man out to show me how to mix it all. From then on, they did not pay any attention to me but to fill my orders. It is a special oil that they make. I do not know how they treat it, but they take oil and treat it with steam some way. They mix it up, it looks like a dark oil. You can pour it on the road anywhere, and it rejects the water.

I got a concrete mixer, and we found that we needed to put in a quart of oil to make a certain number of bricks. We put in the dirt and the sand before we started the thing a-whipping. We would then take our hose and start putting water in and kept putting water in until we got the mix just right. We would then put it in a wheelbarrow and go out and pour it into forms that we made out of wood in the shape of a brick. We placed the form on the ground. We shoveled the mud in and packed it down with our hands. When it got stiff enough to stand up, we would take the form off. If the mix was too thin, it would just run away, but I learned what the right mix was. We would leave them out in the sun, and the sun would dry them. Meanwhile, we would go back to the mixer and add some clay, some oil, and some sand, and take some water and mix again. We mixed it all until we got thousands of bricks. We made 60,000 bricks in the end.

Jack Webb digging with a pick and Thompson Webb working on the foundation and excavating the soil for the adobe bricks. The beginning of the rendering of dust to brick to chapel in the transformation of the hill.

Some of my first bricks, I hauled down and put in the fish pond. I left them in a whole year to see what the water would do to them. After they had been soaking in the water for a year, I took them out, wiped them off with a towel, and used my hammer to crack them open. They were just dry as a bone inside. The oil had kept the water out. So that convinced me that it was good stuff, and we made all the bricks that we wanted that way.

Q: Did you get the soil right here on the premises?

TW: Yes.

Q: Is it a good adobe soil or did you have to mix that emulsion? There's an emulsion that sometimes is mixed with it.

TW: We used that oil emulsion.

Q: Yes.

TW: Our soil was too rich in clay, so we had to bring in sand to mix with it, to thin it down. But we got the sand right here in the wash from our own campus and the clay from our own campus. Bought the oil and it took a team to work. . . . I had some Mexican laborers help me get the bricks made.—*from oral history, p. 80.*

We had some blueprints drawn up of what we wanted to build. We then had to get permission from the Building Department of the County of Los Angeles. While I waited, I staked out my foundations. [According to Bill

Webb, this was 1939 during his senior year at Webb.] We had already leveled the hill. We cut off the top and put the fill way down on the side to make a level spot. The brick and walls had to be on sound ground. Where we had scraped off the most in the middle of the chapel area, we were way down and right on ground rock, so to speak. So in the middle we just dug a little way down,

Diana Stimson, soon to be Thompson Webb, JR's wife, shovels dirt for the foundation.

[but] as we got out where the fills were, we had to dig all the way through that loose material. On this end on the front, the ditch was 12 feet deep. The same thing at the other end. It was only 2 feet deep in the middle where we had little loose dirt to go through. Moving that dirt [for the foundation] was hard work. A faculty wife would come and shovel a little while. A member of the faculty would come and shovel away before break-fast. Gradually we got this hole ready for this foundation that was to be built of cement. We went in with our plans to the county of Los Angeles to get permission to build, and they wouldn't let us build. It was crazy. I kept working at it and went in to see them, but I couldn't get a permit to do it. The ditches were wide open all around while we waited for the permit, so I could pour the concrete in. I was afraid the rains would come and melt down the sides, and we would have to dig out again.

Then one day a gentleman came by. He was a Dr. Milbank Johnson. He had been a very popular doctor over in Santa Monica and that part of the world, in Bel Air. He had gotten pretty old. This was a Saturday morning, and his wife was attending some lectures down here at the college. He had driven her out in the car. While she was at the lectures, he just came in here. He just wanted to see what this was. He had never heard of Webb School, but saw our sign. My wife was here. She talked to him. Then she said, "Would you like to meet my husband? He is up at the chapel there." So they came up there. She got in the car to show it to him, and they got out, and he got terribly interested in this adobe he was seeing. He knew all the old missions. Finally he said, "You better fill this all up before it rains." "Why," I said, "I can't get permission from the Building Department of Los Angeles County. They have not said that I couldn't build, but they won't let me go ahead." "Oh," he said, "you got some good blueprints on this?" I said, "Yes, we have had them drawn up." "Let me have them. I'll get your permit." That was Saturday afternoon. Monday morning at 9 o'clock, I got a phone call. They said, "Go ahead. [laughter] Pour your concrete before it rains." The old doctor was president of the Taxpayers Association made up of wealthy people who try to work the politics to keep the taxes down. Lots of people belonged to this organization.

We arranged with a cement company to sell us cement. It came in 50-pound sacks. We got a truckful of it and mixed it with our sand and gravel. We got our foundation all laid before the rains came. But we put a lot of steel [rods] in it. [inaudible] And then we had to put steel in a couple of

Thompson Webb laying a brick.

structures. The bricks were a foot wide. We put a row of them like that and another one like that. In between we put bars of steel and concrete. These walls served as a form for the purpose of pouring the concrete. We never bought any lumber to make the forms. We just put it inside there. We made some pretty tough walls there. Three feet thick, two feet of adobe like that, and a foot of concrete and steel. I don't think it is going to fall down very easily.

Occasionally people would come by: "Can I help you lay a brick?" Everyone in the school laid a brick. Every Saturday afternoon and Wednesday afternoon, I'd be up there laying a few bricks. In summertime I had more time. I had to stay here during the summer to meet people who came to talk about enrolling their boys. I found if I got out there early in the morning at 6:30 or 7, I could work to 11 o'clock before people began to come. Then I went down and dressed and went into my office. I had several summers of that plus all the Saturday and Wednesday afternoons. One Saturday, the Kiwanas Club I belong to down in Pomona all came up in a body. They all wanted to lay a brick. And so they did. They went up and laid a brick in the wall. One time the governor of Tennessee came out. He'd been to Father's school. We were old friends. He laid a brick. We kept on until we got those walls up there.

Then the question arose of those big timbers that go across—the cross beams. I was afraid if I got a lot of boys up there to help me to push them up, something might slip and kill a boy. I decided that I would get a man who was familiar with that kind of work. Over here at San Bernadino the Santa Fe Railroad has a workshop. They are all equipped to build trestles for railroads. When a big storm washes them out, this crew will go out there with lumber and whatever and rig up a bridge and get the train running. They weren't working the time I went there. So they let me have one of those bridgemen to work with me. He came out and got up on top. The wall is 3 feet wide. He walked along the top all the way down. Now he said, "I see that this building is 110 feet long. And I guess it's that long in the foundation, but how long is it up here?" We were 20 feet up in the air. I said, "I guess that it is 110 feet." "Haven't you ever measured it?" "Well," I

Work by the Santa Fe bridgemen who put the roof beams in place and then scalloped them with the adz.

said, "no I never measured it, but I did measure the foundation, and I got it right. I have just gone on building on top of it." "Well," he said, "a professional will be 2 to 3 inches off. You may be 2 to 3 feet off. There is no telling if you haven't measured it." "And," he said, "when we go to put in these cross beams, we want them to be exactly the same distance apart. Not take up all the slack in one spot. We want them to be evenly spaced. We will have to measure this." And he got out his tape, drove a nail in the corner right at the outer edge of the wall. He went down there 50 feet. "Now bring that down." We went on until he got through. He went down there on that first wall and looked at it. He said, "Well, I'll be damned." I said, "What's the matter?" [chuckling] "You ain't a quarter of an inch off." [laughter] He said, "No professional would be that perfect. How'd you do it if you didn't measure it?" "Well," I said, "you asked me if I had measured it. And I said, 'No.' You didn't ask me if I'd used a plumb bob on it. I'd used a plumb. . . . I used a plumb and always saw that the wall was plumb, and I knew that parallel lines never got any farther apart. If they are really parallel, they are equidistant all the way. I got that from teaching geometry." "Well," he said, "I never saw anything like this before." So we measured off places and drove in nails where each beam should sit. Then he got an adz, and we chopped up the beams to give them that rough look. They look pretty good. Then he put little rollers under each end of the thing [beam]. We had a sloping bridge, and we pulled some ropes across the way. Some of us would push it. We would get it up on the wall. Then he had a little bridge across, and he would run it across to the other side. He had the beam that way [pointing]. Then he put on some more rollers that went this way. And we moved these rollers so [the beam] could go in the right direction. When we came to the right place, he stopped them. Then we went and got another one. That is the way we got those beams up.

It took a good many years to build it. It was a lot of exercise and recreation. I had a lot of fun out of it. It has been a very useful building— a very happy building.

In a different telling, it was the building inspector who was up on the wall with TW when the measurements turned out to be so precise. The inspector was annoyed at finding nothing at fault and said, "If you did this for a living and did it all the time, you wouldn't be so gol damned careful." —JLW

Building the Chapel 2

from hand-written page with p. 7 at the top that must be part of a longer document

Monday morning before 9, I received a phone call to pour the concrete before the rain, and the permission would be in the mail that day. In a few days, the concrete foundations were all poured. I put heavy steel rods in the concrete.

From then on, I would take my exercise every Wednesday and Saturday afternoon laying brick instead of playing golf.

The 3-foot-wide walls with steel rods to reinforce the concrete that was poured between the two brick walls. The chapel was designed to withstand earthquakes.

The bricks were 12 inches x 18 inches x 4 inches. I laid two rows on the foundation, 12 inches wide, skipping 12 inches and another 12 inches wide. This made the wall 3 feet wide with an open space 12 inches wide in which I later put steel rods lengthway and at close intervals poured concrete. When I had built the walls all around six bricks high, double row, I put a heavy hog wire fencing 3 feet wide on top of the two rows of brick all the way around the building. This tied the two walls together with the hollow space between in which at intervals I poured concrete to keep the walls separate.

Horse in the Foundation Ditch

from Howell Webb's "Story of the Vivian Webb Chapel," given as a chapel talk in 1982

Before the wall could be started, foundations had to be dug—3 feet wide all around, 3 feet deep at the west end, and 12 feet deep at the east end where there was filled earth. In the year 1938, Dad dug it out with a pick and shovel and wheelbarrow—more exercise than golf ever provided, to be sure. There was more adventure in the excavation than might have been expected. One day he looked up from his work at the bottom of the 12-foot ditch to see a UFO approaching fast and on a low trajectory. There is an old cowboy song entitled "Ghost Riders in the Sky." This was it. The ghost horse teetered for a moment on the edge of the precipice and then somersaulted down at the retreating headmaster. In a fleeting glimpse he recognized the "ghost rider" as a Webb School student [Gerald Oppenheimer '40]. His horse had gone loco and was uncontrollable. The boy fell first and the horse on top of him into the ditch but upside down with all four hooves kicking hysterically. Dad crawled belly down to avoid the flying hooves and grasped the boy's arm. There was mud at the bottom, and Dad pulled out the frightened but incredibly undamaged rider. Oversized western style stirrups had jammed against the walls of the ditch and held the horse about one and a half feet above his prone rider.

A considerable excavation ultimately freed the steed, also undamaged. If he had broken a leg in his fall, he would probably have been shot and have become a part of the foundation. As it was . . . for his misconduct the horse was summarily expelled from Webb School without any counseling or being given probation or a second chance. The ditch was filled with steel rods and

The open foundation that was three feet across and up to 12 feet deep at the east end.

concrete to keep out any other flying horses, and incidentally to provide a firm foundation for the adobe walls which surround you here.

Tennessee Governor Lays the Cornerstone
from the Blue and Gold, *January 12, 1940*

Tennessee, Mr. Webb's native state, managed to produce a football team which was so adept at bone-bruising (football playing) that it defeated all of the eastern elevens that it opposed, and consequently, was invited by California to compete in our annual Rose Bowl classic at Pasadena. With that ensemble came Prentice Cooper, governor of Tennessee and graduate of the Webb School there.

On January 4, 1940, Governor Cooper, attended by a group of film notables and by his parents and a few friends, arrived at our own Webb School of California on our headmaster's invitation. The entire student body had awaited his coming with great expectations. The treasured hope was held that we would be excused from a class in order that we might derive the benefits of his presence.

At last the great moment came. The governor's father spoke first, informing us that he was "deeply honored to be here," and that he had always been extremely thankful for his preparatory school experience as a student at the Webb School of Tennessee.

Then, Mr. Webb arose and introduced the governor, naming him the chief executive of the state of California! Amid much laughing and clapping, Mr. Cooper arose and expressed his thankfulness for having been a graduate of a Webb school. He proceeded to point out how the moral training he had received there had aided him to follow the wisest path during his career as a statesman and a governor.

At his conclusion, he stressed the fact that to be successful, one must do what he knows is right, and that to go by the decisions of the crowd, regardless of the validity of the idea, is a serious mistake.

Despite the rain, the governor, Mr. Webb, and most of the students sped to the hill on which the chapel is being erected. There, amid the flashing of floodlights and the clicking of cameras, the visitor deftly placed a brick. It was a proud moment for the school, and that block of adobe holds an honored position in the erection of the chapel.

January 4 was a great day for Mr. Webb and the students, and we feel that it was also a happy one for Prentice Cooper.

Comments on Building the Chapel
TW III

During his 50s, my grandfather spent over six years building and supervising the building of the chapel. The work began in 1938 when he measured the old chapel that Father Junipero Serra worshipped in at San Juan Capistrano. William Brandt of Arcadia, California, a former mining engineer, and designer for other school buildings (see p. 82 in Chapter 3), drew up the plans. According to the logbook, my grandfather laid out the foundation and began clearing the ground on New Year's Day in 1939 (see p. 137). A *Los Angeles Times* article in August 6, 1940, says that "the educator broke ground for the foundations in January, 1939, [but] because of county building regulations and other factors was unable to begin laying bricks until January of this year." If so, then Prentice Cooper, the governor of Tennessee, was one of the first to lay a brick in the chapel. According to Jack Webb, Cooper's brick is near the base of the wall by the portico near the side doorway into the main chapel.

The plans called for the main building to be 18 feet high and the altar to be 24 feet tall, which would allow "sunlight to flood the pulpit," according the *Los Angeles Times* article. In 1940, my grandfather hoped to begin using the chapel for worship and school activities in the fall of 1943, and he seems to have been right on schedule because they held the 1943 graduation in the chapel after the roof was on but before the tile floor was in place (see p. 139). The portico was constructed in 1944 (see p. 135), but according to the *Los Angeles Times* article the original plans called for "archways leading down the hill to the campus to provide for a cloister similar to that at the Capistrano mission." This part of the plans was never completed but the bell tower was added in early 1950s and the chapel was dedicated in November, 1955 (see pp. 136-146).

Lumber Delivery
story of Vivian Webb's recollected by Jack Webb, March 15, 1998

Mother did not sleep as well as Dad, and one night at 2 or 3 a.m. she was awakened by the noise of a large truck in the driveway at Webb. Soon she heard the front doorbell, and she went to answer it. The truck driver greeted her saying, "Ma'm, I have a load of lumber that was ordered. Where do you want me to unload it?" She said for him to put it just at the base of the hill and that the boys would run it up to the chapel in the morning. The truck driver's answer was, "No boys are going to run this up any hill in the morning." He had the two-ton cross beams for the chapel ceiling.

The challenge then was how he was going to drive up to the chapel. He took a two rut road that wound up the west side of campus from Webb Canyon. It was not designed for a big rig like the one he had. At some point the truck had to leave the road and travel across the sloping chaparral hillside. The truck was able to do this after a slow painstaking climb up hill. The truck got up the hill but one lock released on the chains holding the lumber. At some point the other chain burst and some of the lumber came tumbling off. Ultimately the lumber and beams were placed on the earth at a location close to the chapel but above the roof of the chapel today.

The lumber itself was a gift from a father of two Webb students, Edward Middleton '39 and Richard Middleton '41. Middleton's father saw or heard about the building of the chapel and wrote Dad, "I want to give the lumber for the roof of the chapel. Please send me a copy of the blueprints." Thinking that Middleton did not understand the size of the chapel, Dad wrote back a brief description of the building and indicated that it was no small structure. But he did not send the blueprints. Middleton had to write back and ask again for the plans before they were sent. Nothing further was said about the matter until the truck showed up in the middle of the night.

Chapel Floor
from oral history, p. 83-85

Q: I wonder if you could put on tape a few remarks about the floor of the chapel as you explained it to me when we were up there the other day.

TW: We had made all of our adobe brick, but when it came to tile that had to be burned in kilns, we had no facilities. We bought our tile for the roof and then we got to the floor; we wanted tile there. I went in to Gladding McBean's, manufacturers of tile in Los Angeles, to pick out a tile. The war was on. They laughed at me and said they weren't making tile anymore, that they were doing things for the government in connection with the war. I asked if they didn't have some left over from before the war. No, it had all been sold.

Then he said, "I don't think you could find a tile in the United States, all over. We contacted all the tile companies for our big customers. "Oh," he said, "you could get one tile or two tiles or something like that from our scrap pile. Sometimes right at the end of a certain type of tile, we just throw away a few good ones to clean it up."

I asked to see the scrap pile, so we went out there and it was a huge pile, as big as the whole chapel we intended to build, just scrap and thrown out there for years. He said he wanted to get that moved and he would make me a great bargain if I'd buy the pile and guarantee to clean it up.

Q: The whole pile?

TW: The whole pile. I looked it over and I could see a lot of good tile in there, but you couldn't make a pattern, because you couldn't get any definite number of tile of a size; they were all mixed up. A great many broken things and seconds but there was some good tile in it. So we made a deal and I bought the pile and hired a truck company to move the whole thing out here in a corner of the campus. We sorted it out; all the good tile in sizes so we could count them. We knew just how many we had of this and how many of that and the useless things we threw off to the side. Then we took the drawing board, and we laid out a floor. The biggest tiles of all, there were just enough to go the length of the room, and we made that the middle row. Then we got other rows to match it when we got a certain number. We took the squarish tiles, and there mightn't be enough of any particular square, but there's lots of squares, and we put them under the spot where the pews would go. Didn't have enough to go the entire length, so we used a diamond-shaped tile as a crosswalk between the two doors and the middle, and we adapted those tiles in that way until we got this pretty fancy pattern of a floor. Hadn't occurred to me how beautiful it would be; but, after we got it in, got it waxed, we were so thankful we hadn't had it all one size tile. It's an interesting floor.

Q: I know I remarked that if you hadn't told me the story, I would have thought that it was purposeful.

TW: Guess everybody thought that was designed. [laughter]

Doors and Furnishings in the Chapel
from the diary in the chapel

[The] doors were made by Alec Miller and Frank Poole. Edward and Susan Price had given gifts for the doors with their names carved over the south middle doors. The north middle doors were named for Emma and Susanne McLean, who also gave gifts for the chapel. [The] pews were built of Honduras mahogany during the summers of 1947 and 1948. They were built by Percy Johnson and John R.C. Sumner under the direction of Alec Miller, who designed them. The pulpit was moved in on February 10, 1945, and was a gift of the Catalina Island School for Boys. It was made by E.E. List of Claremont out of Brazilian walnut. Bill Webb drew the

Alec Miller, the English sculptor, who made the chapel doors and designed the pews for the chapel.

design and made blueprints, using the design he had seen of a pulpit in

Guatemala. It was built by Alec Miller. [The] altar rail and lectern were installed May 27, 1945, and were planned to connect to the pulpit. Also hanging for the first time on the same day—a red velvet hanging of Flemish plush in two pieces, the valance embroidered with silver design. This was a gift of Mrs. John Treanor of Los Angeles, [who was Diana Stimson Webb's (TW, JR.'s wife) sister's mother-in-law]. It was then very old.

Obtaining the Wood for the Doors

from Howell Webb's "Story of the Vivian Webb Chapel," given as a chapel talk in 1982

It was wartime, and some of the materials were hard to come by. An elderly English sculptor named Alec Miller came to live at Webb and carved the doors by hand and the Latin inscriptions as well as the small wooden portraits of my parents on either side of the front door on the inside. They were placed there after their deaths. Alec Miller was particularly eager to build the great front doors out of seasoned walnut, but walnut was hard to find in those war years. My father found a man who had a supply of fine walnut but would not part with it for any money. Dad happened to mention this to the father of one of his students. In those days of the Battle of Britain, Scotland was no longer exporting its most famous product. The Webb father whose name escapes me had laid in a case of Scotch at the start of the war and was willing to contribute it to the cause. The walnut man was willing to trade. My father was a teetotaler all his life, but he was amused to think that his chapel doors were purchased with Scotch whisky. "God works in wondrous ways," he said with a twinkle in his eye.

Earthquake in 1971

from letter to Sigurd Andersen '41, February 19, 1971

We had a pretty shaky time here about a week ago, with that earthquake. It did tremendous damage in certain quarters in Los Angeles County, but as far as I know no particular damage was done in Claremont. We had a minute of very hard shaking, and why something wasn't hurt, I don't know. I ran to the chapel at first to see whether our adobe building would stand up, but I see no cracks or indications of damage having been done. The janitor said he saw the bells swinging in the tower. I didn't get there in time to see that, and they did not ring when he said they swung. The coyotes had a fit. All over the hills they began to sing in tremendous volume and woke people up, and then came the earthquake. They must have known something before we did; I don't know how they detected it. But in talking with the head of the Audubon Society in Claremont, who has now become a national official, he told me all the birds became excited before we knew there was an earthquake.

Construction of the arches and portico in 1944. A separate mold in wood was made for each arch as had been the practice at the California missions. That way no two arches are exactly the same.

Dedicating the Chapel and Tower

The first story summarizes what appears after it in this section which is the transcript of the talks given at the dedication ceremony on November 6, 1955. Each talk or prayer has its own subsection and title, and Fred Hooper's sounding the alarm appears in the place where he had to interrupt the first talk.

Reverend Little and the Burning Bushes
Paula Pitzer in The Webb Schools Alumni Bulletin, *1988-89, p. 53*

Thompson Webb began working on the Vivian Webb Chapel in 1938, and the first service held there was the graduation of 1943. [The first wedding held there was that of Thompson Webb's niece, Suzanne McLean, daughter of his sister Emma Webb McLean, to Robert Owen in 1947.] The original building did not have a tower. The tower was given in 1955 by Mrs. Mary Kimberly Shirk, who was a friend of Thompson Webb's on the Board of Trustees of Scripps College.

A dedication service for the tower was scheduled for November 6, 1955, a beautiful sunny day. Alumni, trustees, and friends of the school gathered from across Southern California. The chapel was filled to capacity, with students sitting outside in the cloister. Cars were parked on the hillside above the chapel, where the Longley House and the President's house are now located.

The service had begun when suddenly Fred Hooper came into the building and announced as calmly as he could that those with automobiles should go move them as quickly as possible because the hillside was on fire. Imagine the scene as trustees, faculty members, and students in their Sunday best rushed about, beating at the fire with shovels from the shop, taking the cars away, and helping with the fire hoses. Charles Scripps '37, then a trustee, was photographed holding a fire hose, and the picture ran in the national news.

After the fire was out, the crowd reassembled in the chapel. Taking the podium, the Rev. Ganse Little of the Pasadena Presbyterian Church began

Thompson Webb standing below the chapel in 1944.

to speak. "You will see in the program that the title of my sermon is 'The Place Where Thou Standest.' Those were God's words as he spoke to Moses from the burning bush!"

Words of Recognition
from the dedication service for the Vivian Webb Chapel and Kimberly Tower

I have tried very faithfully to keep a log book of the chapel on its construction. I tried to put down every incident worth remembering, the speakers at our services, the voluntary gifts that were made, the weddings, christenings, everything of significance. I might take a great deal of your time telling you of things of great interest that happened here. Today I can only touch on the highlights. I notice that on January 1st, 1939, I went out for my exercise and began grubbing the sagebrush off the top of the hill in order to see how clearly to stake out the foundations for the chapel. Fred Engel '41, a student in school at that time, from Guatemala, voluntarily joined me and helped me clear the space. You may see from that, that we

have been over 16 years
from the beginning to the
completion.

This morning I felt we
should be so thankful for
good weather on this
occasion when all our
friends were invited to
rejoice with us, and I know
that you have followed the
Scripture and come today to
rejoice with them that
rejoice. I am so happy to
have you here on this

Thompson Webb in the pulpit in December, 1943, when the chapel was first used for services. Photo by Bill Webb, then a photographer in the Navy.

occasion. It is primarily to do honor to Mrs. Shirk and Mrs. Paine, who made this tower possible, but in dedicating [the tower] I realized that we had not dedicated the chapel, [because we were] waiting until its completion, [which] that tower represents. And so today we dedicate both the chapel and the tower.

Before we held our first meeting, and after the roof was on, I then definitely decided upon the name and caused the name to be chiseled over the front door. All during those years, digging foundations, making brick, laying brick, I used to hope and pray that it would be so beautiful that I might name it for my wife, but I didn't intend to disgrace her with an old shack, and so I never voiced that idea until I saw the walls and the roof over it, and then I decided it was beautiful, and so I had Mr. Alec Miller, the English sculptor, instructed to put the name, Vivian Webb Chapel, over the building, and I told my sons about it. Someone said, "Well, certainly she deserves it," and I said, "Oh, there is no question about that. That's not why we did it. We have given it the most beautiful name we knew, made beautiful by the one who gave it to us." And so the boys got together and they said, "We think there should be an inscription inside of the chapel." And they also instructed Mr. Miller to make the inscription and place it in the chapel, and so that is how its name became the Vivian Webb Chapel.

I want to read you something from the first meeting. The roof was on and we decided to have commencement, though it was far from finished. That was a war year, and we had speeded up our work

Front half of interior of the Vivian Webb Chapel.

in order that those youngsters might get out and get into their military service, and so the first commencement held in this building was on May the first, 1943. The log book says: "The first public meeting held in the Vivian Webb Chapel was the graduation exercises of the class of 1943." The chapel was far from finished, but the roof was on, the glass in the windows, a cement subfloor was down, the walls were painted. The pictures, the chandelier, and the sconces were hung temporarily. A table was used for an altar, on which were that cross and candles.

. . . .

Mr. Hooper: Dr. Webb, I am sorry to interrupt, but there is a fire on the hill, and all these people who have cars parked on top of the hill should go up there and move them off just as fast as possible.
(A short recess followed when the cars were moved.)

. . . .

We didn't intend for the bonfire to start so soon. Continuing with the log, we find that chairs were used for pews. Outside there were no arches and cloister and no tower, though these were in the plans for the finished building.

The faculty and students assembled at the foot of the hill and marched up to the door and down the aisle to their places, led by the choir in red robes. The choir, faculty, Dr. Harland Hogue, and Mrs. Mary Kimberly Shirk, then acting president of Scripps College, took their places in the chancel. All remained standing while we sang the national anthem. The Scriptures were read by John Fleming of the senior class. We were then led in prayer by Mrs. Shirk, the first public prayer in this building. The valedictory address was given by John Reynolds of the senior class. The address was given by Dr. Hogue, his subject being "The Search for a Man." There was a violin duet played by one of our students, Ray Sanders '44, and his sister Betty. The diplomas were presented to the seniors bound in the usual Bibles.

A very beautiful and specially bound copy of the Bible was presented to the headmaster just before we marched into the chapel, to be the chapel Bible, as the gift of one of our students, Bobby Cook. During that winter and spring our boys had assisted in picking the oranges because there were no laborers to be had. Bobby picked more than anyone else and used his earnings to buy the Bible.

Following the graduation of 1943, Mr. and Mrs. Charles Skouras gave the great pipe organ to the chapel. I never imagined that we would have such a fine thing.

Following the late war, a memorial was carved in memory of our 20 former students who gave their lives for their country. The chapel was the appropriate place for it to be hung. You can see it at the back of the room.

The work progressed over a number of years. The tile had to be placed on the floor and the tile on the roof, the building of the arches and the roof over the cloister on the south, and everything was completed but the tower. We met difficulties with the Building Department of the county on the plans as originally sketched. Mr. Roland Coate, a great architect in Pasadena, asked if he might be allowed to take over the replanning of the tower as his gift to the school. The requirements were so rigid and required so much concrete and steel that the school could not afford to build the tower, and all construction stopped in 1949, awaiting the time when we should see our way clear to finish it. As you know, building costs have gone up rather than down. The school was a proprietary institution and could not ask for gifts. That situation has been remedied this summer, but before the changeover occurred, Mrs. Nathan Paine and Mrs. Elbert Shirk invited my wife and me to lunch and asked the privilege of providing the funds to build the tower. I wanted to name the tower for them, for one of them or both of them. They objected to that, but finally conceded that we might name it "Kimberly Tower" in memory of their father, and so you will find that name on the tower and also carved by the same Mr. Miller who did the carving over the door. We regret very much that an unhappy accident has prevented Mrs. Paine from being present here today, but Mrs. Shirk is here, and Mrs. Paine is being represented by her niece, Mrs. Lytle, and by Mr. Lytle.

Prayer of Dedication
written by Dr. Ganse Little and read by Donald Kerr, JR. on November 6, 1955

To Thee, O God, the refuge and the home of the children of men in all generations, we dedicate this chapel; that in it in days to come students and faculty, their families and their friends, may worship thee and meditate upon thy goodness and thy truth; that in it they may learn to know thee, the only

Chapel Interior.

true God and Jesus Christ whom thou has sent; that here in the gladness and the strength of life that now is, and in the hope of life that is to come, they may abound in love and helpfulness toward one another and in trust and submissions toward thee, the father of spirits and the saviour of souls.

To Thee, O God, the bringer of glad tidings through Jesus Christ, our Lord, we dedicate the tower of this chapel with its bells. Grant that as their voices call successive generations of boys to study, to meals, to recreation, and to rest, they may proclaim the presence and the grace of God in every experience and relationship of life, and when they call to worship, may hearts respond in faith and praise. Through Jesus Christ, our Lord. Amen.

Fire Announcements

made during the dedication service after the above prayer, November 6, 1955

TW: I want to make a statement to you about the fire. There is considerable brush on fire out there, but all the cars that were near it have been moved. I think those that are on our parking lot are perfectly safe, but any of you who are uneasy about it, feel free to leave.

Dr. Little: I can't help but feel myself that we'll all feel a lot happier during the rest of this service if we know what is going on. And I've got a car out there, too. I heard those fire engines coming, and I'm responsible for suggesting to Mr. Webb that I know a little about mass psychology, and I didn't think any of you were going to be very happy trying to listen to me when those fire engines were buzzing around outside. Let's have a 20-minute recess and go out and see what the fire is doing and then come back and worship God.

The Place Where Thou Standest

sermon by Dr. Ganse Little to dedicate the chapel, November 6, 1955

I bet the boys will not forget this one. Particularly will they not forget it when, according to the irony of fate or the providence of God, the text I have chosen for my brief remarks in this dedicatory hour are the words of God to Moses out of the burning bush. Believe it or not, this is one for Robert J. Ripley.

The place where thou standest is holy ground. It comes completely equipped with a ready-made fire.

The place where we are at this present moment is holy ground, not because it is a so-called house of God. Every place where man, made in the image of God and called into conscious existence in the world, stands is holy ground.

I don't know how many of you have already seen a very interesting article in the very last issue of *Life* magazine. The article, with some scientific background and a little bit of understandable speculation, takes us back to the dim distant past when some higher order of animal first stood upon his two legs and walked. But man made in the image of God does more than simply stand and walk. He stands on holy ground because he is made in the image of God. He is called of God into a set of relationships which he cannot escape and did not ask for. He is called upon to endure experiences often painful, often frustrating. He is called upon to make his own mistakes and to know the bitter sting of failure. Eventually, he is called upon to die to this life and to all the things of this world. And in every one of these experiences and relationships, God is present.

That does not mean that everything that happens to us in life is according to the will of God. This brush fire, for instance, did not happen because God Almighty said, "Well, on Sunday the first Sunday in November in the year of our Lord 1955, November 6th, at whatever o'clock in the afternoon it was, there is going to be a brush fire up near the new chapel at the Webb School." I don't believe that for a moment.

I do believe that the first boy that came tearing up here with his wits about him and grabbed this fire extinguisher off the wall and dashed out there and prevented it from being a much worse conflagration than it was, I do believe that he is made in the image of God. And that the insight and the understanding and the courage and the intuitive reaction which made him do the right thing at the right time was part and parcel of the image of God in him. He may be just a kid standing up there on the brow of the hill with a fire extinguisher in his hand doing it all by himself until the fire department comes. The place where he is standing is holy ground. That's the difference between a man and an animal—one of them.

We are in holy ground right now, not because we are in the house of God, but because we are made in the image of God. But we need to come together at times to remind ourselves that this is so. Don't you see, that's the reason for a church and a chapel. It is a means to an end. It isn't an end in itself. I was the one who selected the brief Scriptural passage which was read as our Scripture reading a few moments ago. It was the prayer of Solomon when that magnificently beautiful temple in the Old Testament days was completed. And Solomon was wise enough to know that God wasn't going to be present in that temple any more specifically or particularly than He was going to be present in any other area of life. But men and women need to come together into a house of God in order to remind themselves that God is everywhere in life, because we don't find that out unless we give ourselves to it, unless we remind ourselves of it.

When Moses saw the burning bush in the wilderness of Sinai, he was having an experience of God, not in a chapel built with hands but in the house of God, built by God himself, that which we call nature. God can be found in nature. But God is not apt to be found in nature, except by the man who goes to church over and over again in order that he may there be reminded that God is in nature. I have heard a lot of fellows tell me in the course of my ministry that they could worship God just as well in nature as they can in church. The only answer to that is that I don't believe it. And that doesn't mean that I am against golf on Sunday morning, but I just don't believe that you necessarily find God in every sandtrap no matter how much Old Testament language you may be using with your lips.

Moses recognized God in the burning bush because Moses came out of a kind of family where he had been reared in a tradition that convinced him that God is in human life. Prehistoric man didn't sense God in nature. This is imparted, this is revealed, this it taught, this is exemplified, and that is the reason we have churches and Christian schools and a program of Christian education, that the next generation may grow up to remember that God is everywhere in human life.

Moses was also enduring a very frustrating experience when he found God in that burning bush. You remember he started out throwing his weight around in the land of Egypt. He was going to do great big things. He was going to liberate his people, take them out of the house of slavery where they had suffered for 470 years. And here he was in the back eddy of life. He had drawn his sword and killed an Egyptian and had to flee from the court of Pharaoh and his royal patrons for his very life. Here he had been in the wilderness of Sinai for years, of all things herding sheep, and of all things working for his father-in-law, which is not necessarily a happy experience either, though there is no reason why it can't be. The point is that Moses was in a period of frustration (what is ahead of him?) and at that very moment God revealed himself to Moses, "The place where thou standest is holy ground."

There isn't one of these boys who will attend services in this chapel from time to time that before they are grown to adult manhood and finally finished their earthly pilgrimage that is not going to stand in the presence of God . . . .

(The sermon is incomplete because the tape recorder ran out of tape and Dr. Little did not have a written copy.) [This note was part of the original transcription of this sermon.]

Memories of the Dedication

from interview with the four Webb brothers at The Webb Schools in December, 1988

Bill: Mrs. Shirk of Redlands and her sister gave the money for the tower on the chapel. It was a beautiful addition to the chapel and quite expensive at that time. The occasion for its dedication was very important to the school, and guests came from all over Southern California for the occasion. So many cars arrived that the brush hillside above the chapel was used for parking. (The headmaster's house and others houses are located there now.) During the service Mr. Hooper came running into the chapel and shouted that there was a fire. My friend, Charles Scripps '37, and his wife were attending the service with Doe and me, and we all ran out to see the hillside in flames where all the cars were parked. We ran up there, and I vividly remember seeing the front of a Cadillac on which the plastic linings around the headlights were just balls of fire.

Howell: All of those cars were driven out, and not one had been destroyed. Quite a few had the paint on the front fenders blistered, however. A lot of cars had to have paint jobs, but little more had to be done. But they were pulled out in dense smoke.

Bill: It took some time for the fire engines to arrive. We tried to beat back the fire with shovels and various things until the engines arrived. Faculty, students, and guests then helped the firemen by carrying and holding hoses. I believe that Charles Scripps was photographed holding a fire hose in his good suit, and I know that I ruined a good suit in that fire. When it was under control, we all went back into the chapel. Dr. Ganse Little, the minister from the Hollywood Presbyterian Church, revived the audience with his wonderful remarks by turning to the Bible and reading from the section where God was speaking to Moses from the burning bush. [laughter] That story got on the wire services and appeared in newspapers all across the country.

Howell: There was reason for that publicity because Charles Scripps was from a newspaper family. When Ganse Little started to speak after the fire was put out, he said, "Nobody is going to believe my next statement, but I prepared this sermon in advance and took as my text the voice from the burning bush." [laughter]

Jack: At least it wasn't the voice from the burning Cadillac.

Beliefs and Use of the Chapel

Methodist Church

from tape interview of TW by TW III on March 16, 1973 in Claremont, California

We have a Methodist Church, and I go to that. We were all Methodists in Bell Buckle. And I married a Methodist, so Vivian and I went to the Methodist Church. When we first came here, there was only one church in town, and that was the Congregational Church. We'd frequently go to the service. We had our membership in the Methodist Church in Pomona. [The church in Pomona had been built by a Methodist minister and missionary named Eldridge Knott, who had gone to Webb School in Bell Buckle and whose mother ran a boarding house for school boys there. Knott's son Walter developed and ran Knott's Berry Farm.]

Comment on Beliefs and Prayer

V[ivian] and I built this school to teach children the finest qualities of character above everything else, then the desire for learning and excellent scholarship. We built this chapel as a proper place for the teaching of the virtues that represent the finest character, honesty, dependability, trustworthiness, strength to do one's duty, courage to uphold the right and fight for it. To acquire these virtues, we must continually keep them in mind and work for them. We felt that everyone should always hold before them a longing for these virtues, and the best way to acquire them was through prayer. We have always believed and felt that there is a great spirit that hears and in his way helps. If you have doubts about a god who hears you, rehearse your prayer to yourself and maybe you will help yourself to answer your prayers.

From hand-written notes on a sheet of yellow paper from among the papers in the folder "Father's and other early stories" of Thompson Webb. It is neither but rather a misfiled piece from a chapel talk in the 1950s (?) or later.

Philosophy on Use of Chapel and Prayer
from an interview of TW made by two Webb students in January, 1972

Now to me the chapel is what I call a classroom. It is a sanctuary for meditation and prayer, not connected with any church. The school is not connected with any church, and the chapel is not a church. Some people call it a church, but it isn't a church at all. It is a place for meditation and prayer. I wanted a place where we would meet every morning, say for 15 minutes, and try to emphasize some of the great virtues that everybody should have. I didn't try to convert anybody. I didn't want to take a Catholic or a Jew and make him a Protestant. I am glad if someone belongs to a church. That is a sign of good character. But it doesn't make any difference to me which church or religion it is. I just think that every day each person ought to pray about the great virtues and the themes they want a child to have: honesty and the strength of character to do the right. Those are the virtues, and we pray for them. If those virtues are engrained in a boy, he will grow up to be a man.

There was one lady who said to me, "Why do you do that? Why do you go through that prayer? You know there is no God. Nobody listens." I said, "How do you know nobody listens? [chuckle] I don't really know, but I want your son to pray." "Why?" "I want him to mention to himself every day these virtues that he wants to get. If he doesn't talk about them, and he doesn't practice them, he won't be a father. But if he keeps praying, it will give him strength to tell the truth, to do the honest thing, the unselfish thing. It becomes part of him as he grows, as he becomes a man." It must be rehearsed. In my mind, the chapel service is a place to rehearse the virtues that we want to obtain. We get everybody together for just a few minutes and talk about those and tell about heroes. That is the purpose of the chapel in my mind. One thing that we want to teach in our school is this quality of integrity and honesty. That is how we teach honest men and good men, and then they do their schoolwork so they will be smart enough. That's our original plan for our school.

A funny thing about that lady. She said, "I don't believe in prayer. Nobody hears that." I said to her, "Well, I may disagree with you, but I am not going to argue that with you. I want your boy to pray every day just to remind himself about honesty and the other important virtues. He can accomplish a good deal even if the Lord does not hear him. He is talking to himself, and he'll be a better man for it. It is very important. He will memorize things and say them over and over again."

I noticed that some months later this lady, her husband, and their two sons joined the Episcopal Church [chuckle], which is almost the Catholic Church. I don't know if my talk had anything to do with it. They certainly did change their ways. Their two boys went through our school. Both she and her husband are dead now. Those were two fine boys.

Confession and Prayer
from the ending of a chapel talk given in May, 1959

I make my failures and do things that are wrong every day. But thank God that we can go to Him in prayer and ask forgiveness and start all over again every day and a hundred times a day. If we are only frank enough to admit to ourselves that we made a mistake, that we did not quite tell the truth about this thing—maybe the actual words that we said were true but the spirit wasn't, that we didn't use wisdom, that we didn't use our resources, that we wasted time, we can ask forgiveness, we can ask for strength. We have the promise that if we go on and never get weary but keep striving, we shall reach, even if we think we won't.

Let us pray. Eternal and unchangeable God, in whom alone we find rest for our weariness and comfort for our sorrow, and from whom alone cometh all true joy we keep in our hearts, we beseech thee to keep us ever fixed on thee through life and death, waiting patiently for that glorious day when we shall rejoice in the fullness of thy love forevermore. In Jesus Christ, our Lord. Amen.

An Ecumenical Outlook

from a talk by Jack Webb given in the Vivan Webb Chapel, December, 1988

Here at Webb School of California one of Mother's and Dad's goals was to focus attention on the great values in religions, and particularly on the values that religions have in common. They looked out at a world of religious diversity and in that diversity they rejoiced. For Mother, Native American cultures pulled like a magnet. Two summer vacations, Mother and Dad devoted to field work in New Mexico learning all they could about American Indian culture. Here at school, students heard from Protestants, Catholics, rabbis, priests, professors. If it had seemed reasonable to arrange for a Hopi shaman or ritual dancers to conduct a kiva service here, I believe that our parents would have made the overture. Their outlook was Ecumenical with a capital E. A conviction that our parents shared was that no matter what our religious commitments, it is essential to keep some degree of an open mind, some receptivity to new thinking.

Dad told with great respect about his father's response to a famous court trial in Tennessee in 1925 [one year before Sawney Webb died]. It was the Scopes Trial . . . . Under questioning [at that trial, William Jennings] Bryan admitted that he was an expert on the Bible. In the meantime over at Bell Buckle, many people there thought they had their own expert on the Bible. They wanted to know what Old Sawney thought about the furor at Dayton. Old Sawney declined to take sides until he could secure a better understanding of Darwin's information and interpretation. He bought Darwin's books, *The Origin of Species, The Descent of Man*, and several books by others about evolution. Then he went into a kind of reading hibernation in his study. Many perhaps assumed that Old Sawney would side with William Jennings Bryan. . . . Well, if that is what some thought, they again were in for some surprise. When Old Sawney had read those books, he made one of the humblest comments of his life. He remarked, "If what Darwin says is right, then nearly everything that I have ever thought in my whole life is wrong, but I think now that he probably is right." To Dad, Old Sawney's willingness to stretch his thought and his frame of reference even in advanced years was a valuable trait, one to emulate. An open mind, the power to adapt. Dad and Mother both believed in holding on to the best of the old, but also in making room for the best of the new.

Bible Reading by Seniors
from oral history, p. 126

Q: Did you here at Webb, as was done at Midland [Paul Squibb's school—Paul taught at Webb for eight years until the early 1930s], ask the seniors, or should I put it this way, require the seniors to read from the Bible in chapel services in rotation?

TW: No, I invited them to, and anyone who didn't want to didn't have to. Most of them did.

Ringing the Changes

Signals for the Daily School Schedule
from interview with the four Webb brothers at The Webb Schools, December, 1988

Bill: The siren [which was sounded daily in the '20s, see story at the end of Chapter 2] was then traded to the town of Claremont's fire department for their fire bell. That bell was then hung up here. It was hung over the kitchen and presented a problem at the end of each class period. Someone would have to be sent over to the kitchen to ring the bell. Then the electric bell ringer was installed. A button could then be pressed in the study hall room and the bell would ring for 6:30, 6:55, and for 7:00 and for the changes in classes. Later a bell that Dad had bought from the scrap heap went to the Alamo. The old fire bell was left in the kitchen. Many years later when I had become headmaster at the Dunn School, the old dining hall and kitchen at Webb was torn down [in the mid 1960s], and the original Claremont fire bell was given to the Dunn School and it is ringing there today.

Howell: The first real bell was hung in the Alamo. That was the school bell until the chapel was finished with the construction of the tower. Some really big bells were hung there that Dad had acquired from the Hearst's

Vivian Webb Chapel in the 1950s.

collection in San Jacinto when those were put up for sale. Those are the bells that ring today.

Jack: On the subject of sound effects on the Webb campus, this discussion of bells reminds me that particularly for use during vacations when the boys were away and the bells weren't ringing, there needed to be some signal from Mother to summon Dad to the telephone. He was often out on campus somewhere working with men, or she would need to signal us kids when it was time for lunch. We could get lost as far as Mother was concerned. On top of Mother's and Dad's house, up on top of some shingles, they installed an old Model-A auto horn that sounded "ahugga, ahugga." It was sounded by a button in the hallway next to the telephone. The code was: two long blasts on that horn was a signal for Bill and me to come on in, perhaps for a meal at the house. A continuous long number of blasts was a signal to Dad that a phone call was waiting for him. That would imply more of a rush.

The Chapel Bells

Before I started building our chapel I knew that I would need a bell, and one day, in going to Los Angeles in a roundabout way, I saw a tremendous pile of scrap iron and a huge crane that was loading trucks with the scrap. Up on the top of the pile, I spotted a big bell and went in and asked if that bell was for sale. The man handling the big crane said, "Well, we contracted all this scrap to the Japanese government and they're loading out a ship now." I asked him if he'd weighed it out to them, or could he weigh it to me. He said I could have it if I'd give him what those Japanese were paying, which he said was 8 cents a pound. I said I'd take it if there was no crack in it. He had the crane pick it up and bring it to me and give me a hammer and let me hit it. It had a beautiful tone.

I asked him to send it to me c.o.d. Then he told me he had several other bells and I told him I'd take them all if they weren't cracked. Finally, four or five bells were delivered to me. He said that they wrecked buildings and they always got all the scrap material from that. I asked him if a bell was scrap. "Oh yes. Anything metal on the building we keep and sell separately."

Two or three years later I started the work on the chapel at our school, copying a California mission, largely. It was quite a few years before I got the tower up. There were four large openings for bells and above that there were four small openings in the tower. I wanted to be able to run the school by the bells and found that I could get an electrical ringer in Los Angeles that we could control with a button in the office and also by a tape set to ring the different periods. We bought that ringer, and the man said that he would have to install it as it was a little different from the usual things that electricians did. When he came out and saw the bell he said it was a Meany Bell. I asked him what that was. He said that was the finest brand of bell ever made in America and there was quite a price on them. He said that he sold bells and he had an order for a Meany Bell and would like to buy it from me. I asked him what he'd give me for it, and he said $2,500. I assured him I'd have never bought it if it had cost that and that it was sold to me at 8 cents a pound which came to about $112, but that I wasn't about to sell it! So for many years that bell has rung the program at Webb School.

I had three more bells to go in the larger windows, but nothing that would fit in the smaller windows above the large ones. Shortly after we had our bells going Mrs. Shannon, Mrs. Richard Armour, and Mrs. Doheny of Los Angeles told me that they wanted to supply the small bells, if I could find some. I told them I knew where there were some, but I hadn't had the money to get them—that I'd seen them in Mr. Hearst's collection in his warehouse at the bottom of the hill on which stood his castle. Since he had died, I understood they were for sale. I'd been told that Fred Harvey, in the early days of the Santa Fe Railroad, had put up trading posts with the Indians of the west and that these Indians did occasionally bring in an old mission bell which he would buy and when he got his collection, he sold it to Mr. Hearst.

So these wonderful ladies bought four of those mission bells and hung them in the top of our chapel tower.

5

Running the School
1922-1962

The Partnership

There were no articles of incorporation in their partnership, only the marriage certificate. But that was all that was necessary. If there was ever a partnership, in every sense of the word, it was the one formed by Thompson Webb and Vivian: a partnership in the Webb home and in the Webb School.

Richard Armour, in Vol. 22, p. 20,
Webb School of California Alumni Bulletin, 1974-76

Vivian's Role
from oral history, p. 6-8

Q: You would certainly have a great deal to say about the contributions of your wife. So I wondered this morning if you could for just a minute or so detail some of these contributions of your wife.

TW: Well, my wife had taken postgraduate courses at the University of California in Los Angeles when it was known as [the Los Angeles State] Normal School. She has a teacher's certificate, the only one in the whole school that I ever knew of [who] had a California teacher's certificate; I didn't, but she did. But anyhow, we came out here with this lease to start

Thompson and Vivian Webb
in 1943 in the office.

this school and we started out with 14 boys, scattered over the curriculum. I taught eight classes and she taught five that first year. We had three small children; before the year was over we had four. She had to run the dining room, hire the servants, look after the domestic type of life, see how the boys' rooms were and that everything was cleaned up and in proper shape. She was a very busy woman. After that first year, she did not have to carry classes again; the next year we had a larger school and more help. But she always looked after the domestic side, the happy side of living in a home like this. She gave the boys birthday parties on their birthdays, let them come down after study hall with their intimate friends, not to exceed 10, and she'd serve them ice cream and cake and they'd have a happy birthday in the evening. She frequently would have parties for them in our home. My wife was continually busy with these social functions and keeping the home and the home atmosphere and watching the infirmary and the care the nurses gave the students. That was the nice side of the school that we looked after.

Then subsequently my wife offered to teach the boys woodcarving, if they would like to carve a panel in the library. Our new library has panels in the oak work. So she would teach them how to carve and then let each one carve a panel of some design of his choosing and put on it his name and the date of his class and that way we filled all the panels in the library.

from a talk by Howell Webb at the Vivian Webb School on September 11, 1981

Dad and Mom were a great team, each with very different talents. He was director of admissions, business manager, director of studies. Mother's role was less precise. She saw to it that each year the place was more beautiful than the year before. I followed her about as she planted a hundred eucalyptus trees, each two inches high. She led me to believe that I helped her, but in late years I have begun to wonder.

*Vivian Webb in 1963
next to the chapel.*

My brothers and I grew up here, but those trees grew faster. They are here today and account for the continuing narrowness of the roads. In those days cars were smaller, and the roads fitted them.

Mother's role in the Thompson and Vivian partnership was never clearly defined. Perhaps her job description should have shown her as head of Webb's Department of Beautification. But mother had an even more important occupation. She also had sole charge of what might be called the Mothering Department. Teen-aged boys, trying hard to be men, don't think that they want to be mothered, at least not publicly. They love having a mother, but that is a secret failing which they do not want their friends to discover.

Away from home, they missed being mothered—or would have if Vivian had not been here. She was the one who sewed on their lost buttons. Her job description should have listed her as head of the all-important Button Department. She knew all their birthdays and at the appropriate time invited each boy to invite seven friends to come to her home for ice cream and cake around her dining table. She was the undisputed head of the Birthday Department.

When a boy had a great longing for a special privilege that might not be quite within the restrictions of the Webb School rules, she always told him, "Don't worry, I'll talk to Thompson about it." Couldn't the rules be bent a little bit? Sometimes they could, sometimes they couldn't, but every boy knew that he had an advocate before the Supreme Court. She loved them all with an affection that was reciprocated. You might describe her as head of the Department of Tender, Loving Care.

When Dad with his own hands built the school chapel out of the adobe clay on which it stands, he cut an inscription in stone and placed that stone in the east wall of the chapel for all to read. Since you may not yet have visited the chapel, I will tell you what it says:

This chapel is dedicated to the glory of God
And is named by the builder in honor of his wife;
"Her children arise up and call her blessed;
Her husband also, and he praiseth her.
Many daughters have done virtuously,
But thou excellest them all." Proverbs 31:28

On her Golden Wedding [Anniversary, June 23, 1965], one of her grandsons [Robert Howell Webb, JR] put those words to music, and her 10 grandchildren sang this Biblical tribute to her in the Vivian Webb Chapel. Her face was wreathed in smiles; she seemed on the verge of laughter, but tears streamed down her cheeks.

[Uncle Thompson] married a Los Angeles girl, Vivian Howell. This union was to be known far and wide as one of the most successful of all marriages, for they were truly partners in everything which occurred later.

Robert Webb [W.R. Webb III], Vol. 22, p.18,
Webb School of California Alumni Bulletin, *1974-76*

Headmaster Experiences

Choice of a Profession

from tape interview of TW, JR. by J. Pierotti, Waunakee, Wisconsin, February, 1996

Q: Had he always wanted to be an educator?

TW, JR.: He had always wanted not to be an educator. He always said that the one thing that he didn't want to do was to be a teacher. And he didn't want to have anything to do with schools. But when WWI came, the bottom dropped out of real estate in the desert, and he was left with debts that he had a great deal of trouble meeting. He also had a big loss in a crop of onions. [These setbacks led him back to Bell Buckle and then ultimately to Claremont.]

. . . .

Q: What did he want to be, a farmer?

TW, JR.: I don't know. Howell once remarked to me a few years ago that Dad had a great admiration for a good deal. We were talking then about selling a piece of land that Dad had left us. In Dad's telling about his camp in Tennessee, he ends by saying that he had all those teachers who were senior to him and who came up to the camp to teach the boys who needed coaching of one sort or another. He said, "I left all the academics to them, and I took care of the management of the camp." In a sense that pretty well answers the question you asked. He was a good manager. If it wasn't agriculture or the real estate business, he was the kind of person who could run a school, run it well, and be admired for it. He was not a scholar. In fact, he really did not know what scholarship was. Scholarship was good grades to him. There is a lot of difference between his view and what scholars do. He had the grades in his pocket for every boy in school at all times. He was a man of good taste and a man I admired, and I do not want to criticize him, but he did not understand what a scholar did. He did not know the difference between a grade-school teacher and a college teacher. He didn't appreciate it. He did not have the concept of a college professor in mind. He never wanted to be a schoolman, but when he got into administration, that was what he understood and did splendidly.

Professional Activities
from interview with the four Webb brothers at The Webb Schools, December, 1988

Howell: Dad was asked to serve on many committees and boards. He served for many years on the board of the California Junior Republic, the Pomona Valley Hospital, and the Norton School. He was president of the Pilgrim Place Board for some time. He was on the founding board of Scripps College, which was founded in 1927, and he remained on the board until he died in 1975.

The organization that asked him to join them and really gave him the greatest pleasure was when he was asked to become a member of the Headmasters Association that meets annually at Rye, New York. It is a very old organization of headmasters. Old Sawney was asked to become a member as early as the 1870s, maybe the '80s. Old Sawney took great pleasure in being in an association with the heads of the most famous private schools in New England and the Middle Atlantic states, when he was the only representative of the Southern schools there. He made many many friends, and Dad heard a great deal about it. Then Uncle Will, who succeeded Grandfather as the headmaster of the Bell Buckle Webb School, was asked to take his father's place when his father had retired. Later Dad was asked to join them too. More recently our cousin, Robert Webb, who founded the Webb School of Knoxville, Tennessee, also joined, and when he did, it was stated to the applause of the association that it was the only time that four members of the same family had served in this association of the leading heads of independent schools in this country.

Recognition and Service
from Mother's Day letter to Emma Clary Webb, May 8, 1928

The school is doing nicely. Our enrollments for next year are far ahead of any previous year. We will have to add to our dormitories this summer to meet the demand.

There is a new school for boys opening in Claremont next year. It is for little boys. The headmaster asked me to go on his list of references to which I consented. His catalog came today. He has President Blaisdell first,

Dean Norton of Pomona College next and I am third. Following me comes Dean Briggs of Harvard and Dr. Stearns of Andover. I couldn't help but laugh at that situation. Another boys school in La Jolla gives only two references in their catalog, Mr. Thacher and me. I have felt this was quite a compliment from the other schoolmen.

I think the funniest situation occurs when we have a meeting of the board of the Junior Republic and the president does not come. I am vice president and have to preside. The rest of the board are very distinguished people. It amuses me to preside over Dr. Millikan [head of Caltech] and such people. In fact it embarrasses me.

View of the Great Depression
from interview with the four Webb brothers at The Webb Schools, December, 1988

TW, JR.: I remember two conversations with my father about the Great Depression. I remember riding with him alone in November or December of 1929, and he talked to me long and seriously about what the stock-market collapse meant and that we would be facing hard times. He was aware of it. Of course, the newspapers were full of the collapse, but as a youngster, I was 12 years old then, it didn't mean much to me. He talked to me for half an hour or so about this and his concern for what was about to come upon us. As I watched later events, I had an understanding of why people were out of jobs and why banks were closing.

Some years later, perhaps 1934, we had another conversation on this subject. What he said then was that we have been going through hard times. "I am proud of the fact that I did not have to discharge a single employee. No teacher was discharged because of the depression. We have not been very generous with what has been paid for things, but the school has survived. Its enrollment has declined somewhat, but we have been able to weather the storm and maintain our staff."

Jack: The impression I gathered from talking to my brothers was that if the school felt the financial effects of a depression, it happened at an earlier period than 1929. The school's depression and the nation's depression were not in synch. By the time the nation was in full depression, the Webb

School of California was getting into a better financial position than it had been.

Q: How do you account for that?

TW, JR: This school was started in 1922 when the nation was in an expanding market and economy. In 1929, the bubble burst. It was fortuitous that Dad started the school at the bottom of that incline. By the time 1929 came, he had reached a point where the school was self-sustaining. As he pointed out afterwards, the school felt the effect of the depression, but the effect was not severe enough to prevent the school from surviving that period of national economic depression.

Howell: In 1922, the Webb School of California had no reputation at all, and anyone looking at the place then would think that it never would have a good reputation, but my parents in the course of those years established a remarkable reputation. They went into the Depression with that asset.

Thacher School – 50th Year

In March, 1939, the Thacher School, in celebrating the 50th year of the school, issued many invitations to their friends for a special gathering. It started with an opening sermon by Mr. Curtis Cate on Sunday, the 19th. On Monday . . . I was very much honored in being invited to pay a tribute to a "Fellow Headmaster," a man whom I had loved and admired above most men I had known.

Arthur Brisbane

Many years ago, Arthur Brisbane, writer of a syndicated column in the Hearst papers, placed a young son in our school while he was working in the West. He owned a ranch on the Mojave Desert.

Quite frequently he would visit the son and come in to see me, usually around 9 or 10 in the morning. After talking a few minutes, he would ask to borrow a typewriter. I offered to lend him my stenographer, but he said all he wanted was the machine on the table in my office as he did his own typing.

He would peck on the machine with two fingers for a bit, and then talk some more, sometimes ask questions and get me talking. Then he would bring up some question of the day on education or any other subject and ask my opinion, and either agree or differ with me. Then turn and peck. This occurred a number of times during the year the son was here. The day after his visit I would buy the *Examiner* and read his column. It would always be about what we had discussed the day before. Sometimes he would quote me "as a teacher friend had said," never by name, maybe agreeing or maybe differing. It was interesting to see how Brisbane worked. He needed a whipping post on which to try out his thoughts.

Twenty-Thousand-Dollar Salary (Part 2)
see Chapter 3 in Vol. 2 for the first part of this story

As the years have gone by I am glad Mr. Rand told me to stick to my school teaching. [Rand was a graduate of Webb School in Bell Buckle and was president of a shoe company.] I think, maybe, life has been sweeter and more interesting in the work with boys than it could have been in a great industrial plant. But Mr. Rand did this much for me, at any rate. A few years later he sent to my school his own Frank, JR., but he didn't pay quite $20,000 a year for that.

I was never able to forget that desire to go out after a 20,000-dollar salary, and now in the light of subsequent events, I have to chuckle when I think about it.

A few years ago, one day out of a clear sky, I received a long-distance call from a distinguished college president, asking Vivian and me to meet him in a very luxurious country club for luncheon. There was to be present also a distinguished importer and merchant whom I knew. I knew him to be one of the great businessmen of our nation, and aside from his own distinction and his own business, he was then holding a public place of great prominence and responsibility and honor. The college president's wife was to be at this luncheon and the merchant's wife. We felt very much flattered and pleased to receive such a distinguished invitation, and needless to say, on the appointed time we were there. It was a delightful occasion and we enjoyed the luncheon together; though frequently during the luncheon I somewhat marveled that I had been included in such a delightful affair and in such distinguished company; I secretly suspected that it was really a compliment to my wife.

At the conclusion of the luncheon, the distinguished merchant asked me to go aside with him. We went into a deserted corner of this lovely country club and sat down together. The merchant then told me about an institution in which he was interested, one which I knew and toward which I felt great respect, because it was distinguished. He told me of its past history and of its future plans. He and the other men who were concerned with it had some beautiful plans for its development and improvement with the possible expenditure of a million dollars or more in additional buildings and equipment immediately. He then told me of the resignation of the head of this institution, which had come suddenly, and of their quandary in regard to the right man to fill the place. They had been casting about over the country, trying to locate the right man to fill that place.

I then suspected that I had been called possibly to advise about someone to take that position. You can imagine my astonishment when the gentleman turned to me and told me that I had been chosen for that position if I would consider it; that both he and the college president felt that I had the qualifications to head this enterprise and carry it through in its expansion and development. He further said that I had exactly the right wife to make a team at the head. He emphasized the fact that Vivian was included in this offer quite as much as I.

I am quite sure that the old expression of "knocking one down with a feather" is not an exaggeration when I think of my feelings and sensations at that moment.

Of course I was tied up with my school. I had an investment and at that time considerable debt, but it was a going concern. I was frank in saying that I did not see just how I could turn loose even if I were fitted for the position.

He told me that there had been no action by the board of directors but he was confident that because of his position they would follow his advice and that if I would consider the position he felt sure that he could notify me in a few days of my appointment.

I felt greatly complimented, and frankly, greatly flattered. But it was an entirely new idea, something I had not thought of, nor longed for, nor considered. It simply had never entered my mind. The gentleman further explained to me that inasmuch as he had not been given authority to make any definite offers to me as to the position, neither could he take the authority to state what the salary would be, but that there would be a very nice salary in it. Still I could not see just how I could turn loose in the middle of the stream on my own enterprise.

He then inquired if a 20,000-dollar salary would be of interest to me.

Despite the fact that I was considerably surprised and shaken, I told him without batting an eye that I could not consider it.

Through the course of these stories I have given names and people but inasmuch as this offer was never formally made, I never felt that I could connect the names and people in speaking of it.

The gentleman urged me to think it over, and talk it over with my wife, and not decline it hurriedly, but to give the matter ample thought. This I agreed to do, and after a day or two of thought and discussion with my wife, we declined it without further thought. It was an impossible situation for us at that time in the development of our school. But I always feel glad that this offer came, and when I lie awake at night, I chuckle about it.

Sometimes when I think back to the old days and the dreadful struggles to make ends meet and how big a 20,000-dollar salary looked to me when Mr. Rand was talking about it to those boys at Bell Buckle, I think of how the time came in my own life when out of a clear sky I turned down an offer of $20,000 without blinking an eye.

I think it is rather curious how many coincidences there are in life and how many queer quirks of fate there are. I think over the time in the summer when I traveled to get boys in my own school and the number I interviewed, but particularly of the two who were exceedingly discourteous and rude to me and how both of them in the next few years came to me in my own place, begging me to accept their boys.

I think of the struggle to raise a little money with which to start the school, and after my friend [Rayford Alley] in New York had to withdraw and leave me stranded without money and without an organized school but with a doubly large indebtedness hanging over my head. Later in that year my friend did send me $1,000. Two or three years later I returned this to him. And the time has come since when I have had to lend him $1,000 to meet his emergencies.

I think how I went out to see three people to request them to take partnership with me and help me finance it, and get it on its feet. I would have been glad to have accepted any one of them as a partner or anyone else who was respectable and had money enough to get it going. But there were three whom I thought were the type of men to fit in ideally to the scheme and who could possibly raise enough money to help me get it going. These three I approached, one at a time, with my proposition, and begged them to consider it, and yet each in turn rejected it. The amazing part of it is that two of those men have actually come to the school and taught for me after the school was on its feet. I have wondered through the years what became of the third one. It has been nearly 10 years since I have heard anything about him or had the least idea where he was, until since Christmas of this year he drove up to my office one day and asked for a position to teach. I could not give it to him.

I cannot help wondering if the chances of life are jokes that fate plays.

One of my most cherished articles which I keep down in the bottom of my safety box is a certificate of stock in the First National Bank of Banning. Yes, it has intrinsic value and pays a 24 percent dividend, but it is not for its worth that I value it. It means something far more than that to me. It means being a partner with that grand old country banker, John M. Westerfield. He was the man who told me he would take up my checks personally when I was "broke" and badly in debt at a time when my wife and baby were in need, on his own suggestion. [See Chapter 2 of Vol. 2, end of oral history entry under "Overview."] I am glad that fate has allowed me to own stock in that man's bank, and not until the "grim reaper" has taken one of us is that stock for sale.

Some of these coincidences have brought tears to my eyes, but when I think of the $20,000 salary I get only a satisfying chuckle. I still think that potentially I am a good shoe man.

The School's Reputation

Hall Martin '30 Trip to Key West

One summer when Hall Martin was about a sophomore in my school, his mother took him to Florida. He wanted very much to take the train ride to Key West. The railroad in those days went over wooden trestles from small island to small island, all the way to Key West.

Hall went out on the back caboose and sat down alone to see what he could see. Soon two nice ladies came out and sat down. They had a great argument as to which was the better school, father's school in Bell Buckle, Tennessee, or my school at Claremont, California. One lady had a son at father's school and the other had a son with me.

They did not know Hall and he did not know them. Hall never spoke to them, but came back telling me about the big argument. He claimed that they really got heated up over that argument.

Hall Martin later graduated from Stanford and then taught at Webb from 1936 to 1942, when he joined the Army. According to The Webb Schools Alumni Bulletin *in 1984-85, he founded the Drama Club, and students in his classes remembered his flair for the dramatic. My grandfather wrote that he doubted Webb School would have been the same "if there hadn't been a Hall Martin as pupil and a teacher in those tough old days."*

Japanese-American Soldier Claimed Webb School Was in California

During the second World War, there was a big [Army] encampment at Tullahoma, Tennessee, about 15 miles from Bell Buckle. From there they held many maneuvers all over middle Tennessee.

One day my brother Will, then headmaster of the Webb School, walked over to the gates of that school marked in big letters "Webb School." There were eight or 10 soldiers standing there having an argument. One of them, a Japanese, approached him and said that he was telling the boys that the Webb School was at Claremont, California, and this sign was not right. He said that he had cooked for the Webb School and knew where it was.

My brother explained to him that there were two Webb Schools, that he ran this one, the old one, and that I ran the other. Then the Japanese soldier asked Will if this one did fine work like the one in California, for he knew that the one in California was considered the finest school in the country. I loved having my cook put Will in his place. Will was amused too.

Two Richest Men

In *Time* magazine of March 7, 1957, under the heading of "Business," there was a write-up of two men, Mr. Paul Getty and Saudi Arabia's King Saud. The article stated that they were the two richest men in the world. I had had in my school at one time a son of each of them. I assumed that they were rich men, but until then I did not know how rich. I still wonder how a little country school like this should have had those boys. We had never solicited students nor advertised since the first year of our school. The Saudi Arabia boy remained only one year, but George Getty '42 remained three years and graduated. He made a splendid record and was much beloved by students and faculty. He is still a loyal alumnus and a member of our board of trustees, a very wise and able member.

Entertainment at the School

Will Rogers

I never knew how Will Rogers found this school. He brought us his younger son, Jim, who stayed with us three years and graduated in 1935. He was a fine boy after he settled down. For a few days, Jim was homesick. When the first Sunday came, Jim decided to go home and started on the way by the back entrance. One of my seniors, a conscientious boy, came and told me that he had tried to talk him out of it to no avail, as Jim had just left.

I ran down the front way and intercepted him. We had a good talk, and I told him that I did not want him to leave without his father's permission, and at least to come back and telephone him. He returned with me but did not call his father. From then on, Jim was an obedient, fine boy and added much to the fun of the school.

We allowed the boys to have horses, and many did. Jim was an expert horseman and easily took the lead in that sport. At one time, the boys rented a dozen young steers on which they practiced roping. Some years later Jim's own son [Jim '58] attended the school.

While Jim was here, his father and mother came out very frequently. Will always stirred up fun. He sometimes would tell me that he had to give a talk in Washington or New York and had some new "gags" and would like to try them out on the boys. We would call off study hall for the evening and gather in the Commons Room to hear him. Several times we had a preview of some of his most famous talks. He would wind them up with all his rope tricks. When he got the rope spinning a circle and began jumping through it, the boys would begin counting out loud. Sometimes the count would get up to 40 or more jumps. Will's face grew red, and his breath was coming hard. I was frightened his heart would fail, but those counts from the boys brought out all he had.

Will Rogers was a lovable man and most thoughtful and considerate of everyone. He did many kindnesses for my family and me. Once, he invited me to bring my family and guests, Will and Louise Webb of Bell Buckle, to the studio to see him making a movie. He entertained us for the whole day on the lot and introduced us to many of the famous movie people of the day. "Step 'n' Fetchit" had a part in the picture Will was making. The short act would be repeated time and again when something was not perfect, such as the hen and chickens running out of the scene despite efforts of several people assigned to direct them, out of sight of the cameras.

One time, Mr. and Mrs. Rogers invited us to bring our sons and see a polo match at his estate and remain for dinner afterward. The polo was exciting, with Will showing great skill before several hundred spectators of very fashionable society of Hollywood and Beverly Hills. Will and the other players were correctly dressed in polo uniforms. When the game was over, Will rode up to where Mrs. Rogers and my family were standing. The rest were leaving in their automobiles. He told us he had to take his horse to the stable and care for it, but for us to go into the house. With Mrs. Rogers, we went into a large living room, beautifully decorated with paintings by famous Western artists and a number of trophies and silver-decorated saddles. In a short time, Will came in from the stable. He had changed from polo clothes to blue jeans, boots, and an old leather coat.

At once, he asked to show us his saddles and trophies. He put his arm around our Bill, who was about 7 years old, calling him "Honey," and together we went around the room as he told us about every item. Then in came the butler, dressed immaculately in dinner coat, and announced dinner. Mrs. Rogers sat at one end of a long table and Will at the other. She was beautifully dressed and he was in his cowboy clothes. The butler served us a beautiful dinner, but if he didn't get around to replenish food or drink, Will would bounce up and lavishly fill our plates. I was drinking hot tea. Will saw that my cup was getting low and rushed around before I knew it and added coffee to the tea.

Our California Association of Independent Schools [not yet formed, see Chapter 8, so some earlier association] was scheduled to hold its annual meeting at our school one year, and I had to provide the visiting speaker.

I asked Will Rogers to be the speaker. He graciously accepted. Mr. [Morgan} Barnes was headmaster of the Thacher School [1931-36], following the death of Sherman Day Thacher. Barnes had been outspoken in his criticism of Will Rogers because he affected colloquial bad grammar in many of his published remarks. I arranged to seat Mr. Barnes by Will. During the dinner I watched the guests. Will had his arm around Mr. Barnes talking to him earnestly.

At the proper moment, I introduced Will for the address. He began his talk by saying that when he moved to California the only school here was the Thacher School—at least, the only one he had heard about. He said on the day school was to open, he had taken Will, JR., to the Thacher School and told Mr. Thacher he wanted to put Will in his school. Mr. Thacher told him that all the spaces were full and there was no room for Will. Rogers went on to say that he found out that if you wanted to enroll a boy in Thacher you had to reserve the place before the boy was born. He turned to Mr. Barnes and asked him if he could reserve a place for a boy, since he and Mrs. Rogers never knew what might happen in their family. Mrs. Rogers was sitting at the table with them. After the dinner, Mr. Barnes was nice enough to tell me he had never enjoyed anything so much and that Will Rogers had won him over.

One day our track team went to Carpenteria for a triangle meet with the Dean School and the Cate School. The Cate School was not a member of our California Association at the time; so Mr. Cate had not been at the meeting where Will Rogers had spoken and had not met him. I was talking with the other two headmasters, Mr. Hewitt Reynolds of Dean, and Mr. Cate, when I saw Mr. and Mrs. Rogers come up to watch their son Jim compete in the pole vault. I went over and spoke with them and asked Mr. Rogers to step over and meet the other headmasters. I said, "Mr. Rogers – Mr. Reynolds," then, "Mr. Rogers – Mr. Cate." Mr. Cate said, "How do you do?" and strolled off to watch the events. Reynolds and I remained, chatting with Will, who was highly entertaining, until Jim had done his act. Then Mr. Rogers took Mrs. Rogers and hurried off. When he left, Mr. Cate joined Reynolds and me. Reynolds said, "Will Rogers is a fascinating man." Cate said, "Will Rogers, Was that Will Rogers? I would have loved to talk to him."

One day on our athletic field we were having a football game in which Jim Rogers '35 was taking part, and out came Will. It was shortly after we had been at the polo game and dinner, when Will had called my small Bill "Honey." Bill ran over to him and told him that we had been to see *State Fair* the night before, in which Will had the leading part, and in which the largest hog in California was part of the fair exhibit. Will asked Bill if he liked it. Bill replied that he liked him and the hog just fine, but he didn't like the love stuff.

A framed telegram from Will Rogers to the 1934 graduating class hangs in The Webb Schools office and was printed on p. 5 of Webb: 75 Years of Building Character *by H. Stephens.*

Sir John Adams

When our school had grown to about 40 boarders, we had an opportunity [in late October, 1925] to secure Sir John Adams to talk to them. He was from England on a lecture tour of America. I told my little sons that a real knight was coming to talk. When Sir John arrived at my home, I introduced him to my small sons. Howell looked him over and said, "Where is your sword?"

When Sir John addressed the school, he began by saying that he wanted to talk on deduction as is so well illustrated in the stories of Sherlock Holmes. Then he said if he came home in the afternoon and found on the hat rack a bowler hat, walking cane and gloves, he would say, "My son, Johnnie is back from school." The whole school roared with laughter. Sir John stopped, turned to me and said, "What have I said or done to cause this mirth?" He gave us a delightful talk and won our hearts.

Goodbye, Mr. Chips

For several years Sidney Franklin, JR. '42 was in our school until he graduated in 1942. During that time his father was making films. One day Mr. Franklin told me that he had a film that he wanted to show to our boys and teachers, but it would have to be a complete secret as it had never been released for public showing. He stated that he would show it in our library on a certain night, provided no information about it leaked out and no outsiders were invited in.

I called our assembly of the whole school, boys and teachers, on short notice without a hint of anything unusual. A truck loaded with projection machine and screen pulled up and unloaded. In came Mr. Franklin with a few introductory words, and on the screen came *Goodbye, Mr. Chips*. Mr. Franklin said this was its first showing. In a short time, it took the movie-going people by storm over the whole nation.

Mrs. Miniver

One year we had planned a Parents Day at the school, with athletic events for the afternoon, dinner, and a play by the students for the evening in the gymnasium. When the day came, all the leading men in the cast came down with German measles. There could be no play, and it was too late to call off the invitations. Sid Franklin, JR. '42 phoned his father and asked him to bring out a film, something to entertain the parents that evening. He said he would find something and help us out.

That evening he put on the first showing of *Mrs. Miniver*, a delightful show. The plot worked up an intense moment when the hidden German soldier sprang forward with a pistol aimed at Mrs. Miniver. We were all tense, when suddenly from the back of the room a large dog let out a ferocious bark and rushed down the middle aisle up to the screen. Everyone's hair was on end. I suspect that the parents went home far more pleased than they would have been had they seen our own amateur performance.

Movies and Movie Stars

from interview with the four Webb brothers at The Webb Schools, December, 1988

Bill: We could not drag Dad to a movie theater. He couldn't see why anyone was interested in going to a movie. Of course, during those years, there were always people from Hollywood who had children here. The only star that Dad recognized as someone that he knew was Will Rogers. World War II came on, and Greece was overrun. At that time, Charles Skouras, a Greek immigrant who owned the Fox Theaters, had a son in school. Mr. Skouras hired Grauman's Chinese Theater, and he was able to get every major star in Hollywood to volunteer services for a supershow that was given for raising money for Greek relief. He gave the Webb School faculty tickets that he had bought from his own pocket for this great event. So Dad and Mother were sitting with Mr. and Mrs. Skouras in the center of Grauman's Chinese Theater, and on either side was the entire faculty. At the beginning of the show, every glamour girl, every great star of Hollywood including Jean Harlow, Shirley Temple, Mickey Rooney and Clark Gable walked out together. At that time, as Mother told it later because she thought this was so good, Dad leaned over to Mr. Skouras and said, "And Mr. Skouras, are these people connected to the motion-picture industry?" [laughter]

Howell: Mother was embarrassed for about the only time in her life.

Bill: Oh, she wasn't embarrassed. She thought this was so funny.

Dining with a Local Dignitary

TW, JR., from a phone conversation, April, 1998

After being retired for a good number of years, Dad was invited to eat in the Price Dining Hall and was seated next to a gentleman of some prominence. The place was noisy and his poor hearing had prevented him from hearing the man's name when they were introduced. At some point, Dad turned to this man and asked him, "And what do you do?" The man replied that he was the governor of California. He was Ronald Reagan. Dad was never one to know dignitaries of all kinds. He paid little attention to their pictures in the newspapers.

Fay Bainter, Mother of Reginald Venable, JR. '41

When I go back home in the South and in many other parts of the country, old friends and acquaintances so often ask me if I have sons of movie actors and actresses in my school. They want to know if I know the movie people and what impression different ones make on me.

I have known many of them, and had sons of quite a few in my school for longer or shorter periods. Many of them have been delightful to know, and their sons have been fine boys, but there have been a number whose sons have been spoiled brats and would not or could not adapt themselves to the somewhat rigid discipline of a boarding school. In talking to their parents about their shortcomings, I usually found why they were what they were. Usually that type dropped out very shortly, on their own, or by my decision. We granted no special dispensations because of the family name. I leave the unpleasant ones out of my stories. The less said, the better. There are some I like to talk about and of whom I am very proud.

I felt sorrow this morning when I read of the death of Fay Bainter, Mrs. Reginald Venable. She and Commander Venable were here frequently while their son Reginald, JR. '41 was in school. We admired them and enjoyed them. They had done a fine job in bringing up their son. After graduating here in June, 1941, he went to Stanford University.

Arthur Cahill, Artist

Mr. Arthur Cahill was a cartoonist for the *Examiner*, a Hearst paper, at the time he enrolled his son Jim '39 in our school and shortly afterward he entered his second son [Richard '43]. He told us that he had painted the portrait of President Herbert Hoover, which had been placed in the White House, and was to do a portrait of Dr. Millikan, president of Caltech, for the college. He and my wife Vivian did some whispering from time to time and finally told me that he was going to make a portrait of me for Vivian, which he did when Dr. Millikan was too busy to sit for him. When he was waiting on Millikan, he would come here and work on me. That picture hangs in our school office. He painted in a low corner the faces of his two

Thompson Webb, James Easton '58, and Will Durant at graduation ceremonies.

sons listening to me. After he was through, I tried to get him to paint a portrait of Vivian, but he begged off by saying he did not enjoy painting ladies. I am sorry that I did not get that one.

Will Durant

For three years we had in school the grandson [James Easton '58] of Will Durant. Mr. Durant would come to see the boy very frequently and often come in to see me. My wife and I became very fond of him and great admirers of him. We knew Mrs. Durant slightly, but she did not often come into our home. To know Mr. Durant was one of the great experiences of our life in a school.

I needed his help with Jim, for Jim was something of a handful academically. He had an amazing mind given entirely to math and physics. My problem was to get him to do his English and history. One year on the College Boards, Jim made a grade of 800 on Math and 800 on Physics. Eight hundred is the perfect score. Jim could have done as well on everything if he wanted to do it. He spent much time searching for problems on which to stump his grandfather.

For the commencement speaker in June, 1958, we were able to secure Mr. Durant. He gave one of the finest commencement addresses that I have ever heard. The newspapers all over the United States picked it up. Many of them gave it in full, while some others gave parts of it. We received hundreds of letter requesting copies of it.

With his consent, we printed it and sent them out on these requests. That was nearly nine years ago, and we are still getting occasional requests. One of the most prized books in my library is a copy of the VI volume of *The Story of Civilization*, written while Jim was here and given to Vivian and me by Will Durant with an appropriate inscription and his signature.

Henry Koster, the Movie Director

It was my good fortune and most of all my pleasure to know Mr. and Mrs. Henry Koster over a period of 11 years. The first son, Robert '56, came to us in 1953, Nicolas '61 in 1958, and the youngest, Peter '64, in 1961, all going through to graduation. They were fine boys, good students and superb musicians, all going on to college. Peter is in Yale now. In June, Yale notified the school that Peter had been graded as "Ranking Scholar," which I am told places him in the top two percent of his class.

When students do well, their parents become friends, which may not be true if the boy does not do well.

I think I am correct in saying that Mr. Koster directed the first Cinemascope picture, and I believe *The Robe* was that picture. At any rate, Mr. Koster directed *The Robe* and won world renown. He came out one Sunday evening and told the faculty and students about making it, the problems and ups and downs. He brought pictures which he and his sons had made on the side and behind scenes, illustrating the problems and solutions. It became an informal show as well as an exciting talk.

Mr. Koster writes me from time to time about the boys, which is thoughtful and kind, for he knows I love to hear. I appreciate it, for I know he is a busy director.

Faculty and Faculty Decisions

Teachers and Trapping at Webb

from "Webbs Remember Webb" by Paula Pitzer in The Webb Schools Alumni Bulletin, *1988-89, p. 17*

The earliest masters at Webb School included Ernie Powell, Glenn Vedder, Ed Price, J. G. Hirsbrunner, and Paul Squibb. Before the Webb brothers left Webb, Raymond Alf, Horace Boynton, and John R. C. Sumner had joined the staff. Old-timers have their favorite stories of early Webb teachers. The one most often mentioned is Ernie Powell, who taught Latin and Spanish and is renowned both for his demand for rapid-fire recitation and for his rapid-fire chalk missiles, which penalized those who might have made the mistake of gazing out the windows or chattering in the back of the room.

Ed Price and Thompson Webb himself are remembered for their use of the "trapping system." In trapping, the classroom seats were ranked, and the objective was to stay in the first seat for as long as possible. Correct responses guaranteed that one could hold one's seat, while a mistake meant that the next person to get the answer right moved ahead of whoever had missed the question. Ed Price and Thompson had experienced learning by the trapping system at Bell Buckle. Susan Webb, one of

Edward T. Price

Sawney's daughters, is famous for trapping Ed Price, not only in the classroom, but in matrimony. In California, Price used "trapping" in his English and Latin classes, and Webb used it in algebra. Thompson Webb taught algebra in the southeast corner of the "Old Schoolhouse." From that vantage point he could watch the driveway for visitors to the school. Bill says, "I was surprised and delighted to find that my father was an exciting and entertaining teacher."

Teachers at Webb early 1930s
by E. T. Price, JR. '33

My teachers included Ernest Powell (Latin I, II, and IV), Leon Scales (English I, Ancient History), Thompson Webb (Algebra I), Mr. Hirsbrunner (Algebra II, Geometry, Trigonometry), my father (English II, Latin III and IV), Glenn Vedder (Physics, Chemistry), Paul Squibb (French I), John R.C. Sumner (French II), and Horace Boynton (English III, U.S. History). The enrollment in Latin III was only three boys, and that in Latin IV was I alone.

John R.C. Sumner

Trapping occurred only in Algebra I and II in so far as I remember. Other than the final exam, Uncle Thompson graded only on trapping. I remember when he gave me a 95 one month when somebody else I thought had missed as many as I had got a 99.

Faculty Employment
from oral history, p. 120-123

TW: I just got a man that was very smart and a whole lot better student than I was and turned him loose.

I have a remarkable faculty. Now you take this man [Raymond M.] Alf, that museum boy, he was offered the head of the Department of Geography at Pomona College; he was offered a professorship at Princeton and one at Yale. And others who've been here. Why, I had a much better faculty than

Pomona, Occidental, Whittier, USC. I don't know what, what Berkeley and UCLA or Caltech did, I never knew how to compare that, but I was getting top men.

Q: What were you paying then, in the '30s? During the depression.

TW: I'll have to look back in the books; I don't know, because the whole family [of each faculty member] got their board and room and lights, food.

Q: Could you guess at approximately what, what it was in the '30s?

TW: I really couldn't.

Q: I see.

TW: Now I know this, that I was paying better than the public schools all along after the first year or two. I employed Dr. Blaisdell's youngest son for my first year at an absurdly low salary; I paid him $100 a month and took care of his wife, gave him food and housing. During the spring he told me he just had to have more money than that the following year. I told him I'd love to have him back the following year, but I didn't see any way of promising him more unless I had the students and I didn't have them yet. But I said, "If you want to go to another school, I'll try to get you a job." I got him one at the Harvard Military Academy in Los Angeles at $1,800, just twice what I was paying him. I did that over and over for different teachers then. After we got up to where we were having 40 or 50 boys and most of them paying, I could pick up salaries and I did. When the Great Depression came, '29, people would come to see the school, but they wouldn't sign the contract and when we came to the first of September, I didn't have a reservation. We were opening the middle. I told all the teachers, "Go get a job, for heaven's sakes. I can't promise you a thing; I can't pay you unless I get it out of these boys. If you can find any kind of a job that you're willing to take, take it." Not one of them took it, but on the 15th of September, the school was full. These people that had been here didn't want to sign something until they knew it; well they have to settle it now, they came and—

Q: I suppose many of them wanted to go home, talk it over with the boy, try to convince him that he would want to come, too.

TW: I don't know anything about that, but they paid, and I was able to pay every teacher on time the full amount of the salary. As we went along we'd increase it, we never had a written contract with any teacher.

Q: Never had contracts?

TW: No, I wasn't giving a contract.

Q: Why?

TW: What good would it do? It protected him but it didn't protect me.

Q: If you didn't like the way he was teaching, he had a contract you couldn't say —

TW: Then I couldn't get rid of him. And if he decided he'd quit, as two or three of them did, they would just walk off.

Q: You had some that quit in the middle of the year?

TW: Oh, sure, I've had that happen. Unless you have a good man, takes a man with character, you know. I've had them come in and say, "Well, such and such a school offered me a hundred dollars a month more than you are paying me. Will you beat it?" And I said, "No, we've had the agreement." "I'm quitting." "All right, if you're that kind, I don't want you. You don't keep your word; I want a man that is honest and I'll keep my word and I want you to keep yours." You're always tied. I guess these big public school systems have to have—But what could you do, this fellow with nothing in the world just said, "Well, I'm done; I'm quitting." You can't sue him. But if he wasn't satisfactory and I said, "You've got to go," he'd say, "Well, I'll sue you." And I had property.

Q: Sue you for the rest of the year's salary?

TW: Yeah, anything he saw fit. Damn it, he might sue for a million dollars for damaging his character; you don't know what they could do.

School Rank and The Faculty

from oral history p. 115-118

TW: One of the big foundations, Carnegie or something of the kind, put out a team to study the private schools of America and it came from schools of education. Asked 18 private schools to participate and the rest were public schools; they studied a total of 100. The first week of school they had a committee of three people here, and they gave all our boys aptitude and achievement tests and then during the year the committee came back and studied and quali-

John Pettley

fied our equipment. How many toilets we had—everything was that kind— the number of books in our library, what we had. A very detailed study, and put it all down and gave us thermometers on everything they studied. Then when the year was over, towards the end of the year, they came back and gave achievement tests again, so they had the beginning and how much the boys achieved at the end. They studied our faculty, and if you were an A.B. you were nothing; if you had an M.A. you got so much; Ph.D., you got a lot. So many hours of education, the more education you had, the more you could get. Well, I was a member of that study [and] was a zero; I just had an A.B. degree. When the whole thing was finished, they gave each school a book, . . . showing exactly how you rated in comparison with a hundred schools. Now when we got our letter, I mean our numbers, we were number one in shopwork and our shop was under a tent out in the yard. We were number six on IQ of the hundred; on achievement we were number three; on our faculty we were number 100. We had the bottom faculty of any, a hundred schools, and yet we got the achievement for third place.

Q: How do you account for that?

TW: Well, they rated faculty on the number of degrees they had.

Q: I see.

TW: We didn't have a lot of Ph.D.'s and most of them hadn't studied in the field of education. I never brought a man and asked him whether he's got any background in the field of education, I never believed in them.

Q: What do you believe in?

TW: Being a scholar. I got that from Father. Pick out scholars for your teachers, Phi Beta Kappas, they don't have to be trained in method, they're smart enough to do it. He never cared a fig for what degrees you had if you could teach, if you were a scholar and knew your stuff. I always picked top scholars.

Gordon Wilson

Seated: Molly Wilson, Mary and Ramsay Harris.
Standing: Vivian Webb and Gordon Wilson.

Q: Well, then you would be looking at the grades; would you ask a faculty member, a prospective faculty member, for his transcript, or would you get the transcript from the college?

TW: You always got it and looked at it, his dossier or whatever you call it.

Q: Including a transcript of his academic record wherever he went to school?

TW: Yes, yes, and how he did in them and if he seemed to be the type of person that could put it over. I have had top faculty out here, no doubt about that. Now for instance, one year down here at Pomona College, we had four boys in the senior class—had others in lower classes, but they only appoint seniors to Phi Beta Kappa—all four of ours were Phi Beta Kappa. Out of only 10 men that made it, four of them were Webb men. In 1965, just four years ago at Harvard, we had four boys in the senior class, all graduated cum laude and one of them is the top boy. We've done that kind of thing over and over. And yet we got our failures, too. The most brilliant boy I ever had flunked Stanford the first quarter. He never attended a class, did a thing.

Warner Marti

During the war, men teachers were hard to get as so many of the younger men had gone to war. In my search, I found a blind man by the name of Warner Marti, who wanted to teach history, and we employed him. He was married, and he and his wife lived in one of our dormitories with the boys. He was quite a successful teacher. He had a connection by which he could get a tremendous amount of library material on recordings for his phonograph, and he kept himself posted, and he was very much beloved by students and faculty.

One day he left the schoolhouse and went to his room in the dormitory, and as he came in the hallway, he smelled fire. He followed his nose down the hall until he came to the door where the fire was. He opened the door, and there was a brisk fire started in a short circuit on a radio. He instantly closed the door and went down the hall where he knew there was a fire extinguisher, came back, made a crack in the door, and discharged the fire extinguisher into the room and closed the door and ran up to the schoolhouse and gave the fire alarm to which, of course, the entire school responded. But when we got there, the fire was out. The room was very much disfigured, but he'd saved the whole dormitory by his quick action, which proved to be a very amazing thing to us, that a blind man could be so well able to take care of a situation like that.

After the war, he went back to college and acquired his doctor's degree and has been a very successful teacher in one or two of the state colleges since.

According to Jack Webb on the interview tape (#9) from December, 1988 at The Webb Schools, Warner Marti lost his eyesight in an injury sustained while playing football in high school. After obtaining his Ph.D. in history, he went on to be the chairman of the History Department at California State Polytechnic University in Pomona.

The Baxter Incident
from the second part of the story about Jim Wiggs in Chapter 2

There was another incident in which Jim Wiggs '25 figured, but was not his fault. I'd employed that year a man named Baxter, whom I'd picked up in Pasadena, a man of charming personality and evidently fine education. He'd come in to teach for me, and I thought I had a great find. The first week went beautifully, and then Sunday night I was reading in my room when there was a knock at the door, and I said, "Come in," and Baxter came inside the door, and when he spoke there was something peculiar about it. His voice was not normal; it was a much higher voice than he ordinarily used, much louder, and he started out by saying, "I demand that you require the boys to stay in bed in the mornings until 7 o'clock." I asked what he was talking about. He said that the boys were getting up at 5 or 6 o'clock in the morning, waking him up and disturbing him, and he just couldn't take it, and again he said, "I demand that you require them to stay in bed and be quiet until 7 o'clock."

"Well," I said, "Mr. Baxter, you heard me talk to them the other day and tell them that the early mornings were the brightest times of the day and that they could learn their lessons in half the time if they'd get up at 5 or 6 o'clock and study." I said, "I think that's what they should do." But he said, "I demand that you stop that."

I said, "Demand all you want, but I'm going to tell them to get up. That's my policy and I'll stand by it." So he closed the door and went out.

We had another pleasant week. And the next Sunday night, again there was a knock at my door and I said, "Come in," and Baxter was there again and he had that same strange voice which I'd never heard but once before, but the minute he began to speak I knew that there was that same queer thing about him. This time he said, "Did Jim tell you?" referring to Jim Wiggs. I said, "Tell me what?" "Didn't Jim tell you?" I said, "He hasn't told me anything. What are you talking about?"

"Well," he said, "I tried to kill him."

"What do you mean?"

"Well, I was sitting in my room and I got to thinking about how much trouble Jim had given me in study hall and I just got so mad I sent for Jim, and when he came in," he said, "I grabbed him and threw him down on the floor and I piled down on him and tried to choke him to death. And I wanted to kill him. I was just determined I would kill him. I did my best to kill him. But," he said, "he was too strong for me and he shook me off and got out and ran. Didn't he tell you about it?"

And I said, "No, he hadn't told me anything about it." I said, "Are you serious?" And he said, "Yes. I want to kill him more than anything in the world. I know you won't approve of it, and if you don't want me here I'll get away." And I said, "Go pack your stuff as fast as you can, and I'll take you off of these grounds within a few minutes." "Oh," he said, "I don't want to go until morning." And I said, "No, you're going right now. Now go get your stuff and pack it."

And I had to go up there with him and help him throw his things in his trunk, and I said, "Come get in the car and I'll take you to Pomona to the hotel, and I'll ship your trunk tomorrow." So I took him and left him at the hotel. The next morning, he called me up in a normal voice and said he was sorry for the way he'd acted, he didn't know why he acted that way, he was all right now, he didn't care anything about Jim Wiggs and that he'd come back and go on teaching. I told him, "Never come on my grounds again."

It was a very unusual experience. I didn't know what caused it or brought it about. But subsequently I was told that he was a drug addict, and about once a week he went on one of his sprees.

Honorary Degrees and Retirement

Doctor of Pedagogy
from oral history, p. 109-110

TW: Subsequently, some several years later, what was then the College of the Pacific, known as the University of the Pacific, that's the oldest college in California—that's at Stockton—invited me to come up and have a doctor's degree. Well, that was legitimate and I accepted it. I presumed that they'd give me an LL.D., what they usually do with these complimentary degrees. So I went up and [was] entertained by the president of the university and the chancellor who was then retiring—I can't think of his name at the moment—and governor, just retired as the Supreme Court justice—

Q: [Earl] Warren.

TW: Governor Warren was at the dinner and Bishop Somebody of the Baptist church. Governor Warren had already had a doctor's degree from them, so he sat by me when I got mine and mine wasn't an LL.D.; it was a Doctor of Pedagogy. Did you ever hear of one? Neither did I. I thought that was the darndest fool thing I ever heard of; I don't know why they did that. Anyhow, when I got home the secretary at the office was making out the calendar for the following year; we always put in the names of the new teachers and their degrees, and they put behind my name D.P., Doctor of Pedagogy. I looked at it, D.P., displaced person. [laughter] You got it! But I made them spell it out, Doctor of Pedagogy. [laughter] Never had pedagogy in my life. It was sometime later [1962] that I picked up a couple of LL.D. degrees: one from Occidental [College] and one from Pomona [College].

A different telling of this story is as follows (from last part of "Helicopter Ride")

[In 1949], I was invited to come to the University of the Pacific in Stockton and receive an honorary Doctor of Laws Degree, which I was very proud to accept. After I arrived, President Burns told me that they had decided to change my degree from Doctor of Laws to Doctor of Pedagogy. When I came home, the secretary was making out a new calendar for the next school year. She was including a list of the faculty with their degrees indicated behind their names. She had my name in usual form, but had added "D.P." for Doctor of Pedagogy. When I saw it, I roared with laughter, and said "exactly right, displaced person." I thought back to the old days at Bell Buckle when I was the "Bonehead Teacher."

Helicopter Ride

At the time of my retirement in 1962, I was much surprised by two letters. One was from Arthur G. Coons, president of Occidental College in Los Angeles, saying that it was his pleasure to inform me that the board of trustees had voted to confer upon me the honorary degree of Doctor of Laws. They requested me to be present to receive it at their commencement at 7:30 p.m. on June 10th. Of course I was pleased and flattered as I thought back to the days of the Bonehead Teacher. I accepted.

A little later the other letter came from Wilson Lyon, president of Pomona College, informing me that his board of trustees had voted to confer on me the honorary degree of Doctor of Laws, and requested me to be present at their commencement to receive it at 5 p.m. on June 10th. This was a great surprise from our nearest neighbor which I must admit gave me great satisfaction. But how was I to do that at 5 p.m. and keep my appointment at Occidental College, less than two hours later, through Los Angeles traffic. It seemed impossible.

A fortunate incident occurred. Before I had answered the last letter, a meeting of a committee on which I was a member met at the California Club in Los Angeles, and present were the two college presidents. I went over to them and told President Lyon I appreciated his invitation to come to his commencement at 5 p.m. to accept the Doctor of Laws degree. However, I did not think it was possible since I had agreed to accept one from Dr. Coons at 7:30 p.m. the same day. The two presidents looked at each other in surprise. Then, Dr. Lyon said he would have the conferring of honorary degrees first on his program, and I might slip out the back door of the stage after receiving it. Dr. Coons then said he would schedule his program to confer honorary degrees at the last, and give me time to get there. I thought I could make that work with a fast car and driver.

Mr. Bob Reynolds, president of the Board of Trustees of the Webb School, heard of this. He was director of KMPC, the large broadcasting company, which owned a small helicopter and was operated by Captain Max Schumacker.

The captain flew over the freeways leading into Los Angeles and reported on accidents and congestion by radio to the traffic officers and to the broadcasting company. He rode in a bubble for two people in the front of the helicopter. Mr. Reynolds arranged that Captain Schumacker would have the helicopter on the Pomona College football field behind the Pomona auditorium and deliver me to Occidental College on time.

I have always been scared of high places and do not enjoy conventional flying, though I do fly when I have to and can find no other way. In the jets I take an aisle seat in order not to look down, but in the bubble, I could see everything. It was like drifting on a cloud.

I asked the captain how long he had been flying a helicopter. He said 20 years. Then I asked him how long would it take to Occidental, and he said 20 minutes. I cheered up and figured maybe I could take 20 minutes if he could do 20 years, but I was a scared rabbit. I suspect that it might take three honorary degrees to get me into another helicopter with a bubble. A few weeks after my ride in the helicopter, it fell and killed the Captain and passenger.

Comments on "Selling" Honorary Degrees

One time the *Los Angeles Times* announced that one of the California colleges had awarded several honorary degrees to several men and women who were known principally for their great wealth. Shortly after that I was at the board meeting of Scripps College where we were discussing some new appointment to our board. The doings of the other college were mentioned, and Mr. William B. Munro spoke up and said this university was building its endowment by degrees.

The next incident was not a compliment to me. Maybe I should not tell it. I will leave out names. A president of a university not in California was very anxious to work out a situation which he thought would be to his advantage. By coincidence, I was very close to the people involved.

The president called on me and asked me to advise them to grant his request. I told him that my influence would have no weight. He was convinced that it would. My convictions were opposed to his plan, though I didn't have to tell him that, and did not. When he stood up to leave, he invited me to come to his university at commencement and receive an honorary degree. I declined, and it was the first one ever offered me. I am sure the degree would have been of advantage to me at the time, as I was struggling to put my school on a firm foundation.

Comments about Pending Retirement
from letter to Mr. and Mrs. Walter Stokes, board member of Webb School, Bell Buckle and former classmate, December 21, 1961

I am closing my 40th year as headmaster in June and giving way to a very choice person to take my place. Fred Hooper has been with us for 28 years. I have been itching for a long time to do a lot of things for which there was no time in a school life. I shall miss the school, but I shall enjoy other things which I want to do.

from the Webb School of California Alumni Bulletin, *1974-76, Vol. 22, p.18*

. . .I know I am retiring with both sorrow and joy and face a new way of life. My dear wife refuses to retire. She says she will stick to me in the future as in the past, for better, for worse, for richer, for poorer, in sickness and in health 'til death do us part . . . .

Views about the School During Retirement
from letter to Hall Martin '30, January 18, 1971

I cannot tell you how much we appreciated your lovely Christmas card with the writing on it. It's one of the most delightful things that's come to us in many years. We treasure that card and the beautiful way in which you write to us. Vivian and I read it with a great deal of pride.

We've talked about you every little while and we're wishing you'd come down some time and bring Rosamond and Chris. It would be lots of fun to see you again and to have you here and to show you some of the new things that have come up on the campus.

Since we gave the school away, the people of means have been very kind to us and have given us many delightful improvements on the campus. I never had the privilege of teaching in such beautiful classrooms, with rugs on the floor, and great expense has been put into equipment by these lovely gifts of the wealthy alumni. Yet we never get enough, you know. The trustees are still combing around hoping to find some more money, a few extra things in the way of equipment—almost everything is here that's really needed. We have several nice playing fields, but we've outgrown the gymnasium that was built when we had about 50 boys; now we have 230.

I take no part in the school. I don't ask questions or criticize, and I don't know the students and I don't know many of the teachers. But the old-timers, of course, I know, I see frequently. But I don't want Fred Hooper to be annoyed by an old cranky headmaster sitting around. And the fact is I'm very seldom annoyed with any of his decisions. I've admired his administration tremendously. He is a great person. And some of them would have distressed me very much if they had had power to run the school, such as these people that think we're too old-fashioned and they want us to keep up with the other schools, put in coeducation, and all sorts of things like that. Well, I don't know why we all want to imitate somebody, especially when they've gone on a cranky procedure as so many of our colleges and schools have done. I like our school to stand out solidly for what it is, and if they don't like it, don't come to it. That's my attitude.

6

Student Issues

Student Life at Webb School

Selection of Students
from oral history, p. 126-128

Q: I wonder now if you'd—I have a number of other points here that I'd like to ask you about. One of the things that always, I suppose, plagues the headmaster of a private school is the question of selection of boys, and if you can select good ones, you'll pride yourself in this. You can only take so many after all now—not right in the beginning when you were crying for students. What was your philosophy of selection?

TW: Well, the first year, I just had to take anybody I could get, and they were pretty good boys, no trouble. So I went on the same way, as they'd apply, I'd take them if they'd fit into our program. I got these 12 boys that were rascals, out of 28 [in the second year of the school]. The rest of them were good boys. I didn't select any teachers until the last minute when I knew I had boys, got them all [the boys] in the last two weeks. Then I hired two teachers. When they got here they were terrible. Went off for a weekend north. They'd ask for a certain amount of time off, and every other weekend one of them [would] get off and get drunk and couldn't get back for two or three days and get back bleary-eyed. I saw what they were doing. And the boys, they sided with these tough boys that weren't going to chapel, and they weren't going to do this and they weren't going to do that. They were going to tell me how to run this school, and so I said, you won't either. Just go on home, get out, you're done. [See "Shoestringing" in Chapter 2 for details.]

I learned my lesson. Get a good boy. I quit questioning their IQ or achievement. I didn't say what they had to be academically, but I would look up their character, what their teachers and their ministers and their neighbors said about them as to whether they were mean kids or whether they were gentlemen in their conduct. I picked only good ones and sometimes I'd turn away a dozen boys before I'd get one, but I'd get the class of boys I wanted in behavior. Then as we went along I began to add to that, academic achievement. I didn't give them tests in the beginning. I got to the point later when I began to give IQ and achievement tests, but I wouldn't believe much in the IQ; don't still. If he can achieve, that's what I want. And I watched that very carefully, and we still do.

The Boy from Phoenix

One year I received an application for a boy from Phoenix, Arizona, and they gave me some references, one of which was a bishop of the Episcopal Church. I wrote a letter to him saying that I had an application for the boy to come to our school, and they'd given him as a reference and I'd greatly appreciate it if he'd tell me if he was a boy of fine standards. I could give him tests to see about his academic standing. Immediately the bishop replied and stated the boy's father was a very prominent and successful banker, and he wrote me quite a long letter about the family, never mentioning the boy. I read it two or three times and came to the conclusion that the bishop wasn't taking the chance of telling me the truth about the boy and he was sidestepping the issue. I wrote to the father and told him I was sorry I could not take the boy. I put that letter in the outgoing mail box.

Shortly thereafter a man came to my office looking for my secretary [Mrs. Tyndall, who had worked for me for a number of years]. He was Mrs. Tyndall's brother, ... and he was a U.S. attorney in Phoenix, Arizona, so he was evidently a very substantial citizen. In a little while Mrs. Tyndall came and found her brother and there was a joyful meeting. But while he was waiting for her to come, I said to him, "I have just had an application for a boy from Phoenix by a certain name who gave me as reference an Episcopal bishop of the city. Is it possible that you might know that boy?" He said, "It certainly is. He belongs to my Boy Scout Troop and we've been camping and all sorts of things together for several years. He's one of the finest boys I ever knew."

I reached over and got the letter declining him from the outgoing basket, and I wrote another letter accepting him. He proved to be a great find and a joy to have. I have often wondered what was the matter with that crazy bishop that he didn't say a word for the boy.

Work and Scholarships
from oral history, p. 50-51

TW: So then [in 1922] I looked up seven of the boys who wanted to work their way through, boys that looked to be of fine character and able to do schoolwork. I agreed to take those seven, provided they would do certain work in return, such as janitor or dishwasher or yard man. We signed the complete contract that I'd give them the schooling and they would do this particular work for me.

Q: I was going to ask you at this point, there was then an aspect of the self-help idea there in the beginning, similar to Midland and also to Kent. Has this continued, or was that just in the beginning?

TW: That's continued.

Q: To a certain extent do you still take—

TW: Oh, we always have. There was only one year we didn't have a scholarship boy. That was the second year.

from a letter dated June 4, 1964, to David Rosenbaum, director of the Milford School in Connecticut

We've had many scholarships for many years. Before we turned it over to the trustees, I budgeted $25,000 for scholarship aid each year, when I could have filled the place entirely with fully paid boys.

Philosophy of Studying
from oral history, p. 118-120

Q: Thompson, what would be your philosophy about study? Now I remember that at Midland we were always told that when you go to college nobody's going to be sitting right in back of you—your mother or your father—and telling you you have to study, but that the thing is to develop good study habits during the time that you're in high school, and this is one thing, I guess, that is not easy to do. What's your philosophy about study?

TW: I have the same feeling. If they come here, they got to study; if they don't study, they can go anywhere, that's all right. That's why we had study hall.

Q: You put them in a study hall?

TW: If they didn't work themselves out of it.

Q: Well, now, when do you let them out?

TW: First month, if they come out all As and Bs, right then they're out. If they get a C during the next month, they're back.

Q: In other words, anybody that maintains an A or B average throughout the school year doesn't have to study in study hall, right?

TW: That's right. He mustn't have a C in anything. Then the seniors we're not so severe on; we want them to get used to not having somebody holding a ruler over them. But these younger boys, we come right down on them; they never had to do that in the schools that they'd been in before.

Q: You let the boys out of study hall in their junior year?

TW: Not unless they earned it. No, they keep up that B average, and our B wasn't easy to get.

College Boards and Grading

Our first year 1922-1923, we set our academic standards on the basis of College Board Examinations. In those days the examinations were given at the end of each school year for each subject the student had taken. On these, the student would accumulate the number of credits he would need for admission to the college of his choice. A score of 60 or above was required by the Ivy League colleges for admission. In giving grades monthly to our students, we based our grade on what we thought the College Board people would require.

For instance, we did not give a grade of B unless we felt sure that the student would pass the College Board Examination at the end of the year at the 60 level. If the student was excellent, he could get our A, but the majority were below our B grade. He would pass our course with a C or D, but he did not get recommended grades to college on those subjects, unless at the end, he surprised us by getting 60 or better on College Boards. Some did.

Our boys thought that our grades were too hard and unreasonable, but our system of lower grades stimulated them to put on more effort, and greatly improved our scholarship. It was not popular with many boys who came from schools with easier standards, but resulted in giving us a good standing with the colleges both east and west.

A Student's Speech

Some years ago I wanted to train our students to speak in public. I told them that I wanted every boy to speak before our assembly at least once during the year. I asked them to write on some subject that interested them until they thought they had a good speech. Then I wanted them to memorize it and give it to the assembly. Several of them had trouble with their memories under excitement and embarrassment. I conceded that they might have notes to use as reminders.

The day came when John Shields '34 was to give us his speech. He was going along too well, with eyes on his notes. I spoke up and said, "John, are you reading all of it?" He said, "No, Sir, I am skipping some of it."

The Popcorn Prank
by Paula Pitzer (and Bill Webb) from The Webb Schools Alumni Bulletin, *1988-89*

Demerits were the penalty for pranks, of course, as well as for missed commitments, and the usual follies of youth. But Thompson Webb always said that he would give no demerits for a prank if it were totally original. Bill Webb says that the only prank he remembers (and we gather that he remembers quite a few) which Thompson ever accepted as totally original was the following:

At the time, the late '30s, everyone in the school was required to be in study hall from 7 to 9 p.m. on school nights. The study hall was held in "the old schoolhouse," with a master presiding from the elevated desk in the rear, a situation in which the master had the advantage—any deviation could be observed without the student having the advantage of counter-observation. Though much was generally accomplished, study hall was not the students' favorite occupation, and was the butt of more than one prank.

On this particular occasion, a classmate of Bill's, who is currently nameless, sneaked into the room early, armed with a bag of unpopped popcorn. By climbing on desktops, he was able to feed a small amount into the bowl of each of the overhead light fixtures. Later, about 15 minutes after the study hall lights were turned on, the fun began—as a hail of popped corn descended on the study hall—and pandemonium ensued. The study hall was excused, but both Thompson and the surprised master "laughed heartily" at that one!

Accommodations at Webb and Paul Squibb
from chapel talk given in May, 1959

They tell me there are boys who cannot see anything good about this place. Well, it isn't a country club. I do remember the time when Mr. Squibb taught for me. He was here eight years. And he always complained about the luxuries at this school. He thought it was entirely too luxurious. Have you ever thought of it that way? I hadn't. He thought that for building the best character, we should be very primitive and almost have a camping attitude with none of the luxuries. So finally he withdrew and went up to Midland and established the Midland School along the lines which he believed in. And that was magnificent. Because if he really believed it, then he ought to have done what he did. It is a great school. I have been on that board all these years. Mr. Squibb and I have remained friends, and I am a great admirer of his. But when I go up there, I do think that we have some luxuries. When I visit your home, I don't feel that we have such luxuries. Those things are comparative. But at the same time, we are not particularly concerned with you being proud of your accommodations here.

Food at Webb and Philosophy of Eating with the Students
from chapel talk given in May, 1959

We do our best to satisfy you in the food, but we will never do that. There will always be some who won't enjoy the food. And there are times when I don't. Living in a community of this size and eating in one dining room, we have to take what comes. There are a few things that I would like to say to the dietitian, "Don't ever put [them] on the table. I don't like them." But if I did, my wife would have a miserable time because she just likes the things that I don't like. And it is a great outlet for her to have this. And sometimes she tries to please my tastes. Puts on things that she doesn't like just because I like them. So I can't complain of those things—the fact that they come on the table when I don't like them. But more recently they put me on a diet. I am having things different from you. I never did that in my life in all these years until the doctor ordered it. I always ordered that my table have exactly what every other table had. And it still does, [mostly]. But I suppose that after living 70 years in a boys school, I might have for a year or two [food that is] a little bit different. I can't live in my own home and have everything my own way if I am going to live with you, and I think that it is essential in a school that I do live with you and eat in the dining room with you.

Extracurricular Activities, 1936-37
from the Blue and Gold, *1937, Vol. XII, No. 8*

Every week someone asks me the question: "How in the world can you keep your boys busy all the time?" The question somewhat annoys me by its frequency and by its insinuation that I have to keep them busy all the time. I feel I give very little time trying to arrange plans by which we may get a little time for all the activities that deserve a place. If the boys were not interested and did not want to do things, maybe I should be concerned. Our boys do not lack desire to do things. I am driven to the limit to find ways and means to provide places and equipment and time by which these boys may do the things they want to do.

This year our *Blue and Gold* has distinguished itself by improving its looks and content. There has been more work put on it than before, which shows for itself. I suspect that the same thing is true of *El Espejo* but as yet I have not seen it. There is no limit to the time and effort that could be put on these publications. It pays well in return to those who work and it deserves great consideration. I should like to say more on this subject but possibly I can do that somewhere else.

Our dramatics have required much time this year. Those boys who have worked on the stage have spent much time. We all know that it takes time to learn and rehearse a play but more than that are the hours spent by technicians in making scenery, arranging lights, collecting properties, running errands and running everybody crazy by upsetting the even tenor of their ways with thousands of unceasing demands.

Nor does the social committee lack in disturbing even tenor when they decide to have a dance. They run hither and yon, collecting everything everybody owns and making the gymnasium a burst of glory for the few short hours in which we are honored by the presence of the beautiful visitors.

Then look at the little group on the hill, making radios, learning codes, striving for amateur licenses, broadcasting; and behind all that, remodeling the shack, wiring it, painting it, and furnishing it. They have converted it into a little radio palace that would take the eye of anybody who peeped in.

One of the most insistent beggars for time and transportation is the fossil-hunting group. Every vacation the whole place is upset by this gang, collecting and assembling equipment, rushing off to bring home more and bigger prehistoric animal tracks and skulls. Just look into the biology room and see what the energy of this group has brought forth; and now they beg for more room in which to store their treasures and upset the place more and yell for more time. I almost wonder if Mother Nature doesn't grumble at the prying spirits that emanate from the Webb campus to break "open a shaft away from where men sojourn." From what they bring home I know they have found "that path no bird of prey knoweth, neither hath the vulture's eye seen it."

Then we have a group of boys who indulge in the use of rouge. They spend hours throughout the year rubbing it into the faces of lenses for telescopes, hoping by the use of cosmetics to tempt the Old Man in the Moon a little closer. They fooled him all right and caught his picture, but how they clamor for time to put up these ruses on the Old Man. They may make old Mother Nature jealous yet.

Then the shop for the boats, starlets and seasleds, dories and canoes, paddle boards and gliders keeps the environment of the headmaster's home resounding with buzz saws, hammers and electric planers—some mornings before 6 and all through the afternoons, even disturbing the quiet of the Sunday afternoons. If that were all, maybe we could abide it, but hours of the precious office time are spent trying to explain and justify to disturbed parents the bills for mahogany and spruce, brass screws, paints and gadgets galore. What troubles that shop can bring to a tired headmaster! How can he keep these boys from being so busy?

In desperation the headmaster turns into his house to shut windows and doors to seek peace and quiet for a few minutes of contemplation. But there all hope is gone. All over the dining table are rows of dignified seniors designing and carving and pecking on oak plaques. All peace is gone. Peck, peck it goes.

With the warmth of home and fireside banished, the headmaster turns for relief to the outdoors and strolls across the campus seeking a spot in the sun, if perchance there may be a bright interval in the California weather. Here they come, the candid cameras, seeking an awkward moment when the headmaster may not be at his best. They are not satisfied with snapping him on the sly at every point of disadvantage, but come from their hiding and ask him to stand here and there, and watch for the little birdie. With this ordeal over, as a committee they present their petitions for more darkrooms, the present three not being sufficient to satisfy the demands for darker caverns in which to enlarge their unholy work.

From this conference, the headmaster is interrupted and called to the office to interview a lady who has come to see the school. Her first question is, "How can you keep these boys busy all the time?" And I as a headmaster think to myself, "And how!"

I have one hobby of my own which gets woefully neglected. That is reading. I should like to make it contagious. Maybe it would bring about more peace and comfort and even tenor to our ways. For years I have worried for fear some boys would leave here without catching my hobby. I have bought all the good books I could afford, and good friends have supplemented my ability and added many books. Some boys find them and use them but still others are too busy working in shops that are more appealing to them. I fear our books have not been in attractive surroundings which sufficiently entice the boys to read just for fun. Now, our good friends, Mr. and Mrs. Willard Jackson, have given the order to the distinguished architect, Mr. Myron Hunt, to plan and build the library of our dreams here on the Webb campus. What a love gift this is: The Thomas Jackson Library. It is named in memory of one of the finest boys who ever lived on this campus, a lover of books and a lover of horses, a student, a gentleman. Tom's life was too short. He made so much of his few years for all that was fine that one feels he must have known that much had to be accomplished in only a few years. I never knew one who accomplished more or lived a fuller or more beautiful life. It is such a joy to have the library of my dreams named and dedicated to Thomas Jackson. I think it is the most fitting gift that could have been made in his name and one that he would have loved. The library will be more sacred, more beautiful to those of us who knew Tom because it bears his name, Thomas Jackson.

Lt. Deuel and his Glider

Along about the late '20s [1928], we employed an interesting young man by the name of Deuel. He had been a lieutenant in the flying force during the first World War, [and was affectionately known as the "Lieut" by the boys]. [He was known for striding about in his army flier's uniform, with the requisite white silk scarf draped jauntily at the neck.*] We put him to running our hobby shop. He excited our boys very much with a suggestion that they make a glider. Everyone rushed to the shop as soon as there was free time. It took them many weeks to make the contraption—a biplane of wooden framework and canvas about eighteen feet wide. [It was called "The Spirit of Webb."*] The flier would take his place in the middle and hold it up off the ground and then run with it and jump off the top of a steep declivity above the athletic field. If the breeze was favorable, he would glide a short distance out into the field and land on his legs, running.

The boys were so full of excitement when they went home for a vacation that the news spread among the moving picture people. Several newsreel companies sent their photographers out and took pictures. They would get close up under the declivity and shoot up as the glider went over, the boy's legs hanging down.

These pictures appeared in newsreels all over the country and in some foreign countries. I received hundreds of letters from boys all over the world wanting blueprints of the glider, and from old friends here and there who had seen it.

A few years ago, many years after the glider, one of our family was looking in the *Encyclopedia Britannica* and discovered a picture of our glider in the *Britannica*. It was labeled "U.S. Army Glider in California." However,

Lt. Deuel with The Spirit of Webb, a glider that he and students built.

it was our glider with our boys and Lt. Deuel standing by it. The background was our old school house. The later edition of the *Britannica* does not repeat it.

* *from the 1988-89* The Webb Schools Alumni Bulletin, *p. 59.*

Deuel was also a well-loved babysitter for my brothers and me and would play games like airplane with us. He also could tell stories like nobody else. —TW, JR.

Photo in the *New York Times*
from letter to his sister, Alla, May 5, 1928

Yesterday, we received a copy of the *New York Times* in which they have a very nice picture of our glider in the pictorial section of last Sunday's *Times*. You probably see copies of it back there [in Bell Buckle]. Do look for our glider.

Crash of the Glider
from interview with the four Webb brothers at The Webb Schools, December, 1988

Bill: The final and last flight of the glider occurred in the summertime long after Deuel had left. Bob Baum '32, who lived locally and was a graduate of this school, had his little Chevrolet convertible up on the gymkhana field and tied a rope to the glider. Ellsworth Bartholomew '32, who was the younger brother of Fred Bartholomew, who was the repairman here, climbed into it. Bob Baum took off with his car, and Ellsworth climbed up about thirty feet before the rope snapped. The plane went up and then straight down and crashed. The tail wiggled a few times, as I remember, and then snapped and collapsed on Ellsworth. He was lucky that he lived through that.

Howell: We thought that he was dead, but he came out unscathed.

TW, JR.: Luckily, he survived but that was the end of the glider. I remember seeing the crash.

Camping on Weekends

TW, JR.

When I was in the eighth grade [ca. 1930], Mother and Dad took the class camping in the desert. I spent an uncomfortable night sleeping on the sand. Probably Mother thought that this was something they ought to do with the boys. Camping was one way to deal with weekends before the school had a fully active sports program.

Camping was not a regular activity for Dad at school, but he did it a few times with the students. It had no other purpose than getting the boys out, though Dad enjoyed showing the boys some of the sights that he knew about in the Coachella Valley. He would show them where the fish traps were or take the boys to see the rock in which J.C. Fremont's name was carved. It was never clear whether the inscription was authentic, but Fremont's forces had been in the area in 1848 during the Mexican War. The site was not protected or part of a park.

Headmaster Talk on Morale

from the Blue and Gold, *November 1, 1925, by a student reporter*

Last Sunday evening at vesper services Mr. Webb spoke to the student body on the subject of "Morale." It dealt principally with the football team, and its showing at the various games. The team, Mr. Webb says, lacks "morale" to the highest degree. If you have no morale in a football team you may just as well stop having one and do something else. "Morale" in one sense means "fight," and where is a football team without any fight? Just where we are now, and that is where we will finish if we do not take a different attitude. When we go out to practice, the majority of the football "hopes" bring into use that well known motto, "Take it easy." By all means don't "take it easy" on the football field. When you go out to practice, don't go at it in a half-hearted sort of a way. Work hard, and if everybody does the same, we will have one of the best football teams in the league.

What we need, fellows, is cooperation. Work together and do it well; at least as well and hard as you know how.

Of course this does not always apply to football and nothing else. It applies also to the activities of the classroom, that is, your studies. Do the same in your studies and you will soon be getting good results. Muster up all the "morale" you can and go to it.

Thompson Webb photographing at a lacrosse game.

Attitude Towards Sports

from interview with the four Webb brothers at The Webb Schools, December, 1988

TW, JR.: The school had regular teams in the regular seasons as soon as it had enough boys to make a football team and a baseball team. After that the athletic program grew. Dad's personal attitude towards sports was that sports were something that boys played. This was good healthy activity for boys to participate in. He, of course, had other things to do than watch the boys play. I can remember on at least two occasions in the years when I was here from 1922 to 1935 that he was waited on by committees of the students saying that they thought that the headmaster ought to attend football games and other sports events and that the headmaster was not showing appropriate school spirit. Dad always listened to the boys solemnly, but he very seldom attended any games because games were for boys. That was his attitude toward sports. He had his activities that were appropriate for him. He saw that coaches made sports available.

Jack: At the time that I was in school from 1936 to 1940, I recall Dad attending every football game. I played in many of them and attended all that I didn't play in. I always noticed that Dad was out there on the sidelines. If there was a bench, he was sitting there usually. It always astonished me that he was so impatient about the games. He was actually talking in a friendly manner to the visiting headmaster or whoever was in charge of the enemy. [laughter] I can see why some of us felt that he did not show enough school spirit, but he was there.

A Great Tragedy

In January of 1938 we had a withdrawal and were very happy to fill the place with Howard Bryan Kindelberger, son of Mr. and Mrs. James Howard Kindelberger. Mr. Kindelberger was president of North American Aviation. In those days, we had a stable where the boy who wished might keep his horse and use the horse as his major athletic activity. Howard brought his mare.

Our rule was that they could ride alone on our campus, but off campus they rode together with a master who supervised the sport. Mr. Kindelberger requested that Howard be allowed to ride alone without the master, if he so desired, as he had done at home ever since he was 7 years old. He assured me that the mare was gentle and safe. All went well that year and the next. In the spring of 1939 the mare produced a beautiful colt which was the pride of Howard's heart. In February of 1940, Howard rode out into the hills alone on the mare with the yearling colt following. He followed a path he knew through a gate into a pasture where some horses were grazing. The loose horses ran up to see the colt and frightened it, causing the colt to run into a wire fence. The colt became tangled up and cried out in fright and pain. Howard jumped down and ran to the colt with horses crowding around. The mare became excited and began kicking at the horses and struck Howard in the stomach. He was alone, but the noise had brought Mr. William W. Clary '35 out of his house in time to see the mare kick Howard. He ran to the rescue and called me. In a short time we had Howard in the Pomona Hospital under excellent doctors and had called his parents who came and took charge. In a few days, Howard died.

We felt fortunate that Mr. Clary saw the accident and could tell us exactly what happened, and that Howard did not lie out there until we made a search for him.

Mr. Kindelberger asked me to conduct Howard's funeral. I am not a minister and never did a thing of that kind before. I begged to be excused, but he and the mother were insistent. Of course I had to do it. I worked over the prayer book and selected appropriate passages with one or two favorite passages from the Bible and a poem or two until I was satisfied with the service. Then I rehearsed but would completely break down with emotions and could not get through, he was so dear to me. I was desperate. I went to my doctor and told him my condition. He gave me a pill to take one hour before the service. I do not know what it was, but it worked. My mind was clear, my emotions were calm. I went through the service.

That was the hardest task I ever had.

The Two Boys Who Could Not Room Together

This story is about two mothers who came to see me about entering their two boys in school. They were very charming and attractive young mothers, each having a son about 14 years of age. They explained to me that they had been born in adjoining homes the same week, and had grown up playing together all their lives and had been in school together in the same class, finally to boarding school and roomed together and then to college and roomed together, and that on graduation they were each engaged and so they decided to have a double wedding and were married, and that they bought homes adjoining each other, and had always lived in adjoining yards, and each had a son the same week. And those little boys had grown up always inseparable companions almost like brothers, and the time had come now to put them into boarding school, and they were planning to put them in the same school and wanted to consider this one.

The short of it was that they enrolled the two boys for the coming year. We tested them and found them well-qualified and were delighted to have them enrolled.

A few days later one of these mothers came back alone, and she explained to me that these two boys had always been together and had almost had no other companions, and she felt it was very necessary that her son learn to mix with other boys. And in order to break up that continual companionship, she would rather have her son room in a different dormitory from the one in which the friend was to room, but she went on to say that if I should ever give that away, it would cause trouble between these two families that had been inseparable friends all their lives and cautioned me that under no circumstances must I ever let the other family know that she had requested that separation. Of course, I promised to keep it in the greatest secrecy and said that I could arrange to place them in separate dormitories.

I don't think she had been off the campus two hours before here came the other mother, and she put me under secrecy and explained that she wanted the two boys separated, but did not want the other family to know she felt that way about it and that I must never betray that confidence but just arrange to have them separated some way and not let them room together under any conditions. And so this arrangement was made, and my wife and I selected single rooms for these boys, each in a separate dormitory.

The opening day of school there was a great group of parents and boys arriving, and the different teachers were going with each boy and helping him find his place and get his things unpacked. These two boys arrived at the same time with their mothers, and I assigned a different teacher to each of these boys and showed them the room chart where these boys were to live. Almost at once the two boys came running back together in great excitement and said that they were to room together, and we didn't have them in the same room or the same building. Well, I told them the school was full and that every room was taken and had been assigned to each boy, and it was too late for me to change it. They tried to argue with me, and said that of course it was understood that they were to room together in the very beginning. I said, "I am sorry, nobody explained it to me that way, and I just put you where I had available rooms." They went running back for their mothers as hard as they could go, and they brought the two mothers in, and the two boys sat down in my room, and the mothers said, "Mr. Webb, there has been some mistake. We understood our boys were to room together." And I said, "You didn't tell me so." "We told you we had always been inseparable friends and had grown up together and lived in adjoining houses, our boys had been born the same week and always been inseparable. It never occurred to us that you wouldn't put them in a double room together." "Well," I said, "I am sorry. I just can't arrange it now. This wasn't brought up in the beginning, and I have made my plans. Every room is taken and promised, and the mothers have inspected the rooms and approved of them, and most of the boys have moved in. There is just nothing I can do about it."

These mothers argued harder and harder, and they got really very angry, and it made the thing exceedingly embarrassing to me. And I began to think I had made a terrible mistake, but I hadn't forgotten my individual instructions, and I had not forgotten my promise that I would not give them away, but they were so convincing, I decided I had made a mistake, but there wasn't anything I could do. I had to leave them where they were, with the result that they went out very indignant and very angry with me, and the boys entered the rooms that were assigned to them. The mothers got busy helping them unpack and get straightened out, and through the crowd here came one of the mothers back and she leaned over and whispered, "Thank you, Mr. Webb, for handling that so tactfully." It was a tremendous relief to me when I heard that. I was sure I had made a mistake, and she went on back to help her son, and in a little while here came the other one, "Oh, Mr. Webb, you were wonderful how you handled that. Thank you so much." And so they went on their way, and those boys never roomed together.

from oral history, p. 131

TW: Well, there's a play outfit that sells you plays [Samuel] French, that sells lots of plays for amateurs; [this story of the two boys is] in one of those plays. The woman who wrote the play heard my story, and she made a very comical little one-act play out of that thing. [laughter]

Maintaining Standards

"He is the only educator I have known who never sacrificed ethical standards in the interest of expediency or the placating of parents. May his spirit never die."

—*Lucille Phillips Morrison in Vol. 22, p. 24,*
Webb School of California Alumni Bulletin, *1974-76*

William Boeing and Horse Racing

Some years after our school had been running, the State of California passed a law permitting gambling on horse races under the pari-mutuel system. I don't believe gambling is right and certainly would not be a wholesome activity for schoolboys. A great track was built, Santa Anita, about 20 miles from us. I announced to our students and their families that we were forbidding our students to go there. I had no difficulty about it for a few years. Then Mr. William Boeing of the Boeing Aircraft Company put his son, William, JR. '42, in school. When the racing season came, Mr. Boeing brought down from Seattle a string of horses to Santa Anita. The day before the much-touted Handicap Race was to be run, Mr. Boeing came to see me and told me that one of the horses belonged to William, JR., and he had entered him in the race. He said that he would come out the next day and take Bill in to see his horse run. I told him that I didn't allow our students to go to the races and couldn't make an exception of one. I was sorry, but Bill could not go. He pulled himself up and told me that Bill was going, and he was going to take him. I looked him in the eye and told him I could not stop him from taking his son, but I would stop him from bringing him back, and to take his trunk with him. He stood there a minute, flushed in the face, and looked me over in silence. Then he said, "Very well, I will not take him."

Bill stayed on several years and graduated. He was a fine boy, and all the school was fond of him. Occasionally since then we have seen him and have always had a good time talking about the past years. I had forgotten about the racehorses until a year or so ago, when a new boy came to the school since my retirement. His father looked me up in my home, for he said he wanted to meet me, that he was a near relative of Bill's. He said that when the family had a reunion someone was sure to tell the story of the racehorse. He said that they all agreed that old man Webb was the only man who ever stopped Uncle Bill. (Mr. Boeing died a few years ago and left a considerable estate.)

Now, the racehorse brings up another experience. I was invited to the initiation of Phi Beta Kappa at Pomona College one year, with dinner following. One or two of my former students were initiated. At the dinner I was seated by a stranger who was considerably older than the other initiates. To start conversation I asked him what school prepared him for Pomona. He replied that he had attended for short time nearly every private school, except mine, in the State of California, plus several public high schools. He said that he was too full of the devil when he was young and he would get "fired" from first one school and then another until his family was completely exasperated with him. Finally he ran away from home and became a jockey for eight or 10 years. He told me that jockeys made lots of money but usually blew it in as fast as they made it. He claimed that he had a stingy streak and didn't waste his money but invested his in "blue chips," with the result that he had an estate that would take care of him. When this was accomplished, he decided to get an education. With the aid of tutors he was admitted to Pomona and, as I could see, had made the most of it.

I told him that I had been told that the betting on horse races at one time was very dishonest but that, since pari-mutuel, it was honest. He told me not to get fooled by what people said, and that there was plenty of dishonesty in the races. He admitted that he could not have said that when he was in the business. Now that he was out, he told me that jockeys were not only well-paid, as they should be, but that a few made the big money on betting. He admitted that some races were fixed by agreement of the jockeys; that most were honest but that others might be agreed upon, and the jockey's agents placed the bets. He admitted that no one could tell when a jockey pulled a horse, but that they knew how to do it and would be fools if they didn't take a good share of the big money. He said he got a kick out of watching so-called good judges looking over the horses and placing their bets, based on their appraisal of the horse, when the winner of the race might already be determined.

A Saudi Student and the State Department

A representative of the State Department called on me requesting me to admit N.S. to our school. They said that he was one of the sons of a prominent family in Saudi Arabia. They said he had been in a school in England for several years and spoke English well. We agreed to take him. Soon he arrived. We gave him a room in the dormitory.

Soon our honor committeeman came to see me. He felt that it was dangerous for N.S. to have so much money in his room as it would be a temptation to someone to steal. I inquired about how much money he had. The honor committeeman claimed to have seen $5,000.

I sent for N.S. and advised him to put his money in a bank for we did not always know our janitors well enough to trust them. He did put the money in the bank and learned to use a checking account. However, he was surprised that there might be a thief. He claimed that there was very seldom a thief in Saudi Arabia, because when one was caught the government cut off his hand. Hence, very little stealing.

N.S. was not a bad boy but he certainly did not intend to bother about studying his assignments. I begged him to get down to work. He asked me why should he work since his father had slaves to do all the work and he had all the money he could use. I asked him if he did not want to go to college. He replied that of course he would go to college. I told him that the colleges would not take him unless he did satisfactory academic work in high school. He shrugged his shoulders and told me that a family member would call the college and they would take him.

He failed his work with us, getting all F grades, and I refused to take him another year. Then the State Department tried to make me keep him, saying they were working hard to establish good relations with Saudi Arabia, and it was very important to them for me to keep him. I had to confess to them that I treated all students on the same standards, that I could not treat a prominent person any differently than any other student in school. On that basis, he was out.

Shortly afterwards, I learned that he was in one of our Western universities. I presume that the prince must have called them for they never asked for a transcript from me.

Conrad Hilton

One morning my receptionist announced to me that Mr. Conrad Hilton and his son were in the office to see me. She brought them in, and we shook hands. I had never seen Mr. Hilton before, nor have I since. He said that he would like to enter his son in my school. He was a boy of about 14. Hanging down from the son's mouth was a lighted cigarette. I told Mr. Hilton that it wouldn't be wise to put him with me since he had acquired the habit of smoking. We did not permit our boys below senior grade to smoke. I felt since the boy had the habit he might break over, and I would be compelled to ask him to take the boy back.

Mr. Hilton took the boy's arm and pushed him out the door without a word. In the doorway he turned to me and snarled like an angry dog and slammed my door with a great bang. That is the only time I ever saw that happen.

Support for Fred Hooper
from letter to Hall Martin '30, January 18, 1971

I am very much amused at an attorney in San Francisco, who called me on the telephone and told me that he couldn't get any sense into Fred [Hooper, headmaster at Webb School from 1962 to 1973], who was head, and he wanted me to see what I could do with him, because he'd sent home a San Francisco boy from a very prominent family. He admitted the boy had acted exceedingly badly and deserved what he got, but the family was too important; anybody of their standing you just couldn't afford to send away; that was ruinous to the school. And I told him I admired Fred very much, I felt he'd done exactly the right thing. "Oh," he said, "you wouldn't have done it back when you ran it." And I said, "Oh yes, oh yes."

"Oh, you never sent home anybody as prominent as that," he said. And I said, "Well, I thought I had. I once sent home a couple of my nephews." "Well," he says, "that's family. You wouldn't have sent home somebody that wasn't kin to you as prominent as this boy is." "Well," I said, "I don't know. You got anybody more prominent than the grandson of the president of the United States?" I said, "I don't think this boy outrates him, does he? I sent the grandson home." Well, he wouldn't believe me. But finally, when I told him who it was, he said, "Well, I give up. If you would do that, then you'd stand with Fred on this."

Now, I thought probably I lost that attorney's friendship. But he sent his boy to the school. And then he wrote me one time and he was president of the Board of Trustees of the California Bible Society, and they were looking for someone to fill an empty place on the board and invited me to join them. And so now I'm a member of the board of the Bible Society, which, by the way, is the oldest Bible Society in the United States, outdates the American Bible Society, and is coordinated with them in the work they do.

Problem Students and Parents

The Dallas Boy and the Fire

Along about the middle of our history, we received an application from a boy to come from Dallas, Texas, to the school, giving us several references who knew the boy and could speak for him, one of whom was a bishop of the Episcopal Church in Dallas. I wrote to them all and inquired about the boy. The letters came back recommending him very highly. Bishop Moore stated that he and his family were very close friends in their church, and that the boy would be an honor to any school. So he was accepted and he arrived two days before school was to open along with two boys from Mexico City who happened to come at the same time, though they didn't know each other. The Mexican boys couldn't speak English but we agreed to take them and let them live here with us.

The other students hadn't arrived and most of the teachers hadn't, but I had one young teacher, so I put the Dallas boy in a room next to the Mexican boys and next to them was the young teacher to take care of their needs in the dormitory. About 6 o'clock the next morning we were awakened by the fire alarm and found that the room in which the Dallas boy had slept was a roaring fire. The teacher had gotten the boy out of the room and up to the infirmary for he was badly burned. The fire company had turned loose water and other things and extinguished the fire and the Mexican boys were all right, but the room was terribly charred. It had fresh paint on the walls that had burned and the curtains and mattress and bed were all badly burned. I went into the room and looked around and on the floor I found a can of cleaning fluid that had been opened and used and it was the type that I knew was inflammable. Then I went around to the infirmary and found the boy in bed and the nurse taking care of him. The doctor came in very shortly afterwards. I asked the boy how that fire got started in his room. He said that when he got to Claremont he bought that cleaning fluid and that morning he'd gotten up and poured it on the curtains, bed, and his pajamas and touched it off—that he wanted to kill himself. He didn't want to come to a boarding school.

I was somewhat amazed and suggested to him that there might be less painful ways of going out if he had to do that. He said he'd gone to Phillips Academy, Andover, the year before and had done that up there and they had to send him home and he hoped I'd send him home.

The doctor sent him down to Pomona Valley Hospital where he had every care and in a few days they could get him in condition to wear his clothing. I called his mother on the telephone and told her what had happened and I thought she ought to come and get him. She said she didn't have time to bother with him, that I should just put him back in school and make him behave himself. I told her we didn't have a psychopathic ward and her kid was crazy. She said, "Oh, he's just spoiled and wanted to make me take him home." I told her I wasn't going to take him back and she said just to put him on the train and send him home. I told her I wasn't going to do that—that boy needed company. He was liable to kill himself. She insisted he was all right and just send him home. I insisted that she would have to send somebody to accompany him and that I'd leave him in the hospital till they arrived.

That boy almost burned up the building with half our rooms in it. It would have ruined the school if that building had gone and I wouldn't have had any place to put my pupils. It was certainly a narrow escape for my school.

I went down and talked to the boy and asked him if the bishop knew that he had done that at Andover. He said of course he did and he told him not to tell anything about it. "Just get out there and make good." I never met the bishop, but for a clergyman I was amazed at his lack of integrity in recommending this boy who might have ruined my entire school.

The mother arrived in a station wagon with a chauffeur and took the boy's possessions and the boy home. I advised her to put him under a psychiatrist for I was perfectly sure he was not sane. She was perfectly sure he was, the bishop said he was all right. I told her she'd make a great mistake if she didn't get him under a psychiatrist at once. So they went away and two or three years later this mother did me the courtesy of writing me a letter of thanks. She stated that the psychiatrist had found a type of insanity and that he had been put in Johns Hopkins Hospital for a long stay, but was now declared sane by the authorities at Johns Hopkins and she felt she owed me thanks.

M.R.

This is the story of M.R. I think it may have been in the early years of the school. It was not a large school, and we were going along very smoothly up till Christmas time. There had not been an incident of stealing reported to me during that entire fall.

Shortly after Christmas, we admitted a boy by the name of M.R. to the school, and placed him in a single room upstairs in the old dorm. Very shortly, there began to be some stealing. The boys would come to me and report different items missing, and sums of money, and one came and said that his gold seal ring had been stolen. We could not help but be suspicious of M.R. as he was the new boy in and no stealing had occurred before his arrival. Consequently, we watched him with some care and investigated quietly, but we found no evidence on him.

Then one of the boys from the smoke shack came in and said that somebody had stolen his meerschaum pipe, that he knew he'd left down there, and now it was missing and he couldn't find it. Shortly afterwards, another boy had lost a Waterman fountain pen. These were objects that we might be able to find. It was difficult ever to discover money.

One time when the boys were all away, I secretly and quietly searched M.R.'s room, but I didn't find a thing in it that didn't belong there. There kept being objects missed and reported to me, but I could get no evidence at all until we came within a month of the end of school, when one of the janitors came to me and said he wanted to show me something. He took me up to the room of the boy who had lost the gold seal ring and pulled up the mattress. Down in the coil springs was tied this ring by a string. That put me to thinking. Well, the thief had tied it right in the boy's own room and the boy didn't know where it was. Maybe that was his way of concealment till the time came to go home. Consequently, I went to the smoke shack and made a thorough search and up on top of one of the rafters, entirely out of sight, I discovered the meerschaum pipe. And then I went to the boy's room that had lost the Waterman fountain pen and made a search, and I found it hidden in his room. So it was very conclusive to me that the same boy had done the same thing, in each case hidden the stolen object in the room where he found it. I decided to watch M.R. very carefully before he went home at the end.

We arranged his examination so he could get away a day early, before the other boys. After he had completed them, I was very much on the alert, but he was lackadaisical. I asked him, "When's your mother coming after you?" He said, "Oh, I'm not going until tomorrow. I didn't want to go home ahead of the other boys, and I've arranged for her to come for me tomorrow afternoon." Then the next day, all the other boys went home ahead of M.R., and his mother came out rather late in the afternoon. He was the last boy to go and it looked very conclusively to me that he had designed that on purpose. I didn't want to search his baggage after he had packed up to go home, so I decided to take his mother into my confidence, and I took her to my office and told her about the situation, and I said, "It looks so conclusively as though M.R. is the thief." "But," I said, "Mrs. R., I could not accuse the boy of stealing until I could actually prove it on him. And I don't want you to ever tell him I suspected he was the thief in any way unless perchance we should discover that he was stealing." I said, "I hope you will examine his baggage when he gets home with a great deal of care, but not let him know. And if you discover the signet ring, the meerschaum pipe, and the Waterman pen, you'll know that he was the one that took them."

She seemed very shocked that I should even think that he would steal. She just thought that he was the most honest boy in the world, and she was greatly grieved and promised she would never tell him, but would examine his baggage with great care. Shortly after dinner that evening,

Richard Sutphen '33 called me from Los Angeles and told me that somebody had stolen a school annual out of his drawer in his room, and he told me that he was suspicious of M.R. He said that M.R. had ordered the annual in advance but when the time came he didn't have the $5 and said he couldn't afford to buy it. He said, "It was a disappointment to me not to make the sale. I was depending on that to make things come out even. But I wouldn't give him the annual. I thought, 'Well, I'll take the extra one home.' But when I went to get it, it was gone."

The following day Mrs. R. phoned me and said that M.R. had not taken those items, there wasn't a thing like that in his grips. She'd gone over them with great care, and he hadn't brought any of them home. And she said, "Mr. Webb, I disregarded your instructions and I did tell M.R. that you suspected him, and his feelings were very much hurt. He wants to come out this afternoon to see you and just convince you that he didn't do it, and tell you all he knew, and to prove to you that he did not take those things." I was very much disappointed she had told the boy, but she insisted that she was making him come out and she wanted to see me that afternoon. So I listened to her a while, and finally I asked her, "Mrs. R., how do you like the picture of M.R. in the annual?" "Oh," she said, "it's a perfectly fine picture, I'm just so delighted with it." And I said, "By the way, Mrs. R. where did you see the annual?" "Oh", she said, "M.R. brought one home with him." I said, "Mrs. R., he didn't buy that annual. He took it from Richard Sutphen's room when he didn't have enough money to pay for it." "Oh," she said, "wait a minute." She talked with M.R. and came back and said, "Mr. Webb, M.R. did pay for that annual. He said he gave Richard Sutphen $5 for it, and brought it home." "Very well, then," I said, "come out this afternoon."

As soon as she hung up, I phoned Richard Sutphen and asked him to come out rather early. I told him the situation, what Mrs. R. said about the annual, and he said, "That boy didn't pay me a penny." I said, "All right. Now, Richard, I want you to be in the closet in my office when he comes in and listen to the conversation." So that afternoon, M.R. began to tell me he didn't take the ring or the pipe or the fountain pen, and he did take the annual but he paid Richard Sutphen $5 for it. I said, "No, you didn't, M.R. Richard told me you didn't pay him, you refused to pay it, said you didn't have the money and you couldn't pay it. And he put the annual back in the drawer in the desk in his room and when he went to get it, it was gone. Now your mother tells me you have it." He began to swear on his honor that he did pay Richard, gave him the money himself, and he let himself out at length and said I was very much mistaken, that it was unjust of me to accuse him because he would swear on his honor that he'd paid for that. I raised my voice, I said, "Richard, come in." He opened the closet door and stepped out and faced M.R. Then all of M.R's bravery disappeared and he then admitted, "Well, Mr. Webb, I lied to you. I did take the annual. But I didn't take any of the other things."

I called his mother and told her he had admitted that he had stolen the annual but said he didn't steal the other things, and that I was quite sure he'd stolen all of those things and I wanted her to get them together and return them. But I never heard from that family again.

Clark Seller's Boy

This is the story of the boy whom Clark Sellers sent to our school, a boy in whom he had taken a great interest. Mr. Sellers was a handwriting expert. It was on the evidence that he submitted that the man who killed the Lindbergh baby was convicted and sentenced to death. Mr. Sellers was a famous man in his field as a handwriting expert.

He came to me and stated that he had taken a boy off of the streets, that he was quite a young fellow, and that he had tried to bring him up the best way possible, and that he was now ready for our eighth or ninth grade, and he asked me to take him. I was very much complimented that a man of Mr. Sellers' distinction wanted me to have his boy, and we took him without much question.

Shortly after school opened, we began to have stealing. Various things were missed by the boys, and our repairman, Frank Gould, reported that someone was stealing his tools. He had a shop full of his own tools and supplied with everything a workman could think of, the very finest and most expensive tools. He took great pride in them in their proper place, properly oiled and cared for. He wouldn't lend them to anybody, and nobody dared bother him about his tools. But he stated that certain ones of them were missing and they seemed to go on a Sunday. I suggested to him that he go in and lock his door behind him and hide in his shop and see who was coming in there the next Sunday.

Well, it so happened I had about a dozen distinguished guests in my living room that Sunday afternoon, when suddenly the door broke open and there was Frank Gould, red as a beet, dragging in this Sellers boy by the neck, and he announced in a big voice, "This boy is the one who's been stealing my tools. I caught him red-handed right in there."

Well, it was quite an embarrassing scene in front of all these guests, and I got him out of there as soon as I could, and inquired. Gould said that he was hidden away in there and had all the doors locked. He said one door he always locked on the inside by a hook, and that while he was in there he heard a little noise and looked around and saw a wire being extended, through a crack in the wall a few feet away, that reached over and lifted off that hook, and then young Sellers had come in and gone over to some of the cabinets and put a lot of his tools in his pocket, and he bounced over there and nabbed him with the tools on him. He said the boy had to admit he'd taken what he caught him with, but denied he'd ever been there before. But subsequently we did find the other tools hidden away in his room. He'd been there repeatedly and gotten various things that he wanted. But he never would admit that he'd taken a thing until we proved it on him.

At any rate, we called Mr. Sellers and had him come and get the boy. He was in our school, I think, only about six weeks.

We didn't hear any more of Mr. Sellers and that boy for a good many years, and then I read in the paper where this boy held up a gas station at the point of a gun, and when the man resisted he had killed him. Subsequently, I read in the papers where the court had convicted the boy of first-degree murder and condemned him to be hung. The case was appealed and he was to be given another trial. That's the last I ever heard of that case.

Difficult Parents
from oral history, p. 128-129, 132

Q: In the matter of parental relations, have these tended in the main to be pretty good, or have there been problems?

TW: Oh, of course you had problems. If you are running a boarding school you have all kinds of problems. I remember one nice boy, he was going along very nicely. One night his mother called me up and she began to curse me, the most profane woman, she called me a horrible son of a bitch, on and on. Just raving, and I, I hung up the telephone on her. Her husband was an officer in the Navy in charge of a naval group at a California college. I called him up in his office and told him what had happened, and I said, "I want you to come get your boy; I won't work for anybody that talks to me like that."

He said, "Well, Webb, you know what the matter is, don't you?"
And I said, "No."

He says, "She's dead drunk. When she gets drunk, nobody can do anything with her; don't pay any attention to her."

And I said, "Well, I'm not going to have her calling me up and talking to me like that."

He said, "Well, I'll tell you what you do. Now, you keep that boy. You look after the boy and I'll take care of the old lady." I never had any more trouble. Never heard from the "old lady" again.

. . . .

TW: I had a world of dealings with parents who were difficult. I had one father that was just so typical. He was supposed to be a minister, he had a doctor's degree from USC and taught over there. His boy roomed with somebody in the old dormitory [that] had some double rooms. We put them in a room together, these two boys, and pretty soon the monitor committee found that one of these boys had a bunch of pictures of nude women in his room. It was not this preacher's son. It was the other one. So we took them away from him and then separated them and said, "You can't room with anybody if that's the kind of thing you want." But the father of the other boy got mad at me for taking his son's roommate away from him, and I explained to him why. "No, but that reflects on my son, that my son isn't good enough to room with him." He just raised cain with me. When he went to renew the contract the following year, I told him, "I don't want to take your boy; you've been so ugly yourself this year. The boy's all right but I won't take him. I'm not going to deal with you anymore."

Boys Not Accepted at Webb School

Navy Captain

When I came to California to start a school, I brought with me a letter of introduction to a famous lady who was very prominent in educational circles and whose family was in the top social circle of Southern California. She received me graciously and referred several families to me, which helped very much in starting a new school. A few years went by before she came to see me about one of her sons. She asked if I could take him, and I could and was delighted to have a son of that family.

Next she said that she should talk to me about some trouble she was having with the boy. She discovered that he had been taking money out of her pocketbook. She had been missing it and blamed it on the servants, until one day she caught him and made him admit that he had been doing it for some time. She had given him a real talk on the subject and thought she had cured him. Then one day a committee of neighbors waited on her, in great embarrassment, to request that she forbid him to go to any houses in their block, for he was stealing them out of money and anything he could pawn—that they had tried to overlook it because of friendship but it had gone entirely too far; so they had to ask her to keep him at home. She admitted that this had been a great shock to her and his father. I admitted that it was a shock to me!

Then she asked if I was willing to take him under the circumstances. They felt they had to put him in a boarding school since he was not welcome in the homes of their friends. I told her that I did not think I should take him, for I never tolerated stealing in my student body and had always sent little thieves home as soon as I detected them. Then she asked where she could put him. I suggested a reform school where there were psychologists who were trained to deal with such problems which I knew nothing about handling. She was indignant about the idea of her son's going to a reform school. She asked if I could imagine her husband holding up his head at the California Club when all his friends there knew that his son was in a reform school. I replied with a question. Could her husband hold up his head with his friends when they knew that his son was a thief and he was doing nothing about it?

She left me in quite a huff, and I thought I had lost a valuable friend. Many years passed by in which I would meet her and her husband at the operas or receptions. They were pleasant, but nothing was ever said about that boy. I asked no questions.

A short time after the close of our late war with Germany and Japan, I was surprised by a visit from this lady with a handsome captain of the Navy in uniform. She introduced him as her son, the captain, with great pride. I knew she had more than one son. She asked if I had someone who could show the school to the captain as she wanted to have a talk with me. I arranged a tour for him. When she and I settled down, she asked if I remembered our conversation of years ago about her son who was a thief. I admitted I did. Then she told me that the captain was the boy. She said that after our conference she went home and told her husband that I had recommended she put the boy in that reform school. To her surprise her husband said he agreed with me and instructed her to enter him at once. She arranged it within a few days.

She said she bought him a fine outfit for going off to school, leather suitcase, silver-backed brush and comb, silk pajamas—everything new and fine—in order to give him a good feeling on leaving home. She said he was delighted and very proud and went off with great expectations.

For three years he remained there, getting good reports, and graduated with honors. Then he told them he wanted to go to Annapolis and be a Navy man. They had to hire a tutor to prepare him for the examination in subjects he had not covered. In the end he went to Annapolis and graduated with honors and went to sea. Gradually he made promotions until he became captain. Then came the war with Germany and Japan. He was captain of one of our great battleships that took part in several large naval engagements in which he won a number of decorations and honors. She and his father were very proud of him.

She told me that the day before was the servants' day off, his father went to his office, and she and the captain were at home alone. At lunch he asked her if she remembered how much trouble she had had with his stealing when he was a boy. She said it embarrassed her, for the subject had never been mentioned all these years since he had gone off to reform school. She admitted that, of course, she remembered it. He told her that she had given him the finest outfit any boy had ever had on going off to school, which had made him very happy, but that within 24 hours after he had reached the school the boys had stolen everything he had. He told her that he was furious and for days would go out on the campus and walk up and down in a great sulk. After some time of sulking he calmed down and thought more rationally. He realized that that was what he had been doing to other people, and no one had ever stolen from him before. He told his mother he then resolved that he would never steal again.

Then the great lady told me that she had come at once to thank me for guiding her to the right place for that boy. Two years later, shortly before her death, she called on me again and whispered, "Now the captain is an admiral."

Billy Burke's Boy

Along in the years when Jim Rogers '35 was in school [early 1930s], the movie actress who went as Billy Burke came to see me about a boy in whom she was interested. She wanted me to take him. As I remember he was something of a tramp or runaway who had appealed to her, and she wanted to get him on his feet and was willing to spend money on him and wanted my advice. I agreed to give him a trial for a few days until I could size him up. He was a more mature youngster and too sophisticated for us. We had a number of conferences. She came out repeatedly to talk to me, but in the end we could not afford to put a misfit in the school. I had to admit my inability to handle him. What she finally did, I do not know. I do want to say that I was tremendously impressed with Billy Burke. She had a big heart and wanted to help that boy. I wish he had been younger and less worldly-wise.

Keith Vosburg's Adopted Son and the Catalina School

There was a family that lived in Azusa by the name of Vosburg. They were people of a great deal of means and I got to know Mrs. Vosburg's son, Keith Vosburg, and came to admire him very highly. I don't know why Keith never married, but he formed an ambition to start a school for boys which he subsequently did. At first he had some plan that he would adopt the boys and he did adopt one little fellow about 12 years old and brought him out to his home to live with him and his mother. It was his intention to add to that until he had a number of boys.

Shortly after he'd brought the first one home, one Sunday Mrs. Vosburg—people who knew her intimately called her Kate—came over here with the chauffeur driving her and with the little boy that Keith had adopted. She told me that the little boy was just impossible and he'd be sweet and pleasant for a while and then he became very disturbed and Keith couldn't seem to straighten him out. Finally Keith got discouraged and decided to go abroad for a few months, and left the boy with her. She said that morning he went into a rage at the breakfast table and threw his pancakes covered with syrup into the face of a fine old cook who had been with them for years. The cook said she was going to quit if they kept that boy. She asked me if I would take him over here at school. I told her I didn't want to enroll him, but I'd let him stay for a few days and see what I could make of him and maybe help the problem until Keith got home. So she left him with me that Sunday afternoon and everything was very pleasant.

The boy did well in school and made no problem at all until the following Sunday morning. One of my students came running into my office and told me that the little boy had tried to kill one of the other students. He said they had all piled on to him and got him down on the ground and were holding him and for me to come out and see what I could do. Well, this had happened in the little yard between our dining room and storehouse. When I got out there five or six boys had the little boy down on the ground and were holding his arms and legs. Finally he quieted down a bit and I told them to let him go, but they showed me a big rock that was half as big as my head that this boy had thrown at another student's head with all the power he could muster. They yelled at the boy and he ducked and the rock just missed him and it had gone through the wall of the dining room building. There wasn't any foolishness about that. He meant to kill somebody when he threw that thing at his head and missed him by only a few inches.

Well, I told the little boy to go up and take a walk on the side of the hill and see if he could calm himself down, which he did. And I called Mrs. Vosburg and told her that I could not keep the boy and that she should not—that he was dangerous, for I'd seen him in his fit. She wanted to know what to do and I told her to take him back where Keith got him. She said he had found him at the Child Guidance Clinic in Los Angeles. I told her that she should not take him alone, that she should have a man or two with her in the car when she took him in, but to come and get him. A little while later she arrived and had another son with her and was being driven by a chauffeur. They took the boy into Los Angeles immediately, to the Child Guidance Clinic.

As they came in, a famous doctor was coming out of the clinic. I don't remember his name, but they called him an analyst, a professional in the treatment of insane people. He knew Mrs. Vosburg and asked her what she was doing with that boy, and she told him she was bringing him back there where Keith had gotten him and that Keith had adopted him. The doctor told her that he was amazed, that he had given absolute orders that that boy was to be locked up every Sunday and that he was violently insane every Sunday and he said, "I have to lock up his mother every Tuesday." That was the last I ever heard of that particular boy.

Subsequently Keith came back from his trip abroad and founded the Catalina Island School for boys, which was a fine little institution until the war broke out with Japan immediately after the Pearl Harbor event. The Navy immediately took over the school plant for the training of their personnel. Keith thought it was the end of his school, but I invited him to bring them all over to my school and camp in our gymnasium, where all of his pupils could sleep, and arrange for the care of his teachers and had them dine with us in our dining room and play with us on our playground. They operated their school in our library when our classes were going on in the schoolhouse. They kept this up for six to eight weeks until Keith had been able to rent a deserted school plant in Santa Barbara and move to that.

Subsequently his old boys reorganized after the war and opened the Catalina School, but by that time Keith Vosburg was teaching the classics at Scripps College and I don't think he ever returned to Catalina.

I was teaching at the Catalina Island School in 1941, when the war broke out. The school closed early for Christmas vacation and then reopened at Webb, because the parents feared sending their boys to an island that might be attacked by the Japanese. — *TW, JR.*

The Lady and Boy from Chicago

My two sisters, living in Claremont, were very much pleased to receive a call from an old college friend whom they knew well when they attended the University of Chicago many years before. She was at the Claremont Inn with her only son, a boy of about 15. They had her and her son to dinner and brought them up to the school to see me.

A day or two later she called on me at my office and asked if I would take her son in school. I do not remember too much about the boy, but I had sized him up unfavorably. I didn't have a place for him. She took him back to Chicago. A few weeks later, our papers were full of pictures and stories about this mother and boy. It seems that he wanted to go out in her car, which she refused. It angered him so that he killed his mother and started out in the car for Florida. He was captured somewhere in Tennessee.

7

Former Students
1922-1962

PRINCIPES NON HOMINES

Former Webb Students: "Old Boys"

He [Thompson Webb] was a friend of Will Rogers. He had educated Rogers' sons and grandsons. Once I talked with him about Will Rogers; and I said, somewhat facetiously, "He is quoted as having said he never met a man he didn't like. Can you, after working with thousands of boys, say you never met a boy you didn't like?" He took my question more seriously than I intended. He hesitated a moment and then gave an answer I have never forgotten. He said, "I have not liked some of the things that some of the boys have done; but, yes, I can say I have liked all the boys I have known."

—Robert Webb [W.R. Webb III] in Vol. 22, p. 21,
the Webb School of California Alumni Bulletin, *1974-76*

Robin Adrian '57

Some years ago Robin Adrian '57 spent several years in our school. His father, Gilbert Adrian, was the famous designer whom everyone knew about. His mother was a favorite and admired star of the movies, who played under the name of Janet Gaynor. They were a delightful couple. It was a joy to know them as persons as well as parents, in no way spoiled by the adorations of the public. They wanted the best in all respects from their son.

Robin Adrian

Robin was a conscientious young fellow in character and scholarship as proof of his upbringing.

Why the movie group from Hollywood sent us their sons always puzzled me. This school is a simple place and our discipline has always been rigid, our academic standards always high. Many of the movie boys did not qualify. Some who did academically, soon [proved to be] spoiled pets expecting everyone to bend to their wishes. The consequence was that they did not remain long. These I leave out of my record. Some others I have told about with pride.

Elmer Bissell's Story

This is the story that Elmer Bissell '35 told me. Elmer had been here in school possibly 30 years ago. He was a marvelously fine boy from Birmingham, Alabama. He had a great sense of humor and we thoroughly enjoyed him throughout his stay of several years. After graduation he went back to Alabama to graduate in agriculture, I believe. I heard very little from Elmer during the intervening years, but one summer day a few years ago up drove a great big Cadillac car and out

Elmer Bissell

stepped Elmer, his beautiful wife and several fine children. They were on a tour of the West and wanted to come by and see the old school. We walked all around the campus. He wanted to show his children the place as he knew it. He seemed very much surprised with the changes in the school that had grown since his time. After our walk they came into the living room and we sat down and talked.

Finally Elmer said to me, "Mr. Webb, do you still talk to the boys on Sunday nights?" I said, "Oh, yes, Elmer, I do a good deal of that still." He said, "Well, I remember some of your talks that you gave us on Sunday nights. I remember particularly the time when one of the boys had put a slug in the telephone box instead of a nickel. Do you remember that?" I said, "No, Elmer, I don't remember anything about that, but it sounds like grist for my mill if some boy did a thing of that kind." "Well," he said, "some boy did do that, and you made a talk to us on Sunday night about it, and it made an impression on me I'll never forget. I remember exactly what you said." And though I don't remember what I said, I do remember what Elmer said that I said, and it was this. He said, "Mr. Webb, you told us that that boy had stolen a nickel from the telephone company for he had put something of no value in there when he should have put a nickel and had gotten a nickel's worth of service for nothing, and that was stealing."

"Then," he said, "you went on to tell us that that boy had stolen something and had a guilty conscience and probably lay awake at night worrying over the fact that he was a thief, and he did it all for just a nickel." He said, "You told us you wouldn't do that for just a nickel, that you would have to have more money than that before you would sell your conscience and your good night's sleep; in fact you would feel as if you had sold your soul to steal a nickel from anybody. You told us you didn't think you would do that for a hundred dollars, and you went on working on that line of thought until you got it up to where you wouldn't sell your conscience and your soul and your good night's sleep for a million dollars. Mr. Webb, that made a profound impression on me—not for a million dollars." He said, "I have thought about that many times through the years, but you know, Mr. Webb, when I read about the Brinks robbery in Boston where those men got over a million dollars, I said, 'I bet you that is one of those old Webb School boys.'"

Paul Brandegee '27 and Prize Winning Students
from oral history, p. 149-151

TW: About the third year of the school, as I remember it, a boy was brought to me by the name Paul Brandegee '27, from Connecticut; he was related to Senator Brandegee of Connecticut. He had one year to do in high school and he wanted to go to Williams.

Q: Good choice.

TW: After Christmas that year—the boy was a splendid student—I wrote to Williams, saying I had this boy that would like to enter Williams. I had a letter from the admissions officer, a man by the name of Eggard, stating he'd never heard of our school and the only possible way he could admit this boy would be by College Entrance Board examinations. I wrote back that was the only way I admitted boys was by College Board examinations.

Q: You weren't accredited at this time?

TW: I was accredited, but I said the only way I'll send them to college is on the College Board, and I would be very happy for him to take them.

So he took the boards when school was out and was admitted.

Q: By the way, were—just to interrupt you for a minute—boards ever given here? Or did the boys have to go to the city?

TW: Oh, no, they gave them right here; they sent people out here to administer them.

Q: So he took the boards here?

TW: Sure, right here at our school. They come from all over the valley and take it here. Until the board sent its people here no one had ever heard of College Boards until we started them. Well, Paul agreed to it. Right after midterms I got a letter from Mr. Eggard, "If you've got any more of those boys like Paul Brandegee send them to us." [laughter] He made it, a junior Phi Beta Kappa. His senior year he was in an automobile accident and killed. Several years later, I had a boy named George Whitney '31 who wanted to go to Williams. So he took the College Boards, was admitted, and he made senior Phi Beta Kappa. So my first two boys to ever go there were Phi Beta Kappas. I've had a good many go since; I don't think they ever made Phi Beta Kappa, but I'm pretty proud of those. That was a good score on Paul Brandegee. Then I've had many, many Phi Beta Kappas; my wife has always put their names up in the dining room; she's kept a list of them, all their names. We've had one Rhodes Scholar; not many applied for that. But Dwight Taylor '49 took the Westinghouse Science Talent Search and came out the number one boy for that year. *Time* magazine gave him a two-page write-up, all there was about him except the school that prepared him; that wasn't mentioned. Twice since then we've had winners

Pat Muffler

David Fleishhacker

George Whitney

on the Westinghouse Science Talent Search. We don't always have anybody to enter it, but when they do we've done well.

David Fleishhacker '55 made it. And I can't think—Muffler, a boy named Muffler made it. I can't think of his name right off the bat; should get it right. Pat Muffler '54. Those three had won the Westinghouse prizes.

Malcom McKenna

Malcolm McKenna '48 got so interested in paleontology here on these trips with Mr. [Raymond M.] Alf; of course we don't teach paleontology, we just play it and go on trips. But he specialized in the field, got a Ph.D. degree, and became a professor at Berkeley. He then was called to be the head of the Department of Paleontology at the American Museum of Natural History in New York where he is now.

Pierre Charpentier '38

Pierre Charpentier

Before the last World War [WWII], Annabella, the French actress, and her husband, Tyrone Power, came to the school and enrolled Pierre Charpentier, her younger brother. He was a delightful and friendly boy. Very frequently she and her husband would come to see Pierre, and sometimes they would come in and talk with me about plans for the boy. All of our relations with the family were delightful.

When Pierre graduated, he returned to France and was very soon in the French Army and in war. He was captured by the Germans and imprisoned in a camp, where he died of starvation.

J. Ross Clark II '27

In the early days of the school, Mr. and Mrs. J. Ross Clark enrolled J. Ross II '27, with me. They explained that they had adopted the grandson at the time his father went down with the Titanic and had done their best to rear the little fellow. They admitted that they had spoiled him. They claimed that they could not say "No" to any of his wishes, for he had a way of talking them into many things that they knew were not best for him. He now had reached his teens, and someone had to curb him. One point they emphasized was that he and they wanted him to conform to our rules and come home only at regular vacations. I told her I would insist on that if he came here. She warned me that he would call her on the telephone and make her request me to let him come just this one time, but I was not to yield, no matter how much she pleaded with me.

Sure enough, every weekend Ross would beg me to let him go. When he could not budge me, he would ask to call his grandmother on my telephone, which was the only one on the place in those early days. Of course, I would let him call home and talk with her. Then he would tell me that she wanted to talk to me. As soon as I took the telephone, Ross would take an instrument in the reception room on the same line and listen to all that was said. Mrs. Clark would beg for Ross to come home and vigorously insist that it was necessary and that I would have to permit it. I stood pat and refused over and again. Finally I would tell her that I could not make an exception of Ross if he remained in my school, and if she took him out he could not return to the school. That would be the end. Young Ross hated me and the ground I walked on, but he never got home once out of schedule until he finished. He never returned to the school as long as he lived.

During Ross's time with us, Mr. and Mrs. Clark invited us to come to their home for dinner on a Saturday noon and attend one of the big football games that afternoon following dinner. At that time, West Adams was the finest residential street in Los Angeles, and the Clarks lived in one of the great mansions on that street. Everything about the place was most elegant. The chauffeur took our car, and the butler escorted us into the drawing room where the Clarks received us. When dinner was announced, Mrs. Clark led us into the dining room, seated us opposite each other on the sides, while they sat at ends. Two maids in proper dress waited on us and remained standing when not serving us. Mr. Clark began carving a beautiful steaming brown fowl. The butler entered and said to Mr. Clark, "Mr. William Randolph Hearst is on the telephone and insists on speaking to you personally." Mr. Clark replied, "Please tell William Randolph Hearst that I am at dinner with guests and to call at a more convenient time." He continued carving.

Winston Guest '54

Some years ago we had a boy by the name of Winston Guest '54 from New York, son of the famous polo player by the same name. He was a delightful little boy and a brilliant student. He was a very much beloved lad by all who knew him. Occasionally, his mother would drop by on her travels.

Winston Guest

When vacations came and all our students were excited about going home, the boys would order reservations on planes, trains, or what not, and have their suitcases packed. When they were gone, Winston would be left with a few others without any plans. We would ask him what his plans were. He would tell us that his mother had written him to come to one of her houses, maybe in Beverly Hills, or her beach house at Corona del Mar, or the house in Arizona.

One day after Christmas when all the boys were back and work was going on, I received a call from his father in New York. He told me that a friend, a Maharaja in India, had invited him to bring his son for a tiger hunt on elephants, and he would like to take Winston out of school for 10 days to go on this hunt. That was a new one for me. Ordinarily, I never let boys out of school except on vacations. I had to do some quick decisions. This was different. Never before had I had that request. I also knew that Winston could make up the work he had missed faster than any other boy in school. I consented and Winston went. At assembly I told the school what I had done, and I would do the same for every boy in school when he had a chance to hunt tigers on elephants with a Maharaja. No one ever called me on that.

When Winston was back, he told us that his father got a tiger and he got a leopard. In a week's time Winston had made up his back work.

Bob Green '34

[Once] we had a nice boy in school by the name of Bob Green. His mother was dead, but his father kept the home open with a splendid Chinese servant. Vivian and I were invited to dinner there on a weekend vacation when Bob was at home. After we were seated, the Chinese cook brought to the table one of the largest platters I ever saw on which were four whole chickens garnished with quantities of beautifully cooked vegetables of many kinds. Mr. Green helped each of us four to one whole chicken

Bob Green

surrounded by delectable vegetables. It was a beautiful and extravagant dinner.

[Later] we read in the paper that one night Mr. Green came home and found a big truck backed up to the cellar door with men taking his stock of liquor. He slipped around to the back door to go for his gun but was met with a blast that killed him instantly. I have never known whether the robbers were apprehended or what became of Bob.

Bob Hepinstall '43

An interesting gentleman named Hepinstall called at my office to see our school. He was an engineer on the Metropolitan Aqueduct bringing water from the Colorado River to Los Angeles. At the time, he was constructing a huge water softening plant on the main line a few miles from the school.

Bob Hepinstall

He told me that he had never married but had secured permission from his brother to educate his favorite nephew, Bob Hepinstall '43, who lived with his family in New Orleans. He said he wanted to give Bob the finest education a boy ever had. He planned to send him to a preparatory school on through college as far as he would go. At this point he wanted to pick the boarding school and would start with us as the nearest one. From here he planned to visit a few Western schools and then a group of Eastern schools. He said he would check the standing of the schools he liked with admissions officers of several colleges, and that he would let me know several months later when he had finished his investigations.

In time, he returned and asked to enroll the boy with us. We made our investigations and later accepted him by mail, sending the contract form. Mr. Hepinstall brought the contract and his check in person. He handed it to me and asked if every detail was settled and he could be sure that we would take the boy. I said that he could count on us. Then he leaned back and said, "Thank God, now I will get him out of that Southern influence." I wondered that he had not seemed to notice my dialect.

Bob came with his mother at the opening of school, and other members of the family came from time to time over several years. We became very fond of Bob and enjoyed knowing his nice family.

There was one very unusual feature about Bob; he was not born with any time sense. He was always off schedule, sometimes late but more often too early to every appointment. He would come to dinner an hour early, or not be dressed in time for the concert. His senior year he arrived from New

Orleans for school a whole week early when there were no cooks, teachers, or servants on campus. Everybody was taking final days of rest after a busy summer of refurbishing the plant. We took Bob into our home and did our best to keep him entertained while we finished the odds and ends before getting down to a busy year.

The 1968 Webb School of California Alumni Bulletin *reports that "The most delicately beautiful carving of all [among those by seniors in the Jackson Library] is Bob Hepinstall's panel of a boat under full sail with straining spinnaker. . . . Few admirers realize that this rare piece of artistry in wood was executed by a boy with only one hand!"*

George Hoag '36

Some years ago George G. Hoag II was in our school for several years. His consuming hobby was the "Peccary Society," which Ray Alf fostered and directed in frequent camping trips in search of fossils. It was named for the first important fossil found, a peccary head from the Upper Miocene period of geologic history, which was found by W.R. Webb IV, my son.

George Hoag

George told Mr. Alf that his father was going to build a science center for our school. He had planned a great building. Mr. Hoag never mentioned this to me. Though George talked about it with Mr. Alf, the boy did not mention it to me officially. We heard nothing officially about it. I did not feel that it was becoming of me to mention it to his father.

Time went by and nothing happened. We continued to teach our classes in three basement rooms, poorly equipped laboratories, but manned by some of the finest science teachers in this country. The evidence of the quality of these teachers comes from the great achievements of their students in later years. Also, the offers of such colleges as Pomona, Princeton, Yale, and M.I.T. to our young teachers, inviting them to join their faculties.

A few years ago I was invited to dinner with friends in Pasadena. There were several other guests. By me at the table was a retired trust officer from one of the largest banks in California. We had not met before. He asked me if I had known how near our school had come to getting a gift of a million dollars. I had not.

He told me that Mr. Hoag, now deceased, had planned to give us a million dollars for our science department, about half for a building, and half for endowment. Mr. Hoag had deposited with this trust officer a million in gilt-edged securities, marked for the Webb School, and discussed it with him.

He had employed an architect to design the building. When the blueprints were ready, he came by the bank to pick up the securities to come out and present them to me. While talking to the trust officer, he said there was one technical item he wanted to check with an authority, and asked the officer to hold the securities until he came back. He was back in a couple of hours. He had talked with Dr. Robert A. Millikan of Caltech. Dr. Millikan had persuaded Mr. Hoag to give the building to California Institute of Technology.

Win some, lose some. See Jackson Library story in Chapter 3 on Building the School. The original typed version of this story listed the student as George Hogue, JR., but no directory lists such a person. The 1982-83 Alumni Directory lists a George G. Hoag II, and we chose him as the likely subject of this story. Our one concern with this choice is that the Peccary Society was not formed until 1937 more than a year after George Hoag graduated. Fossil hunting had gone on as part of Alf's biology program in 1936 and earlier, so Hoag may have participated in that, and was therefore remembered by my grandfather as being someone interested in fossils.

Richard Hsi '51

We had our capacity filled by Easter for the following year and had to decline a large number of applications for boys who applied too late. Many of these were very desirable students and had to be held on a waiting list if they so wished. Not one dropped out. On the opening day all but one was here. I telephoned his home. His mother began to weep and said she could not part with her son, and he would not be here. I called the waiting list and found all placed. This threw me into a slump, for I

Richard Hsi

really had wanted several of those boys, and here this silly woman had held that place and given no warning. I sat in my office and wondered if I would ever fill the place.

After a while my receptionist came in and told me that a small Chinese boy wanted to see me. His name was "Richard See," she said. He announced that he had come to go to my school. I asked him where he had come from. He said Hong Kong. I asked him when he had left Hong Kong, and he replied three days before. I told him that he had not reserved a place for himself nor written us anything. He said that he did not know that it was necessary.

His English was perfect. I asked him how I would classify him if I took him. He said that he wanted to go into the senior class, a thing we did not often do. I asked him if he had any transcript of his record in former schools. He pulled out a big sheet and handed it to me. It was fully made out, all in Chinese characters. I looked at it with curiosity and wondered what it said. Then I took a good look at him and formed a good impression. On the "hunch" I said, "I'll take you."

Richard Hsi '51 was the top man in our senior class, valedictorian and winner of our top English prize. From our school he went to Pomona College, where he won their English prize and graduated cum laude and Phi Beta Kappa. From there he went to the Massachusetts Institute of

Technology for graduate work. The last report I had he was a member of their faculty.

Clarence Huang '49

When the Japanese were fighting China, a Chinese lady took a position teaching Chinese at Pomona College and brought her son Clarence up to go to our school. She told me that her husband had been captured by the Japanese but she and the son were able to escape and get to this country and she was eager to have her son Clarence in our school.

Clarence Huang

He was a very fine boy and an excellent student and remained with us for several years until the war between China and Japan had been settled. His father had been imprisoned by the Japanese; but, when the war was over, he was released and he came here to find his family. He told me that under the old Chinese government before the war with Japan he had been secretary of the treasury of the Chinese government and that when things began to be hazardous he sent his wife and child over here. He said that his signature was on all the Chinese paper money before that war, and he gave me a handful of it and showed me his signature on the bills. He told me it was worthless, that Japan had taken everything over and there really was no Chinese government any more to back that money. I found him a most interesting man and enjoyed my talks with him.

After a few months he told me that he and his wife planned to return to China to see what they might salvage and they wanted to leave Clarence with me. He thought it was quite hazardous for them to go back when things were so upset and he wasn't sure what might happen to them, but he wanted to be sure that Clarence was safe and able to pursue his education. He said that he would like to make me guardian of Clarence and put all authority into my hands as to his plans and welfare and I was to keep him until he graduated from the school and to decide on the college to which he went, and that he was establishing a trust fund in the First National Bank for the upkeep of Clarence, and that I would have full charge of the trust fund to see that it was properly handled for his life and college work. Of course I realized it was a great compliment to put his faith in me. He came back later and showed me the papers in which he had placed a trust fund which I remember was about $50,000. I felt it was a great trust, and I didn't want to be the only person in it, and I asked him if he wouldn't pick out somebody else who would be joint trustee with me. He came back and told me that he had made Stephen Zetterberg, a young attorney in Pomona, joint trustee to handle the money matters and I felt much happier about it.

He was slow in getting started back to China, during which time Clarence graduated from our school, and he'd had time to consider the question of colleges. He wanted Clarence to go to the Massachusetts Institute of Technology and had been in correspondence with them. He found that they were affiliated in some way with William and Mary College in Williamsburg, Virginia, and that Clarence could attend there for three years and MIT for two years and would finish with a degree from each institution at the end of five years. He'd chosen that for Clarence and everything was set for Clarence to do that, which he did. Then Mr. Huang told me that he and Mrs. Huang were leaving for China on a certain date, but he had instructions to go to Washington City, and he was flying back there and would be there about two days and return here, and he and his wife would then start for China. When he returned, he told me that everything was changed, that the allied nations had established a World Bank and they had made him assistant to the president—in other words, second in authority—to the World Bank and that he'd have to live in Washington and not go to China. Well, I was tremendously interested in that and that he should be second in authority to the biggest bank in the world. I then told him of course we would turn over the trust fund to him immediately. He threw up his hands and said, "No, indeed. You are trustee for Clarence's funds," and he refused to remove them, and from then on Zetterberg and I handled the trust until Clarence had completed his college courses.

I always chuckled about being trustee of the funds of the son of one of the top bankers of the world. . . . [After college, Clarence] taught science for us for a time before becoming a chemical engineer for a large industrial plant in the East. After Clarence's graduation, the trust fund was finally dissolved and appropriated as it should be.

Charles Ramsey '33

This is a story of Charles Ramsey. I think it must have been about the third year of our school that Mrs. Ramsey came to us from La Jolla with a bright little boy who was ready for eighth grade, she said, and asked if I could take him. We were delighted to have a student and he looked to be a very likely one. She explained to me that her husband and her brothers all went to the Taft School in Connecticut, that they had never had any other idea than to send Charles to Taft School, but that shortly before he had taken the entrance examinations and failed. She wanted to know if I would take him and get him ready for Taft. I told her I would do my best, and so Charles started in our eighth grade.

He was a bright looking boy, full of life and mischief, and saw everything funny that was going on. I don't think he missed a thing, but he never knew his lessons. We were convinced that he was bright enough, but we couldn't get him to prepare a lesson. He didn't get anything except what he heard in class. Well, I did my best with Charles, but at the end of the first month he was all failure, and we sent his mother a report—four F's. She came to the school very much disconcerted. She talked pretty sternly to Charles, and told me that I had to put on more pressure. Well, I would keep him back after class; I did everything I knew how, but still I couldn't get that boy to study his books. At the end of the next month I sent him a report—four F's.

Mrs. Ramsey came to see me, and this time she was thoroughly indignant at me. Furious that I hadn't made [her] boy work. Well—I suppose it was in self-defense—I began to suggest some possible excuse for it. I asked her if she thought Charles might need some thyroid. Had she had a metabolism test made? No, she had never done that, but he had always been under the very best doctors in La Jolla. She was sure that there was nothing the matter with him. I insisted maybe he needed some glandular tests and advice from a doctor; I suspected there was trouble there. So she asked me if I knew any doctor around here that gave those tests and I told her I did, but I would rather he was under a specialist in that field, an endocrinologist, and that there was a very good one in Los Angeles. So she had me make an appointment, and the next day she took Charles to the doctor. When she came back, she said that the doctor had given him a thorough examination, and when all the laboratory tests were completed, he would notify me. So she went home. When I heard from the doctor, he said Charles was a perfect specimen, nothing in the world the matter with him, no reason why he shouldn't do his work.

Shortly after that the Christmas vacation came, and Charles went home. After Christmas, when he returned, the little rascal went to work. He gave a lot of attention to his subjects and began to make up his back work in addition to carrying on his daily work. It wasn't many weeks until Charles was the best boy in the class. He made a tremendous record from that point on. I never knew what got into him, but he certainly did turn over a leaf after Christmas, though the doctor could do nothing for him. Charles passed his Taft examinations and went there to school. I lost all track of that family for many years.

A few years ago in came Mrs. Ramsey and introduced herself. She said she was passing by and she knew I would be interested to know about Charles. Of course, I was. She said that Charles went back to Taft and was on the honor roll away back there, that he went to Yale and was on the Dean's List and made a famous record for himself. He then went into industry and had climbed from the bottom to the top, and was now the head of a big plant that employed thousands of men. She said she was very proud of Charles, and she thought I ought to know about him.

Then she told me that not long before, she and Charles were having a ride in an automobile and were talking about old times and the matter of Webb School came up and how he suddenly went to work after Christmas and got on his feet when he had given us so much trouble previous to that. She said, "Charles then asked me if I knew what did it. Of course, I did not. Then he said, 'Do you remember when Mr. Webb sent me to that gland doctor in Los Angeles?' And I said, 'Yes, but that doctor didn't recommend anything.' Charles said, 'Well, Mother, when we got there, we had to sit down in the waiting room and wait for our turn and I looked around. The first person I saw was a little girl that had legs as big as barrels.' He said, 'She was the most awful looking creature I ever saw in my life, and after I finally quit looking at her, I looked at the next patient and that was an old lady that had a great enlargement under her chin, and then I began to look around, and,' he said, 'everybody in that room was a monstrosity.' He said, 'I never saw such a collection of people, and I got to thinking, "Oh, my soul, do I belong in this class? If I belong here, it is time for me to dig out," and I made up my mind right then I would go to work on my books.' He said, 'Mother, I had made up my mind before that that no teacher could ever make me look at a book, but that experience shocked me into a change of mind.'"

We sent him to the specialist for physical help and stumbled into a psychological cure.

Gil Roberts, JR. '51

In those beginning years I was invited by a friend to luncheon with his Rotary Club in Pomona. He introduced me to Dr. Gil Roberts, by whom I sat. He was told that I was conducting a private school in Claremont. Dr. Roberts at once said that he wanted to be frank with me and tell me that he did not believe in private schools. Before I could reply, the president of the club rang his bell and called for attention.

Gil Roberts

Everyone stopped talking, and a number of announcements were made. After some time, the president said that we might resume our conversations and eat our lunches.

I had been reading in the papers about socialized medicine. I turned to Dr. Roberts and asked what he thought of the idea of socialized medicine. It hit him in a sore spot, for he hit the ceiling in his denunciation of such an absurd plan. I let him blow his steam for a time. Then I told him that there were almost no private schools in America a hundred years ago, and anyone wanting an education had to go to one and pay a high tuition. I told him that people felt sorry for the poor boy who could not afford to go and decided to tax everybody and open schools free to all children—by which process they socialized education. I told him that they had made a success of that and had the public schools on their feet, and now they felt sorry for the poor little crippled boys who could not afford medical care, and that it looked as if they were going to socialize that.

Some time later, Dr. Roberts came to my office and enrolled his son [Gilbert J. Roberts, JR.]. He was a fine boy who made a splendid record. From our school he entered Stanford University. Even with us, his favorite sport was mountain climbing, scaling up perpendicular cliffs such as the Grand Tetons. I do not like high places and worried about the boy, but he became an expert.

After his B.A. degree he graduated from medical school and went into practice, but he followed his hobby of mountain climbing. Several years ago he was invited to be the medical man in the group that climbed Mt. Everest. He went within less than a thousand feet of the top, but duty required him to stop there, in case he should be needed to care for the two who climbed the last thousand feet to the top. All of our leading journals carried many pictures of him and the victorious two.

William Robertson '31

This story is about William Robertson and his accident with his right arm.

William Robertson

When William Robertson's grandmother brought him to me from Chicago, she stated that she was a Christian Scientist and had brought the boy up as a Christian Scientist and that she did not want any doctor called at any time, even though I might think he was sick; that if I were to give her a ring on the telephone, she would come immediately and take the boy out in case I was afraid it was contagious and might be endangering the other boys, and she'd come and remove him at once, and bring him back when everything was all right.

Well, I think possibly she may have come for him once or twice at intervals; he was with us several years. He became our best tennis player and was a fine boy in every way. But one Saturday afternoon when we were going to have a big football game, and after everybody arrived on the field, Coach Hendricks realized that he did not have a whistle for the umpire and asked Bill if he would run up to his room in the old dormitory and get his whistle. Bill ran in great haste, and just as he was approaching the glass doors to the dormitory he stumbled and fell and ran his right hand right through a pane of glass, receiving two deep long slashes, one on each side of the wrist, severing all arteries and veins. It was a very serious accident. Bill saw the blood spurting and he turned and ran for our infirmary. Orville Hennart, the gardener, was raking around, and after the boy passed him he looked down and saw the stream of blood. He realized that it was something serious and he ran to the infirmary and found that Bill had collapsed on the floor of the infirmary and that the nurse was not there. The blood was going out in great jets as his heart beat. He grabbed the arm and squeezed it with great might and was able to shut off the flow of blood, but there was nobody to help him. So he began to yell at the top of his voice. Mrs. Tyndall, my secretary, heard him calling. She ran over, saw the situation, got a tourniquet, and applied it to the arm. Then she sent for me and told me that boy had to get to a surgeon at once.

I grabbed my car and got him in, and I told Mrs. Tyndall, "First, phone Dr. Palmer that I'm coming. Tell him what the situation is. Then you call the grandmother in Pasadena and tell her where we are."

Well, when I got him to Dr. Palmer's office, he called in an assistant, who gave Bill some anesthetic to breathe, put him asleep, Dr. Palmer operated on the arm, tying off these bleeding arteries and veins, and sewing up the wound. He told me that his nerves had been cut and the boy might lose the use of his hand unless those nerves could be brought together, but that he had lost too much blood to stand so long an operation; and that he had sewn it up for the present, but would be glad later on to reopen it and attach those nerves.

In the meantime, Mrs. Tyndall phoned me that she had been unable to locate Mrs. Robertson, and that nobody at the house answered, and she didn't know who to call. So I brought Bill home, put him in the infirmary, and had him there several days before we were able to get in touch with Mrs. Robertson. It seems she had gone to Palm Springs and left no messages behind about where she'd gone.

But she came by, and I took her over to the infirmary and told her what had happened to Bill, and I said, "Mrs. Robertson, I've broken your rule. You told me never take him to a doctor, but I couldn't let the boy die for lack of having that artery tied up." She said, "Oh, Mr. Webb, that was surgery, wasn't it?" And I said, "It certainly was." "Well, I have no objection to surgery, I just didn't want any M.D." She said, "He didn't give him any pills, did he?" And I said, "No, he didn't get any pills." "Well that was perfectly all right. You handled it just right."

I told her about the possibility of a subsequent operation to attach the nerves and she said, "Well, maybe that would be necessary but we'll wait and see." And Bill learned to play tennis with his left hand. But in the course of time, that right hand got entirely well, his nerves seemed to connect over in some way, and he got the use of his fingers and feeling and all that went with it. And I've understood that he became a famous tennis player with that right hand.

C.W.S.

He was enrolled well in advance from Hong Kong by his tutor. The tutor told me that he had no money sense and among other things I was to teach him the wise use of money, real "money sense." I agreed to try if all of his funds were given me to dispense.

When he came in, he handed me a check to the school for $5,000 as his father wanted to provide for his every need. That seemed generous. Then he said that when he flew into San Francisco he had deposited $10,000 in one of the big banks there and had deposited $10,000 in our small bank in Claremont, before coming to the school. I wondered how I would go about teaching him "money sense."

We put him in his room in the dormitory and assigned him to his classes. Soon the honor committeeman from his dormitory came to see me to say he thought I should do something about the Chinese boy having so much money in his room. It might be a temptation to a student or janitor. I asked how much money he had. The honor committeeman said he left five $1,000 bills on his desk. That was just the beginning.

Before Christmas, his father wrote that his son might spend the holiday in New York City, if one of our teachers would go with him, all expenses paid. Mr. Alf agreed to go, as he was anxious to look up things in the American Museum of Natural History and to see the Metropolitan Museum of Art.

When they came back, Alf was down in the dumps. All the boy wanted to do was to spend every day and evening watching Abbott and Costello over and over. He had no time for anything else.

At the spring vacation Mr. Alf and my son Bill took a large group of boys to the Grand Canyon in Arizona. Everyone took a big pack rack on his back, down into the bottom of the canyon where they camped. C.W.S.

loved it until coming back up. He broke down completely and claimed he could not go further. Mr. Alf phoned for a mule, but none was available for several days. C.W.S. shook hands with all of the party and told them farewell and stretched out, saying he would die right there. Bill added C.W.S.'s pack to his own which was already overloaded, as he had the regular pack plus a large camera on a tripod. He told C.W.S. to get up and go, but C.W.S. would not move, saying he would die right there. No argument could move him. Finally Mr. Alf picked him up and put him on his feet, and Bill began to hit him in the seat with sharp spikes on the tripod until he would go a hundred yards and flop again on the trail. Time and again this was done until he climbed out some time in the night.

All the way home every little while C.W.S. would come up and shake hands with Mr. Alf and Bill and say, "You saved my life. I would have died right there in that hole."

At the end of the year, the father wrote, giving permission for the boy to go to New York City without escort. The day came, and all the boys took off. Then C.W.S. came to the office and called the Campus Cab, about the only cab in Claremont in the early days. When it arrived C.W.S. got in with his suitcase. The cabbie wanted to know where to go. C.W.S. told him New York. The cabbie asked him if he wanted to go to the airfield or railroad station. He told him New York. Then the cabbie came in to see me and we had a conference with C.W.S. He was hiring him to drive him to New York and back. They did it.

Gentlemen (Charles Skouras '44)

Father talked in chapel each morning to his students about many things; not least of his subjects was on manners. He frequently quoted, "A gentleman is as polite to the bootblack as he is to the queen." He emphasized the importance of our relations with the colored people around us, and never to call them "niggers," even though they called each other by that name, and they usually did when I was a boy.

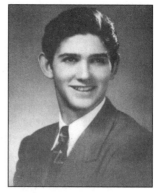

Charles Skouras

One time, Father arranged to have one of his old students, U.S. Senator Ned Carmack, come down and talk to the school. As a boy I remember his talk on manners to us. I so well remember that he told us that we may not be posted on all the best usages, etiquette, and the rules of decorum as we enter good society, but at least we should remember that "the soul of good manners was a kind heart." This training has served me in good stead in a number of situations.

When I was building with my own hands the Vivian Webb Chapel in the style of the old Spanish missions of California out of adobe, I found a use for that. During school term, I tried to get in Wednesday and Saturday afternoons laying the mud bricks; but in summers when every boy and teacher was away, I tried to get in a few hours work each morning early before people came to enroll boys. The school was young, and the enrollments were important. I did all the interviews with parents in those days. I did have one secretary-bookkeeper in the office, a remarkable woman, Mrs. Tyndall. I arranged a little telephone from the office to the chapel walls so that she could call me to the phone in the office. I told her that if parents with a boy happened to come early to see me, she was to give me a ring, and while I was getting into presentable clothes she was to show them the school and library. This happened occasionally.

One morning I was on the wall in my muddy work clothes, having just finished mixing a big batch of mortar which I had carried up on the wall.

The little phone rang. Mrs. Tyndall said, "A man and boy are here to talk to you about the school. I am sending them up to you now." I said, "Let me change my clothes." She said, "No, it isn't necessary." I was puzzled, but coming up the hill I saw the man and boy. They were as dirty as I and wearing work clothes. I understood. The man was very heavy and wet with perspiration.

They made me think of foreign peddlers such as I had seen in my boyhood, traveling on foot to the farms in Tennessee. The man addressed me in a foreign accent and said that the boy's father had asked him to select a school for his son, and they would like to see the school. I knew that they could not afford to pay the price of a boarding school. I looked at my big batch of mortar and hated to let it set before I could use it. I was tempted very much to put them off. Then, I remembered, "A gentleman is as polite to a bootblack as he is to the queen." I knew what care I would have taken if they had been well-dressed, and I said to myself "I shall show them every courtesy." I apologized for my muddy hands and clothes, but explained that I was working on my hobby of laying mud bricks.

The first building we came to was our little schoolhouse, where on the front door was painted "Mens sana in corpore sano." The big man asked the boy if he could translate it. The boy could not. The man said it says, "Strong mind in strong body." Then he said, "It is from a satire by Juvenal, and Juvenal stole it from Plato. You see, all good things go back to Greek."

I took a new look at that man, and said, "You are a classical scholar." He replied that they were Greeks, sometimes mistaken for Jews. Then he told me that he was a professor at the University of Pennsylvania, and taught the largest geography class in the United States. He said that he lectured in nearly all the well-known preparatory schools in the East. He said that Charles' father thought he would know what was the best school for Charles and had given him the job to pick it. He said his father had reserved a place for Charles at a top school in Connecticut, but wanted him to check it. After his trip around our simple place, the professor said he would talk with the admissions officers in the East and then advise Charles' parents.

About two weeks later a big limousine with liveried chauffeur came bringing Charles in dress clothes and one of the most beautiful ladies I ever saw, a classical Greek, to my office. She was Mrs. Charles Skouras. I had not caught the name before. She said they had a letter from a professor saying he had checked with the Ivy League colleges, and found our school had a splendid record, and advised them to send Charles here.

She told me that the professor wanted to see the snake dances being done in Arizona, and had taken Charles over there for a week of camping, sleeping on the ground, and cooking for themselves. On their way back he spied our sign at our entrance and said that was one of the schools he wanted to see. So, as they were, they came in at that early hour.

Charles was with us for three years and handled his responsibilities very well, graduating in 1944. All College Board examinations were first rate. His family was all here for the graduation. When it was over, his father told me that our congressman would give Charles an appointment to West Point, but his acceptance there would depend upon his examination. He said that Charles could take the exam in six months, and if he passed, he would train at West Point and become an officer. Otherwise, he would be drafted and become a private. He told me to get a good tutor and tutor Charles for six months. I told Mr. Skouras that the West Point exams were coming up the day after tomorrow and that Charles should take them for he needed no tutoring, he was ready. His father insisted that I get the tutor, for he had not instructed me to prepare him for West Point. I insisted that he was ready.

That evening, his father called me and said that he had called the congressman and learned that if Charles failed day after tomorrow, he could take them again in six months. He told me that Charles would take the exams at once, but get the tutor, for he knew he would fail, which would put him on his toes to get ready for the tests six months later. In about 10 days, Mr. Skouras came to the school and found me laying bricks. He handed me a telegram to read. Charles was the top man on the exams and was admitted to West Point at once. They wanted him to come at once for the summer course as the war was on.

Mr. Skouras asked me if I had an organ for the chapel. I told him that we did not. He then said he would give us a good one. He said that he had plans to build a theater in Riverside and had ordered the organ three years before. It took three years to build a good pipe organ.

Now that the war was on, he was not allowed to build a theater, and the organ would be delivered next week. He would instruct them to deliver it to us. He said it was a "nice little organ," as it cost him $40,000. He said he had not ordered a console for it as he had several of them and would deliver an old one to us. That was sent out about the time the pipe organ arrived. The grouping of the pipes was reorganized to fit our space. A large truck loaded with sewing machines and other equipment came with a quota of technicians. In a few hours they made a gorgeous Madonna blue curtain to screen the organ.

At that time, I read in our daily paper that Charles Skouras had paid the highest income tax that year in the nation. Later, Charles, JR., graduated from West Point and became a captain in the Air Force. Remember when Charles, JR., and the professor first came up the hill to the chapel, I did not want to stop and show them the school and let my batch of mortar set.

John Stevens '52/Dwight Taylor '49

We had a boy by the name of John Stevens, who came to us from Altadena. His mother was Mrs. Johanna K. Stevens, a woman of definite German descent, and spoke with some German accent. John was a fine boy, fine student, very industrious worker, and he won a great many honors in college after he graduated from our course. But the point of this story is one that Mrs. Stevens told me immediately after Dwight Taylor had won the No. 1 place in the Westinghouse Science Talent Search [in 1949].

John Stevens

She came in one day and said she just had to tell me this story, that she'd never referred to the situation before this, but that in Altadena she belonged to a bridge club that played at regular intervals, and that all the women in that club had been teasing her about having her son in a private school, and made all kinds of fun of her. They said she was trying to be swanky and do things a little more pretentious than the other people, and that they had the finest high school in the world right there in Altadena; there just wasn't any sense in her sending her boy off to a private school, and they'd ask her why in the world she did it. She told them because she wanted him to have an unusually good education. They told her there was no private school as good as their high school. She said that this wasn't just once, that they continued to bedevil her about it until it became a touchy point with her, and she'd really considered the matter of leaving the club just because they were disagreeable over her attitude toward a private school. She said that she had never referred to this to me until now, but she just had to tell me the funniest thing in the world.

She said that the Altadena newspaper announced the great honor that Dwight Taylor had won in being first place in the Westinghouse Science Talent Search, which made him the No. 1 scientist of America in the high schools of America. She said the paper did not refer to what school he attended, but gave a picture of him and a great write-up about his success when he was an Altadena boy. She said at once her telephone began to ring, and these ladies of her club said, "Aha, have you seen what an Altadena boy did? The greatest scientist in America. And you had to send your boy off to a private school. Look what we can do in Altadena." She said she let them talk a little bit, and she said, "Where does Dwight Taylor go to school?" "Oh, the Altadena High School." "Oh, no," she'd say, "you're mistaken. He goes to the Webb School where my boy goes. That's the kind of boys they train out there." Some of the women would snap up the telephone in anger, and then it would ring again and here was the next one; she said four or five of them called, one after the other, before they found out and compared notes with each other. And she went on to say that that was the happiest moment in her life, when she could rub that in to that club that had been rubbing her so long because she was so snooty in having her boy in a private school.

In the next week or two, *Time* magazine gave up their entire chapter on education to the Westinghouse Science Talent Search examinations, and gave the picture of the No. 1 boy and the No. 2 girl. Most all of the chapter was devoted to Dwight Taylor and his great scientific ability, but never mentioned the school that prepared him. And then they had a write-up of the girl who was No. 2, who came, I think, from Oklahoma, but they told about the high school which she attended.

I might add that John Stevens won many honors for himself here and a lot at Stanford and Caltech, continuing until he had a doctor's degree, and became a very responsible person in industry.

At the time of TW's death, John Stevens was quoted on p. 25 in Vol. 22 of the Webb School of California Alumni Bulletin, 1974-76, as writing, "Words cannot express my gratitude to the Webb family for having had the opportunity to attend Webb School and thereby experience the ideals and the character-building genius of Thompson Webb. There are too few men in the world with his capability of inspiring youth and instilling in them a sense of achievement. Rest assured that those of us who benefitted from his genius will try to carry forward his ideals."

Dwight Taylor '49

We had Dwight Taylor in school for several years, a very dependable and forthright youngster who had an active and able mind. Mr. Alf, who taught our biology, found him very apt in science and exceedingly interested in the field trips when he took the boys on camping trips and dug for fossils. We did not teach paleontology as such then, but much was absorbed by all the boys on the digging camp trips in company with Alf. Dwight

Dwight Taylor

was especially alert. Alf asked him to enter the Westinghouse Science Talent Search exams, which were open to all high-school seniors in the nation.

Thousands of students take these exams. Westinghouse rewards the top 40 students with a week in Washington City with all expenses paid and a number of cash prizes.

Dwight went after this prize in earnest and came out the number one man for that year. His picture appeared on the back cover of *Science News Letter* of March 19, 1949, with the picture of the alternate, Caroline Stuart Littlejohn of Oklahoma City. The article stated that Dwight W. Taylor "was the nation's top young man scientist of 1949."

Joe Tyndall '38
Joe was the son of Mrs. Tyndall, TW's office administrator.

In school, Joe was a fine scholar when he could handle the answer from memory. He had his mother's memory. [Joe was a childhood playmate of my son Bill.]

Joe Tyndall

He applied for a job to one of the big airplane factories at the beginning of the second World War. They gave him an aptitude test, along with a few hundred other applicants, and they told him when to come back for his answer. On the appointed day he was there with the others. When he gave his name, the man at the desk said that Mr. Dexter, head of the personnel department, wanted to see him personally. Mr. Dexter told him that they had given that test to thousands of men and women who were applying, and Joe was the only one who had answered every question correctly. He wanted to know how he did it. Joe told him that he knew that one, for he took it four years before at the Webb School. Charlie Dexter extended his hand and said, "Let's shake. I went to the Webb School, too." [He was in the Class of 1927].

I know Joe did not make a hundred the first time he took the test, but when he came off a test he would go around and ask the teachers what the answers were to each question. He never forgot the answers. Dexter put him on a job that involved memory.

Then Joe wanted to join the Navy for his military service. When the Navy examined him, they found that he was 6-foot-7 1/2 inches tall. Their limit was 6-6, and they turned him down. He went back and applied again in three weeks with the same result, but every three weeks he was back, until they all knew him. Finally the Chief said to him, "You surely do want to go to the Navy, but the trouble with you is that that yeoman can't measure right. Let's go talk to him." So the yeoman made his height 6-6, and Joe was in.

The Navy sent him out at once to one of the South Sea islands. He was the last man to go there, very shortly before the end of the war. Then at the end everyone else was sent home but Joe. He was lonesome and wanted to come home but had to wait months before his discharge. Finally the discharge came. He had to take the check-out physical examination. They found that he had grown an inch and one-half and put him in the hospital for three months to see what was the matter with him.

Henry H. Ware '28

Henry was brought to us by his father and mother from Atlanta, Georgia. It seems his grandparents had gone to Atlanta shortly after the Civil War and established a college for Negroes, and the Wares had done a great piece of work in the South working with the colored people, and had built up quite an institution there. After the senior Mr. Ware was dead, his son, the father of Henry, had continued the college for a number of years, but had come to the point of retirement and they moved to Claremont, and they placed Henry in our school.

Henry H. Ware

Henry was an excellent student and a fine boy. We enjoyed having him very much. During that time, his father was taken very ill, and died. Shortly after the father's funeral, Henry was taken with an appendicitis attack. The mother came up and we ordered an ambulance to come and get him and take him to the hospital. The mother got in the ambulance with him and went to the hospital. She stated that on their way down to the hospital, Henry said to his mother, "Do you know that this is the same vehicle that took Daddy to the cemetery?" It's a gruesome-sounding thing, but that's what they said he said. At any rate, when he got to the hospital he didn't want to be given an anesthetic that would put him to sleep and he demanded to have his operation by a local anesthetic and given a mirror so that he could watch the performance. He came through that all right, returned to school, graduated in fine standing, and entered Pomona College.

During his senior year at Pomona College, I began to hear people very much upset about Henry. He had turned Communist and he was so bold in his talk about it, he would get on boxes and lecture, and the students would gather around and heckle him. But Henry was all-out a Communist, just as Red as you can be. And they used to say to him, "Well, don't try to change us to Communists. If you like communism, go to Russia and be one of them." He said that was exactly what he was going to do. And after his graduation, he went to Russia, and I was told that he renounced the United States and became a Russian citizen. From time to time I would hear that Henry was a teacher in Russia in a college.

After some 10 or 12 years, I heard that Henry was back in this country, that he had escaped from Russia, he had all he wanted of that, and had come back and was employed in Washington in government service of some kind. He may still be there for all I know. Anyhow, I read a great book on Russia, and I wish I could remember who the author was. It was something of the type of book such as Gunther wrote on *Inside Russia*. It may have been his book, I don't remember. But in this was given a chapter to Henry Ware. They stated that when there was to be a great conference in Russia between England, America and Russia, over some important points involving the war in which we were in, that our secretary of state, the old Tennessean—I forget his name, but we must look it up—represented us, and he wanted an interpreter to go with him, and that Henry Ware was chosen as the interpreter. This commentator was stating that at this interview with Anthony Eden and our ambassador and the Russians, that there were a great many toasts being downed, as was the custom in Russian affairs, and that Henry wanted to keep his head clear, he knew that the others would get fuzzed up with so many drinks of vodka, and that he arranged a rubber bag inside his collar, and when they'd drink a toast he'd pour his vodka in this bag, and kept his head perfectly clear. And he stated that Henry did a wonderful job of interpreting and sometimes even composed for our representatives, and he saved us from a world of trouble. This commentator was complimenting Henry for having been so honest and straightforward and having gone to Russia as a Communist, learned his lesson, and came back as a very loyal and wise representative of our country.

David Webb '53

I have a nephew (Sawney) Ben Webb, farming in Coachella Valley. [See Chapter 2 for a story about Sawney Ben Webb, when he attended Webb School.] Farming has been difficult in recent years, with the result that Ben has had difficulties with his finances. His oldest son David showed unusual talents as a small boy. Vivian and I decided we would like to see what we could do with David in our school.

David Webb

We invited him to come and live with us and go through our school. He made a splendid record in all respects, scholastically and as a fine character. He won a scholarship at Pomona College, but needed some money to carry his part at the college. His family were not able to carry this expense at that time.

We applied for him to go to the Deep Springs College, a fine junior college, where students could work out all expenses. David became a very satisfactory student there and was head of their dairy for three years while he covered the two years of junior college with credit. He won a scholarship to Cornell from the Telluride Foundation which paid all set expenses. He had to earn enough on the side for clothing and incidentals. This he did and in two years there graduated with honors.

When he graduated he thumbed a ride home in time to be at his sister's wedding. We went to the wedding and saw David. He told me that he had won a fellowship to Berkeley, which would pay his way there for three years, to get his Ph.D. degree. I was very proud of him. He had lived up to our expectations.

Then David told me that he was going to be married in August. I asked him how he could take care of a wife on a fellowship. He said his girl was going to make her own living until he earned his degree. I asked him if she was going to teach school. He said she was going to write stories. I asked if she could sell them. He assured me that she thought she could, but admitted that her father questioned it, saying he tried selling stories and nearly starved on it.

He then began publishing other people's stories and got along that way. I asked him what her father published. He said that her father was Hiram Hayden, one of the owners of Random House with Bennet Cerf, and among other things, published the *Key Reporter*, journal of Phi Beta Kappa. I said, "David, I guess you did all right."

In August he thumbed his way to New York and married Mary Hayden. We received some six engraved invitations to parties given the young couple at the Waldorf Astoria, University Club, and various Park Avenue addresses.

Two years later Vivian and I were in Berkeley and called on David and Mary in their small apartment in Berkeley. Mary invited us to come back that evening to dinner. It was a lovely dinner and she cooked and served it herself. She is a beautiful girl. We found that she graded papers for the English Department and wrote stories. We gathered from the conversation that she had not called on her family for help.

In proper time David took his doctor's degree and was given a position on the faculty of the University of Florida, where he is now. Last year when the American Association for the Advancement of Science held its annual meeting, I saw that David was one of the six speakers scheduled for the Division of Geology. They now have a small son, my great-great-nephew.

George Westinghouse and David Scott '33

David Scott

In the early years of our school we had a very nice boy named George Westinghouse enrolled here. He was the grandson of the man who invented the air brakes for trains. They were evidently people of considerable wealth and his father moved to Canada—we thought in order to avoid the heavy income tax. He was with us several years and a pleasure to have and we were proud of having the son of a very distinguished family.

At that time we had in our school a local boy by the name of David Scott whose father was a professor at Pomona College. Some years later David Scott was serving in the Air Force in the second World War. He had been given the task of assigning duties to the flying squadron that went out and fought in their planes. One early morning he sent out several fliers and one of them was George Westinghouse, and they recognized each other as having been students here at the same time. Among those that David Scott sent out at that time was the author, Antoine de Saint Exupéry, who wrote the book entitled *Wind, Sand and Stars.* He had made quite a name for himself as an author, but he didn't get back from that assignment. We named our trailer park in the desert for that book.

A Richard Westinghouse is listed as a member of the class of '37 in the 1982-83 Alumni Directory, but no George Westinghouse is listed there.

Melvin Young '30

In September, 1928, a Mrs. [Fannie Forester
Rowan] Young from England enrolled her son Melvin
[Henry Melvin Young] in our school. I think he was
12 years old and had been in a good English school
until he came to us. She told me that she was a Los
Angeles girl from the family of Rowan. They were
real estate people of some wealth. I had heard much
about the family but did not know any of them. This
Miss Rowan had married an Englishman [Henry

Melvin Young

George Melvin Young] and lived all of her married life in England. She had
several children. For some reason, the family broke up, and Mrs. Young and
the children had come to Los Angeles to live with her family.

We discovered that Melvin had an excellent education in Latin and
math and other subjects. We had to put him in our junior class with boys
at least two years older than he. I was amazed at a boy so young so well
advanced. I take my hat off to the English schools. Melvin proved to be
equal to the very best boys in our junior class. In two years he graduated
from our school, June, 1930, the youngest boy I have known to graduate
there. He was academically ready for any of our best colleges. His mother
felt that he was too young for college and decided to have him take another
year in school before college. She put him in one of the best Eastern
preparatory schools. I believe it was Kent. Mr. Squibb of our faculty probably arranged that.

I think it was in the spring of the first year Melvin was with us that
Mrs. Young came to me in great excitement to tell me that she had to hide
Melvin. She had received word that her husband had come secretly to this
country to steal Melvin in order that he might continue his schooling in
England. She wanted me to enter him in a good school under a different
name where his father could not find him, and no one was to know where
he was. I arranged this with Keith Vosburg, who was operating an excellent
school, the Catalina Island School. Vivian and I took Melvin and his trunk

to Catalina, where he remained a few weeks until his father returned to England. Then he came back to us.

After the one additional year of school in the East [actually 2 years], Melvin returned to England [in 1932] and [in 1934] attended Oxford, I think, for his advanced work [in Trinity College]. I cannot recall hearing from any of his family since, but through the papers we have learned some of the rest of his story.

During the last World War, Melvin was in the English air force. We read a newspaper account of his rescue from the sea when he was shot down in a fight [in 1940]. He was rescued by one of our naval officers by the name of White, son of the famous editor, William Allen White of Emporia, Kansas. Young White was delivering to England some old destroyers our government was giving to England before we joined the war. Again we read in the newspapers where Melvin was again rescued from the sea. The last and tragic news was of his death [in 1943] when he was one of a small team of fliers who blew up a big dam of great importance to the Germans. I have heard that Melvin Young goes down in English history as one of the greatest heroes of the late war.

Since writing the above, I was able to get in touch with Melvin's sister, much younger than he, who now practices medicine in Whittier, California, under her maiden name, Dr. Young. She is married to Mr. George T. Sturr, a teacher. They have a lovely family.

I called Mrs. Sturr and asked to call on her for accurate information about Melvin. She invited my wife and me to dinner when she was entertaining her aunt, Miss Florence Rowan. We spent the time talking about Melvin. The first two times he was shot down at sea he saved himself in the dinghy until someone rescued him, [William L.] White [among them] the first time. From then on, he was known by his mates as "Dinghy" Young. He was a member of the famous 617 Squadron. Mrs. Sturr loaned me her copy of the book, *The Dam Busters,* by Paul Brickhill, which gives a graphic account of the destruction of three great dams in western Germany, the Moehne, the Eder, and the Sorpe, by Squadron 617. These supplied electric power and water to the industries in the Ruhr and maintained the water level in the canals, supplying shipping to and from the industries. Their destruction was a tremendous loss to the Germans. Two huge bombs were dropped on the Moehne but not close enough to break the dam. Melvin Young took the third great bomb under heavy enemy fire and placed it exactly against the dam where it broke the dam and released a huge flood which swept out towns, bridges and roads below it. He did not get home with the few others in the attack. He is held as one of the greatest heroes in the records of the R.A.F. in England.

The factual information in brackets in this story was supplied by Arthur Thorning of Hitchin in Hertfordshire, England. He has written a short biographical piece about Melvin Young for Trinity College in Oxford. He also wrote that William L. White, a journalist for Life *magazine wrote about the rescue of Melvin in the December 2, 1940 edition of* Life. *White was not a Naval officer, as is related in the above story, but was just a reporter for* Life *magazine who was aboard* HMS St. Mary, *a former US destroyer given to the British Navy. Melvin's aircraft went down in October, 1940 because of engine trouble off Northern Ireland, and he and his crew were in a dinghy for 22 hours before being rescued. He was also rescued from a dinghy in November, 1940.*

The Alumni Association

Greetings to Alumni, 1947
from the 1947 Webb School of California Alumni Bulletin

I take this occasion to wish all you old boys a very happy New Year, and I sincerely hope that you are finding life rich and beautiful. I had the pleasure of seeing many of you at the reunion in June, and I found it a great joy to talk with some of you whom I had not seen in many years. Yet I missed many others.

In the last few years many of the old boys have talked with me about forming an alumni association. I have always felt that it would be a very lovely thing to do this so that we could have gatherings more frequently than we have in the past. I was delighted to know that in December a small group of old boys met in Pasadena with this purpose in mind, and that they are planning to send out calls to all of you for occasional gatherings. It was only the other day that I had a letter from Henry Walcott '32, in which he was saying that the friendships he had formed here at the Webb School were far stronger and dearer than any he has subsequently formed. I suspect that that is true with the great majority of you, and I hope that such an association may meet frequently and be a joyous occasion for you, and that there I may sometimes have opportunities to see you all. We are here publishing a long list of boys who have attended Webb School. I hope that our Alumni Association may include all those 450 who have graduated and a large number of those who were here for a time, and who have indicated an interest in the school.

We have no official register of all of those who served in the armed forces, but it must be a long list; and, of course, much of the information in this directory will deal with the service record of Webb boys. There are 20 names on the memorial tablet in the chapel, and of our older boys who were killed in the war. The list of these boys is in this publication. There may be some others of whom we have not heard. It was only last week that we had the positive confirmation about Barry Campbell '38. He was missing in action over three years ago, and the hope has remained that he would return, but we are forced to place him among those killed.

In writing this directory we have also made a new geographical list of the alumni. You can turn to cities and find those who are listed as residing in those places.

I also want to mention the California Educational Aid Foundation, which was established by some very staunch friends of our school with the main objective of assisting worthy boys and girls in their educational pursuits where there was financial need. It is not limited to those who attend this school, though it was primarily founded with this objective. The central office of that foundation is at the office of O'Melveny and Myers, 433 South Spring Street, Los Angeles. Mr. William W. Clary '35 is the treasurer; and Philip Loomis '33, the secretary. Both are in that office. Mr. Thomas Hamilton is the president and Mr. Leo Chandler, the vice president. The following are on the board of directors: Mr. Stuart Chevalier, Mrs. E.M. Shirk, Mr. Reese H. Taylor, Mr. Will Baughman, Mr. Donald C. McKenna, Mr. Ira N. Frisbee, and I. Gifts to that foundation qualify for tax reduction on the income taxes. This foundation provides scholarship aid for a number of boys and girls to attend this school and other schools when people make donations to it for that purpose. It also provides funds for furnishing ministers and speakers at our chapel service at the Vivian Webb Chapel. I speak of the foundation in order that any of you who may have in mind some charitable purpose, here or elsewhere, may find a way to execute it and get the tax reduction which is allowable by law.

I send my very best wishes to you all for a happy New Year.

*Thompson Webb being presented with a Bible by Al Hastings '42
at his retirement celebration in Los Angeles in April, 1962.*

Inscription in the Bible given to Thompson Webb
presented at his retirement dinner on April 26, 1962

To Thompson Webb, who sent each of us on his way with a Bible, a symbol
of the gratitude and affection of two generations of Webb School students, a
tribute to a friend, unashamed of the Gospel of Christ, never weary in well
doing, who heeded Paul's admonition to "walk worthy of the vocation wherein
ye are called."

8

Accrediting the School

Accreditation

Accreditation, 1924

At the very beginning of our school in 1922, every caller would ask if this was an "accredited school." We admitted we were not for we were too new at the start. With some people, that settled it. They were not about to patronize an unaccredited school. I felt the school should be accredited, and found that the way to be, was to be approved by the University of California at Berkeley. They had a committee of professors who passed on schools.

I put in my application. Shortly there came a knock on my classroom, and I opened the door to find a very formal man, somewhat elderly. He announced that he was Professor Pascal from the university, and had come to examine the school. I said that my name was Webb and extended my hand. He drew back and again said that he had come to examine the school. I invited him in.

He asked for a schedule of classes which I produced. He said, "I will see this one." After 10 minutes he was out and said, "I will see this one." He was German and his English was hard to understand. At that time our classes had never had a caller. Both teacher and pupils were upset by this very formal professor, as they told me later.

When school was out for lunch, I invited him to have lunch with us. He refused positively, as he never accepted any favors from the schools he examined. I told him that the only place where he could get lunch was the Claremont Inn, three miles away and asked if he had a car. He did not, and refused to allow me to drive him. He said that he would return after lunch to examine the library and off he went afoot.

Later he returned and took a look at our library of about 500 books, my personal collection, and again walked off. Later, we were notified that we were not accredited, since our library held less than 5,000 volumes. I applied again next year and stated that our library contained over 5,000 volumes. Vivian's father was a Methodist minister in Los Angeles with a very large congregation. He had retired in bad health and given us his library of possibly 6,000 volumes. [From the oral history: "I hadn't started a library [that] first year. My wife's father was just retiring from the ministry; . . . and he said, 'Well, Thompson, I'll give you my library, five or six thousand volumes.' All religious stuff. [laughter] So we moved it out."]

This time a young professor came to inspect the school, bringing a guitar with him. He phoned he was in Claremont and asked me to come and get him. He told me he made money on the side by giving guitar concerts. He was booked for a concert that evening in San Bernardino and asked me to take him in my car over there after the inspection, which I did. That was a 25-mile drive each way. Later our application was denied on the basis of too poorly equipped physics laboratory. He never inspected the library ministerial volumes.

That year Pomona College received a big gift for their physics laboratory and put in all new equipment. They asked me if I would accept their old equipment, which I did gladly, employing a trucker to get it. We made a clean job of removing all their old tables and all their old equipment.

I applied my third time to be accredited. I knew that it was silly for actually I did not need accrediting. We required College Boards for our boys to get them admitted to college. Every high-class college in America, except for the Western ones, accepted College Boards as blue chips. However, most Western people thought a school had to be accredited to be anything. It looked good in the catalog, though we were on a much higher standard, which the Westerners did not understand.

In due time the university inspector arrived to inspect us, this being the third time. The inspector was Dean Putnam, the dean of the university. He was a gentleman and a scholar. He made a careful inspection of all classes and our humble accommodations. He had lunch with us in the school dining room, and sat down in my home to discuss various questions. [From the oral history: "It was wintertime. He was sitting in this chair by the fire, and I gave him a cigar, and he and I were smoking cigars (I [have since] quit smoking). We smoked that together. It was a very different thing from the way the German professor refused to shake hands with me."] He was impressed that we required College Board Examinations.

In his conversation, he quoted William Elliott on something. I inquired who William Elliott was. He said, "It is William Y. Elliott, a Rhodes Scholar, who is my assistant dean." I told him that I did not know that he was out here. He asked if I knew him. I told him I had taught him as a small boy in my father's school in Tennessee. [William Y. Elliott later replaced William B. Munro as a professor of international law at Harvard and went on to teach Henry Kissinger and advise presidents. Munro had become an assistant to Millikan at Caltech, see later in this chapter.] The next day a telegram from William Elliott told me that our school was accredited.

For some years thereafter the university sent a visitor to inspect us once a year, with no criticism for about five years. Then they hit with a bang! Here was Professor Pascal, the German, who had become chairman of the Accrediting Committee.

It so happened that I had used my privilege of certifying boys to college on two graduates, Jones and Cunningham [S. Austin Jones and Kenneth G. Cunningham '29]. I did it for a very good reason. They wanted to go to the University of California, Berkeley, California.

Jones had done poorly at the Los Angeles High School, earning mostly C grades for two years. He then transferred here for the last two years. He did not want to come, for he was having a good time in high school with his friends. His parents wanted him to do good schoolwork and get away from his play boys and girls. He never was happy here, but he got down to business since that was what everybody did under our rigid rules. He made an excellent record for us, showing real ability.

On his College Boards on work taken here, he was good, but failed some College Boards on subjects he had before he came here. Consequently, he did not have the required College Boards for college.

Cunningham had a full quota of excellent College Boards. I knew that Jones was fine college material and ready to go and was willing to certify him on my privilege of accreditation. It would arouse suspicion at Berkeley if I sent one boy by College Boards and the other by certificate. I simply certified both boys to California and said nothing about College Boards.

At the end of their freshman year, here came Professor Pascal with a gleam of revenge in his eye. He did not inspect the school this time. He asked to talk to me in my office and said that I had forfeited my privilege of accreditation. He said that I had certified Jones and Cunningham to the university, that Jones had distinguished himself as a top scholar and Cunningham had failed every course. He accused me of "prostituting" (his word) my accrediting privilege. I had forfeited my certifying privilege by certifying Cunningham, for the man who could prepare a student such as Jones knew that Cunningham could not do their work.

He gave me a terrible slap in the face, so to speak. It took me a minute to collect my thoughts. Then I asked him if the university would accept a student with a full quota of College Board credits. He said they would gladly do so. I pulled out Cunningham's College Board certificate and showed him that the boy was unusually high on all subjects, fully acceptable to any college in the United States. He read them over two or three times for this was the official certificate.

He was red in the face. Then he asked why I had not entered him by College Boards, and had assumed the responsibility of certifying him. I told him that Jones did not have a full quota of College Board credits, but had done such excellent work for me that I knew he could do well at the university. I wanted him to be admitted.

I told him I thought if I sent one by College Boards and the other on certificate it would arouse suspicion, and Jones might be rejected. I felt that I knew my boys' capabilities, and I knew I had sent him two excellent students which had been proved. I told him that he had accused me of prostituting the trust the university had put in me, but the shoe was on the other foot.

The university had prostituted my trust in them for letting an excellent student like Cunningham fail. I asked him what he was doing all the time in letting Cunningham fail under his very nose. That was the last visit by the university as long as Professor Pascal was head of the Accrediting Committee.

Several years later Dr. Edwards was made director of "Relations with Schools." He was a very fair and understanding man. Our relations were always happy. The University of California no longer does the accreditation.

California Association of Independent Secondary Schools

Formation of the CAISS and Need for a National Council
from a typed text written about 1948 with additions from an earlier (ca. 1945) text

The University of California does all the accrediting of the secondary schools within the state through a committee headed by the director of Relations with Schools. For many years, this department has taken the records made by the members of the freshman class at the University of California and charged them back to the schools where the student originated. On the average of these students, they give to every secondary school in the state a rating. The rating does not have to be very high in order to secure the accrediting privilege; in fact, I am sorry to say it is too low, and there are far more schools in the State of California accredited than should be until they are willing to do better academic work.

Last year I had occasion to ask for some statistical information from the director of Relations, and secured this interesting piece of information. The top 13 schools in the state are independent schools. The best public school comes in at position 14. From that point on down the chart, there are hundreds of public schools, with an occasional independent school appearing; but, after you reach the poorest public school in the state, you find below that 43 independent schools.

In the information published by the University of California, they give only grade averages. For some years, they have made the statement that the public-school average at the University of California was better than the independent school average. It is easy to see where the average would fall between the 13 best schools and the 43 worst schools; however, that kind of publicity has not been very wholesome for the independent schools. There are too many people in California who come out with the fact that the University of California claims that the public schools are better than the independent schools.

Some 15 years ago [ca. 1935-39], a few of us headmasters [Thacher, Squibb, Cate, Vosburg, and Brush] became concerned about that type of publicity and wanted to do something about it. We had the feeling that we wanted to raise the average of the poorer independent schools and make them do work that was not embarrassing to those of us who were trying to do a genuine, fine piece of work. We found some terrible places running as private schools, places where no child should ever be sent. In the beginning of this discussion, there were four or five of us headmasters who had a number of meetings [often in their homes] to discuss this problem and to see what could be done about it and if laws could be framed which would require the bad places to clean up and improve. We called into these little meetings some of the ablest educators in the State of California to help us think these problems out—top men from several of our different universities and colleges and one or two important and thoughtful politicians. We never had many of these together, but invited them to different dinner meetings. We then secured the director of Relations with Schools [Dr. Hiram Edwards] from the University of California [Los Angeles] to come to a number of these meetings with us. [An initial one was at Vosburg's home.] He was very eager to see us do something constructive to improve the standards in a large number of these schools.

[We presented our records to show Dr. Edwards that there were some independent schools in the state that deserved a much better rating, and claimed that there were many more not represented in our meeting where a high class of academic work was done. He told us that there were over 300 private schools in the state, in many of which very poor work was done. Unfortunately for the good schools on independent foundations, all come under the same classification, "Private Schools." There was one other condition that was unfavorable to independent schools. A large percent of their graduates attended colleges and universities outside of California. The university did not feel that they should consider the standing of students in colleges out of the state. Many of the best students of the better schools attend colleges in the East, having been sent here to prepare for these colleges since many of our public schools did not offer the courses required by Eastern colleges. —*from a hand-written version written probably in 1945.]*

We had legal advice in the matter, but we always came back to the conclusion that there was no legal approach to this problem. When we began to make laws, we tied our own hands and could not improve the moral and academic standing of the bad school. All of us were already bound by state laws in regard to health, fire protection, sanitation, etc. We were continually inspected by state officials, but we were unable to frame a law that would make men good or make them do an excellent piece of teaching.

Finally [after several meetings], the director of Relations with Schools proposed that we organize an association of the best independent schools in the state and require that the standard of admission be adequately high to assure any stranger coming to California who wanted to pick a school that he would get a good one if he took it from the association. He then proposed that we give enough publicity to the association so that the general public would know what it was and what it stood for, and that when they had the need of an independent school, they would ask for an association school. We all agreed that the plan was excellent, and we had a very delicate problem in knowing how to select these schools fairly and in such a way that the school who failed to meet the standard would be inspired to try to raise its standard rather than to be embittered and turn against the association. We felt that if we, as neighbor schools, would criticize our neighbor schools, a great deal of hard feeling would come out of it. We settled upon the plan that [the presidents at] five universities or colleges [only three— Pomona, Stanford, and UCLA—at first and later USC and Santa Clara] within the state would be asked to appoint one man from each of their faculties to go on our Board of Standards, and that our association would pay their expenses to meet once a year and give consideration to any independent school applying for admission. We agreed to supply them with a secretary, who would collect all information and material bearing on these schools in advance of their meeting but under their direction. That secretary is responsible only to the Board of Standards, but her salary is paid by the association.

It was difficult to decide exactly upon all rules by which the Board of Standards would make their selection. The basic one, which is easy, was on the grade standing of the individual schools which was given to them by the University of California. The secretary could collect that for every student who had graduated from our schools, and the Board of Standards could then see how the independent schools rated before the Accrediting Commission. We agreed that our standard would be reasonable, but not as low as the accrediting committee of the university would accept. It was agreed that some member of the Board of Standards would visit the independent schools and form his impression of the equipment, the library, the laboratories, etc. of each school applying. It was agreed that they would give full consideration to any ethical policies of the individual schools as might be brought out from time to time. It was further agreed that every school is to be reconsidered once a year; the fact that we belong to it this year does not mean that we will belong to it next year.

[On these major agreements, Dr. Edwards made the first draft of the constitution, a very comprehensive and able document. At a later meeting, only minor changes were made and then the whole adopted. The Board of Standards was appointed by the respective college presidents. A letter of explanation and invitation was sent to all the independent schools we could locate in the state. An executive secretary was employed to receive all applications and furnish forms to be filled out by each applicant. There was a large amount of work to be done in securing the official college records of all students from the schools applying. These records had to be secured from all colleges where the graduates had gone and was not limited to the colleges within the state.—*from a hand-written version written probably in 1945.*]

There were some 50 schools that applied for admission in the beginning. The Board of Standards admitted 25 [actually 21] that first year [1940].

After 25 were admitted, they then met together and organized into an association, formulated a constitution and bylaws and adopted them. These have been changed repeatedly in the past 10 years, as we have learned by experience ways to improve the association. In the beginning we had to assess ourselves $50 per year in order to meet the expenses of the secretary of the Board of Standards and the meeting of the Board of Standards. We also published a small pamphlet explaining the principles on which the association was founded and giving the list of the member schools, as well as the list of the Board of Standards; and we secured a recommendation of the association by practically all the universities and colleges of the state, which was included in the pamphlet. We undertook, as individuals, to distribute that pamphlet, handing it out where we could, and slipping it into our letters and catalogs.

We soon found that that way of making the association known to the large public was too slow and that we needed a general secretary to represent the association and to give it publicity and to work for the association and not the Board of Standards. More than half of the schools felt that that was too expensive and could not be induced to join in such a move. Finally, about six of our better schools agreed to finance this general secretary for a period of three years, with the consent of the other members of the association. We wanted to give it a trial and prove that our method was right. It cost us $1,000 apiece per year. We were fortunate in securing a very able man [Howard Pattee]. For a few years he had been assistant superintendent of the schools of Pasadena, and he knew practically all of the important school men in the public-school system of the state. For 12 years he had been admission officer of one of our best colleges [Pomona College], and through that connection he knew all the secondary schools, both independent and public. We employed him full time and paid full traveling expenses when traveling was necessary. For instance, he called on his very good friend, the superintendent of schools of the state, at Sacramento, and explained to him about our association and what he was trying to do. The superintendent then told him that his office received each year several thousand inquiries about independent boarding schools within the state, and that these letters came from all over the nation and from all over the world, but that he had no provision in his budget to take care of proper answers to them, nor did he dare favor certain schools, and he was too busy to find out which were the good ones and which were the bad ones; but he asked our secretary if he might not turn over to him these inquiries as they came in and allow him to send them the little book giving names of the recommended schools which were endorsed by all of our universities. Of course, that is all that we could have asked.

Our secretary then called on the superintendent of the schools of Pasadena, for whom he had worked at one time, and explained it to him. He told him that he had that year over 1,200 inquiries from people who were seeking boarding schools and who had appealed to him for advice, but that he couldn't recommend individual schools. If, however, we would keep him supplied with our little folders, giving a list of schools that were recommended by all the universities of the state, he could hand them out as an answer to every inquiry; and so his office was supplied with pamphlets; and on and on our general secretary has traveled and visited the city school systems of the state. He goes to the conventions of high-school principals and superintendents and teachers all over the state and chats with them, tells then about the association, and supplies them with information and pamphlets. They have received our association most cordially, and it is now quite the common thing when a stranger comes into our office, to have him ask if this is an association school.

Two years ago the association schools elected a number of primary schools to come in as a branch of our association, and we have put their names in our folders. Within a year, I think we will have so amended our constitution that these schools may be full members of the independent association. [They joined in 1949 to make the CAISS the CAIS.]

Two years ago, we proposed at the association meeting that the six schools who had borne the burden of this demonstration felt that we had proven our case, and we asked the association to assess all members one-half

of one percent of their gross income for tuition, board, and room annually
to support the work of the association, making a minimum of $100 per
school and maximum of $1,000 per school. In the case of the two or three
church schools, the exception had to be made, but the rest voted the assess-
ment upon themselves and have given us a total budget of nearly $17,000
a year. We take care of the general secretary at a salary of $6,000 and cover
his traveling expenses, provide him with an office and stenographer. We
take care of a permanent secretary for the Board of Standards and print
the pamphlets which are distributed in large quantities.

More recently rather radical laws have been passed in the State
Legislature, putting limiting conditions upon the independent schools. One
such law requires us to be licensed and puts the licensing under the Social
Welfare Commission of the state. Another law puts us under the agricultural
code, requiring us to serve milk in individual bottles, which increases the
price of milk about 40 percent. Another law puts us under the Labor
Commission. They come for inspection and require that labor be paid every
two weeks, from the headmaster down, and that the minimum hours laws
be rigidly enforced, etc. Our general secretary has been to see the governor
and various influential members of the state government to see if the
independent schools might not be put under one head and one department,
instead of six or eight different departments, and that all laws pertaining to
us be coordinated. The state authorities grant that that is a constructive
move and appointed a commission, made up of the heads of the different
departments, who have now been delegated to rule over us and our general
secretary. He is a full member of that commission. That commission was
given $10,000 by the state to make a study of the situation and formulate a
plan. They decided it was necessary to have a survey made of the independent schools of the state, and that they would have to employ someone to
make this survey. On the suggestion of our general secretary, this commission has employed a Stanford professor [J.P. Mitchell], who has just retired,
who has been a member of our Board of Standards from its beginning.
He is a man who knows and understands the problems of the secondary

independent schools. He will be sympathetic but thoroughly fair. I give you the inside working of the politics within the state which we, as an association, are able to take part in because we have a full-time secretary employed for the work. As individuals, none of us could have done anything about it.

Now when it comes to the National Council [of Independent Schools], I have felt very fortunate to have been in connection with this little group from its beginning, and I have had an opportunity to attend at least two of its annual meetings and have for two years been on their executive committee. [He served on this committee from 1946-50.] I am terribly enthusiastic about the National Council idea. I don't think I have authority to speak for them, but I should like very much to put in a personal word in their behalf. The work that has been going so successfully here in the West could be carried on nationally with 10 times the telling effect that it can have within one state's boundaries. I can see what could be accomplished by the independent schools of America if we can build a strong National Council, but it takes a great deal of money.

I should like to see standards of excellence set up for membership in the National Council when the time comes that that may be needed. The National Council, through the National Registration Office at Princeton, is definitely offering that to us on a voluntary basis. I have been so enthusiastic about the idea of the National Registration Office that I have joined them in the very beginning and sent in my list of seniors every year who are graduating with us and the colleges which they attend. The National Council, in turn, gets the records of these boys in their freshman year and charges them back to my school. Through that record I have been able to get boys into colleges where we weren't known, and I have had colleges in the West tell me that on the strength of the information that they received from the National Registration Office that they counted on my transcripts my C's to be B's, as compared with B's of other schools.

If hundreds of our schools in this nation will join the National Council, at their present rate of $40 per year, we would have a very good sum to work on, but if more of them would voluntarily take the $100 membership, we would have still greater strength. We need a strong central office; we need Dr. Parkhill very much; and we need to give him several excellent assistants. The field is large, and a strong central office could do tremendous things for our independent schools in bringing out the proper type of publicity and in molding a proper attitude in the minds of the public towards independent education. They should bring out a number of writers to put articles in the leading periodicals in the places where thoughtful people go to read. A strong central office might be able to promote types of legislation that would be constructively valuable to us. I cite one as an illustration. It would be fair for our federal government to allow an individual to deduct tuition from his income tax, as he does taxes and other expenses. There are so many forward-looking things that could be done if we had people to do them, and it needn't cost us comparably much if we united all of our independent schools.

Southern Origins
TW III

The Southern Association of Colleges and Secondary Schools was established in 1895 and John M. Webb, TW's uncle, of the Webb School at Bell Buckle served as its president in 1898-99. According to William O. Bates in his 1957 book *Private Preparatory Schools for Boys in Tennessee since 1867*, this association supported secondary schools in preparing students for college and also accredited the schools including the Webb School and the Webb-Price School of Lewisburg, Tennessee, which was run by Edward Price until it burned down in 1925. My grandfather had to have known of its existence and the help that it provided to the independent schools.

Association of Independent Schools of Los Angeles County
TW III from documents provided by the California Association of Independent Schools

On April 19, 1939, the Association of Independent Schools of Los Angeles County held its spring meeting at the Black-Foxe Military Institute in Los Angeles. Murray Brush, headmaster of California Preparatory School, was secretary; and Major Harry H. Gaver, headmaster of Black-Foxe, was president. Hiram Edwards of UCLA, Florence Brady of Occidental College, and Howard Pattee of Pomona College were speakers. In his talk on "Articulation of the Private Schools with the Higher Institutions in California," Dr. Edwards told of the methods used by the university to estimate the work done by various groups of schools sending students to the university. He presented a chart showing that schools, rated on the performance of their students after admission to college, appear in the following order: 1. High Schools with over 500 pupils; 2. High Schools with 250-500 students; 3. High Schools with less than 250 pupils; 4. Private Schools. He admitted that there were two distinct groups of private schools. The meeting may have led to the meeting at the Glendora School or to the group that decided to start the CAISS.

Thompson Webb's Role in the CAISS

TW III from documents from the California Association of Independent Schools (CAIS)

After working to found the CAISS, TW was elected to a five-year term on its first executive committee on March 26, 1941. Curtis Cate of the Santa Barbara School for Boys was the president, and Miss Burke of Miss Burke's School in San Francisco was the vice president. Paul Squibb and Keith Vosburg were also on the executive committee. At the third annual meeting on November 15, 1942, TW was elected president and served as such until Mr. Anson Thacher was elected president at the sixth annual meeting on June 22, 1945. From then on until at least 1949, TW served as treasurer of the association.

In 1942, five of the schools, including Webb School, hired Howard Pattee to do publicity work for their schools. By July 1944 Pattee had become the general secretary of the association and continued his publicity work. TW, as president of the association, had worked to make this possible by finding the funds from dues and special payments to cover Pattee's salary of $5,000.

Founding the California Association of Independent Secondary Schools
from oral history, p. 102-109, 112-115

Q: Now you said you would say something about the formation of the headmasters' association which then ran into the California Association of Independent Secondary Schools (CAISS).

TW: Well, it was decided that if we could get these schools together, the headmasters, get them to know each other and be friends, we could stop this cat-and-dog fighting.

Q: Could you give me an example of what this cat-and-dog fighting was like? I mean, what were they saying about one another?

TW: Well, the head of the San Diego Naval Academy told me that his football team came up to play Oneonta Military Academy and Oneonta just beat them all to pieces. Then he found out that at the Oneonta Academy, not one of the students played. They had gotten fire companies of men to act as the players with their sweaters on—what a dirty bunch they were—and then they advertised that Oneonta had a great football team, and that kind of thing. Telling about how the catalog would say there's no smoking and yet they didn't stop it. On each other, they just told all the bad tales they could think of about each other and tried to get the boy to come to them, they were pure. They were using that system of trying to get patronage by abusing the other people.

Q: I suppose you might say it was cutthroat competition?

TW: Oh, it was. They'd run all kinds of crazy ads in the papers. The papers were full of them; you don't see them anymore, really. Well, I talked to one or two of the headmasters, and we decided to call them all together and see what we could do. It was a pretty stiff bunch at first. But they began to know each other, other human beings, and I talked to them; I said, "We want to boost this private education, that it's better than the average, so our schools will fill up."

Q: Did you call this meeting here, or where was it called, Los Angeles? Or was it just sort of an informal thing where just a couple of you got together over dinner?

TW: We got together and decided we'd meet at such and such a school. I think it was the Glendora School, the first meeting, long since burned up and gone. Well, we decided on that and then wrote to all these other schools, that we'd like to have a meeting of all the school people . . . on such and such an evening, and have dinner.

Q: Did anybody [come] from up further north at all?

TW: We didn't get that far to start with. We started with our neighbors here in Southern California. There were dozens of little old schools around fighting each other.

Q: You organized this meeting, then, at the Glendora School?

TW: Yes, Mrs. Danzell was running the school there, and we had, I think, the first meeting of six, seven, or eight of them came. We talked this over, that we had to quit fighting each other and boost for what private schools could do, and help each other along. We got a pretty good friendship and organized what we called the Headmasters' Association. We had two or three annual meetings, and the military people [were] so different from the rest of us, I don't know; they finally, we got friendly and just dropped it and quit meeting. Then I felt that we ought to start over again, and there were certain shady people just to leave out. Some of us got together, there was Thacher, and the Cate School, Catalina [Island School], and Webb, oh, I don't know how many more, about six or seven of us got together and decided to start the California Association of Independent Schools, and take in the good ones up north and all. We did a lot of talking about it, and finally [in 1940] we had some meetings, and we wrote our constitution. We decided that we didn't want the low-class schools in there, but if we said they were "low-class," [there] would be war again. We got [Hiram] Edwards, [director of Relations with Schools] from the University of California at Los Angeles, to help us; and he was on the accrediting commission [agency], which was done out of Berkeley, but he was the Los Angeles representative. He met with us and we talked it over. We finally decided that we could not judge other schools; they'd be mad. But we would ask five colleges to appoint a professor from their faculties, ask the president to pick out someone to be a committeeman for this independent association. [The initial Board of Standards was appointed in early 1940 with representatives from just three colleges: Dr. Hiram Edwards from UCLA, Prof. J.P. Mitchell from Stanford, and Dean William R. Nicholl from Pomona College. In July, 1943, representatives were added from USC and Santa Clara.] We had the five best colleges we could pick out, and we paid their expenses and furnished them a secretary. I don't know whether we gave them any income beyond that or not, but we raised enough money to do that. And Mrs. [Katherine] Walker, who was [an associate director at the Office of Relations with Schools at UCLA], was secretary to Edwards [and executive secretary to the CAISS as of May 25, 1941], and they [the Board of Standards] were to judge the schools to enter. We said that if the product [i.e. students from a given school] that went to college didn't average, the school couldn't be there. Their first year's grades had to be averaged, when massed. One [freshman] could fail and another'd be all A's, but if Webb had five boys in colleges over the United States, this secretary got the grades. She gave Webb a grade for its average and the others a grade for their averages. If we didn't make that C average, we were out. A lot of schools couldn't make it. Those that did make it became the association. [Twenty-one schools were admitted at the initial meeting of the new CAISS on March 26, 1941, at the Marlborough School for Girls in Los Angeles.]

We rotated the presidency around. One year [1943-45] when I was president, a man who had bought the San Diego Military Academy, came to me and said he wanted his school in this association, found it'd be of great value to him. Maybe people said that they wouldn't send their boys unless it belonged to the association. And he said, "That committee has turned us down. You're president and I think you can get us in and I want you to do that."

I said, "Mr. R, according to our constitution, the only way anybody can get in is to be approved by this committee. Now you just work on them; work on your students that they get up this grade."

"Oh, no, Webb, you know you can get me in if you wanted to; I want you to do that." He says, "You know, I have a school back in Arkansas that's called R. University, and if you go back with me in June, I'll give you a doctor's degree, and you can say you have one from R. University."

That's the first offer I ever had of a doctor's degree; I refused it. [laughter] Mr. R. never did get in; his schools never came up; he had one over here in Glendora.

Q: What's the problem with the military academies generally? They don't stress the scholastic side of things?

TW: Oh, I don't know. Some people are good teachers and some are not; and some have character and some don't. Why, some of the military schools are fine, and I understand Culver [Military Academy]'s a great institution, things like that, but this one's not.

. . . .

Q: I wonder, after you got the association organized, through the years, what have been some of its major problems, what have been some of its major accomplishments?

TW: We got going to put this requirement of satisfactory production in college as the basis of the whole thing. We got the good schools together, and they had several little short meetings during the winter, but in June they had a longer [all-]day, several-day [meeting] somewhere. It's become a very friendly thing, we've all learned to be very fond of each other and admire each other. It's very helpful, and they have a reputation with some of the best institutions, that if you belong to that association, the school's all right. It helps us that way. But at the time [just before] I was president of the association, I got a letter from someone in New England [Fall, 1942] saying that several of the New England schools had gotten together to organize a national association. They had written to all of the local associations for their constitutions, and they said ours was the best constitution. The little committee of them had gotten together and felt that the California association was the leading local association in the nation, and they were going to have a meeting of about a dozen of them in Cambridge, Massachusetts, that summer to join in the matter of the national association and could I come and represent ours and tell them about how we did it. They had me come back three or four different summers [probably between 1942 and 1950] and we'd sit and discuss these things; oh, they were tiptop men that I was talking with, and it meant a great deal to me. We organized this national association [initially in 1946 the National Council of Independent Schools, which helped found the National Association of Independent Schools in 1950 or so. —*see p. 23 of the* Webb School of California Alumni Bulletin, *1974-76*]. Now there are some thousand schools in it and they have a great meeting every summer, [to] talk over their problems and even introduce legislation.

Q: Paul Squibb told me that I should ask you particularly to tell about the question of dues and how you found, when you went there, that there was a disparity among the various headmasters as to how they were going to pay to support this association.

TW: Well, we had to fight the president of the California association. A lot of people didn't want it to cost them anything. They wanted to give $25, a flat fee a year. But we felt that we had to have somebody to represent us, a paid secretary who would visit the public schools and tell them about the private schools and the requirements they had, so they'd know that a membership in that meant something. And it did. Many high-school principals that never paid attention to private schools began to send problem kids that would come up. I mean "problem," I should say, where the parents had died and the child had no home, and where can we put them? In a boarding school that's a good boarding school. They got to being able to say, "Well, if they belong to that California association, it's a good one." That meant a lot to us, and didn't mean that they made enemies by doing that. So we put up our dues to where we were giving one percent of our gross income.

Q: Whose idea was this in the beginning, if you can recall, that it should be one percent of the gross?

TW: I don't know.

Q: Was that your idea?

TW: I don't know; happened too long ago. We sat around and we came to that agreement [that] this would be perfect; that would give us enough to pay Pattee's salary.

Q: Now this was, could you give his first name?

TW: Howard Pattee [formerly director of admissions at Pomona College].

Q: Howard Pattee. And he was the man that you hired?

TW: We hired him as our secretary, to give us our full time. We paid him a reasonable salary [$5,000] and expenses [$1,500]. [Pattee was originally hired to do publicity work by five schools in 1942. While TW was president of the CAISS from 1942-45, the financing was worked out for Pattee to become general secretary of the association.]

. . . .

Q: Well, now, you have generally been satisfied with Webb's performance in rank within the association over the years?

TW: Yes.

Q: How are you ranked?

TW I don't know, but we've never been questioned as to our eligibility. Our boys have always been above the average.

Q: Now, Paul Squibb said that the way in which the reports were made by Mrs. Walker, it was possible for anybody in the association to see exactly where they ranked, one, two, three, four, or whatever. But over the years, Midland has tended to rank three, maybe, once in a while, one, but how have you ranked?

TW: I don't know. I don't ever remember seeing that.

State and National Associations of Independent Schools
Howell Webb, from the interview with the four Webb brothers, December, 1988

In Southern California, there had been a little association of about a dozen heads of boys schools that had met very informally for a number of years. [This group seems to have formed the Association of Independent Schools of Los Angeles County by the late 1930s.] They met in one headmaster's home or another when the spirit moved them. When somebody felt that it was time that they got together and talked about common problems, he would send out an invitation to the other heads, and they would get together for an hour or two and talk about the problems. I remember when it was in our living room, and I was a child hiding behind the curtain in the hallway that led to the living room. I heard Sherman Thacher commenting, or somebody was commenting, that one of the girls schools had expelled a girl (this was back in 1920s, I think) for the gross sin of wearing lipstick. I was kind of shocked because that was not the kind of thing that nice girls did, at least in school, in those days. I was even more shocked when Sherman Thacher said, "I wonder what they would have done to that girl if she'd done something bad." [laughter] But anyhow, that was a very loose kind of organization, and Dad felt that they needed something more substantial. I won't take the time here to say what the problems were among California schools. But mostly to promote good will between the various preparatory schools in California and to promote cordiality between them instead of a sort of ruthless competition for students and teachers, Dad felt that they needed to have regular meetings. They also needed a paid general secretary who would organize all these meetings and see that they were carried out and keep records of the minutes. He wanted the secretary to start making it into a functioning organization to improve standards in all California prep schools. This idea was rather enthusiastically accepted by most headmasters, but Curtis Cate at the Cate School was concerned about keeping his budget under control. He opposed this organization which became known as the California Association of Independent Secondary Schools [in 1940]. They admitted headmistresses as well as headmasters. Dad felt that the Cate School was certainly a fine school academically and should be part of the association. The Cate School was long established before the Webb School. He felt that it was important to have Curtis Cate in this organization. Cate was fighting it all along the line. Dad suggested to the group that wanted to elect Dad as the first president of the association, "Let's elect Curtis Cate." And they did, and Cate served for one year [1940-42], but his heart wasn't in it. Dad's strategy seemed to have worked, but it didn't really. So he [Cate] dropped out with his school until he retired. Then it rejoined under the second headmaster of Cate School, and it has been in the association ever since.

The association has served a great purpose. When I came home in 1947, Dad took me to my first meeting with the CAISS. It very quickly changed into the CAIS [in 1949]. They decided to admit elementary schools long before I had thought of starting one at that time. When I went to my first meeting, there were 13 schools in the association. When I retired in 1987, there were more than 100. It has been very successful in getting the support of all the leading independent schools in California.

In the late '40s, there were three national associations of independent schools of sorts. They were all doing things that should be done in one organization. A group of the Eastern headmasters thought that they ought to revise any national effort to unite independent schools. The problem was what would the organization be like. They studied regional organizations. The California association wasn't the only one. Many states had them. They decided that the plan for the CAIS was the best of them all, and that they should plan this new broad national association on the pattern of the CAIS. The NAIS has served extremely well the cause of good independent education throughout this country. I would say this is the place where Dad had the greatest influence on education in America.

Bill: Dad was invited back East personally to work with the other headmasters for the establishment of the NAIS. He was a vital force in that effort.

Q: Were private schools accredited and who was the accrediting body?

Howell: The University of California was the only accrediting organization at that time, and accreditation meant very, very little. The CAIS had much stricter guidelines. When the University of California got out of the business, admission to the CAIS was the closest thing that the state of California had to accreditation. Later the Western Association of Schools and Colleges took over the role of accreditation, and the CAIS worked very closely with this new organization. The Western Association adopted the requirements of the CAIS as the state requirements for accreditation.

Advantages of Private Schools

Dr. Millikan, Mr. Kersey, and Dr. Munro

Dr. William B. Munro, who had been a professor of international law at Harvard for some years, was brought out to Pasadena to assist Dr. Millikan in running the California Institute of Technology. Dr. Millikan was giving his time to raising money, and Dr. Munro took over the operations the president usually does. Dr. Munro was also on the board of Scripps College, where I was a member of the board. Someone had given Caltech a beautiful faculty clubhouse known as the Athenaeum. When the time came to use the Athenaeum, they put on a big dinner party and Dr. Munro invited me to be his guest at that party. When we went into the room Dr. Munro placed me at a table with Dr. Millikan and himself and Mr. Kersey, who was at that time superintendent of schools in California.

When we started to talk, Mr. Kersey turned to Dr. Millikan and said he had a grievance to pick with him. Dr. Millikan asked him what it could be. He said, "Dr. Millikan, you said you're sending your son to Phillips Academy in Andover, Massachusetts, when right across the street from you is the Pasadena High School, as fine an educational institution as there is in America. Why do you pay a big price to send your boy to Boston to Andover when you could send him across the street free of charge and give him just as good an education?" Mr. Kersey said, "The private schools are on their last leg. They're all failing and closing and I don't think there will be one left in California in 10 years." Dr. Millikan replied by saying, "Mr. Kersey, you're not very well-informed about private schools. Mr. Webb has one that is thriving and not about to close." This surprised Mr. Kersey and he said he didn't know about Mr. Webb's school. Then Dr. Millikan said, "Mr. Kersey, I sent my oldest son to Pasadena High School and he was a bookworm and wasn't interested in a social life. He was always in the library with his nose in a book—that was just his nature. When it came to my next son, he was an outgoing fellow who loved every boy and girl he met. He went there a few months and was out every night in automobiles running around to parties, with no time to work at books and nobody to stop him. We decided to put him in Andover where he couldn't run around at night: there weren't any automobiles and no girls to divert him." He said, "They were just different types of boys, and your school over there was all right for a bookworm, but not for a social boy. He went through Andover and became a student and accomplished everything we wanted for him, which you couldn't do. There was no way for you to stop his social life in the public schools, and Mrs. Millikan and I were not successful in stopping it either."

In the course of the conversation Mr. Kersey turned to me and said he'd love to see my school—he didn't know anything about it. I invited him to come out and said I'd love for him to address our assembly when he could find it convenient. So we made a date and he came out, and when he came into the auditorium with all the students, Mr. Kersey looked up at the blackboard where there was some scribbling and he said, "Boys, is that Latin?" They said, "Yes," and he said, "Well I don't know but one word of Latin, and that's 'sock it to em.'" Mr. Kersey was a likable man, but I think he belittled the public schools by that kind of an appearance.

Protecting a Boy From His Parents

When a boy finishes grammar school and starts to high school, he may well need protection from his parents. Too often the parents, with the best of intentions, indulge him in too many attractive diversions, too much free time and too much spending money, and do not insist upon homework and necessary chores about the house which develop good habits at an early age. Too many homes have all the comforts and conveniences, with no responsibility for the growing boy, which is a mistake. He should help to provide many of the comforts and have jobs to earn some money and learn to save some of it to produce worthy objectives.

When he gets home from school, here is his television and the automobile and a lot of nice boys and girls to play with. Away they go, having exciting fun before dinner and more parties and dances and movies after dinner, until there is no time to do chores and study the homework assigned by the schoolteachers.

Many fathers and mothers indulge themselves in the joy of their child's happiness without requiring the stern rules that build scholars and good habits of self-direction.

Probably one of the best things in these United States is the public-school system, where every boy and girl can acquire a good education if he or she wants it, without cost. But those children need a stern hand at home to see that they do their part to get it.

. . . .

So often in my teaching days, mothers would say to me that they wanted to send their sons to the boarding school where I was the headmaster, but their sons did not want to come. Should they make him? My reply was, "Yes," that a boy would not want to leave a happy home and all his friends for some far-off school he knew nothing about, but that his mother was older and wiser than he, and should direct him. I told her it would take a while for him to get over homesickness and make new friends, but the chances were that after a few weeks he would be happy and enthusiastic about his schooling. But after some months, if he was not happy, I would request her to take him home, but she should give him a chance to make good.

There are many fine boarding schools, but, of course, there are some that are not. The parents should be careful to pick a good one. Neither can they be sure that all day schools are first-class.

See also stories on "Mrs. Hilton's Views of Private Schools" in Chapter 2 and on "John Stevens/Dwight Taylor" in Chapter 7 for other discussions of the advantages of private schools.

9

Incorporating the School
1947-1966

Incorporation and Gift of Land

Rising Costs and Incorporation after World War II
from letter to David Rosenbaum, director of the Milford School, June 10, 1964

After World War II, inflation and high taxes came in, though we had continued to raise our tuition somewhat each year, and I ran the school in the black, but sometimes with a profit of less than $500 a year. I didn't dare borrow money anymore, because I couldn't see how I could pay it back, since I couldn't make any more. Los Angeles had been growing out our way, and the subdivisions were on three sides of us. The subdividers began to bid for our campus of approximately 80 acres at fabulous prices, stating

The original Board of Trustees from left to right: Mr. Frank P. Barker (Second Vice President), Mr. Leon W. Scales (First Vice President), Mr. Howell Webb, Mrs. Willard C. Jackson, Mr. Millard Sheets, Mr. T. Kirk Hill (President), Mr. Harold M. Ruddick, Mrs. Elbert W. Shirk, Mr. William V. Shannon (Secretary-Treasurer), and Mr. Frederick Hard. Not pictured: Mr. Ira Frisbee, Mr. Philip A. Loomis, Jr. '33, Mr. Donald McKenna, and Mr. Charles E. Scripps '37.

they would destroy the cheap frame buildings the school inhabited and subdivide it.

My four sons were then through college and supporting themselves. We held a family conference as to whether we should take a large sum of money and close out or try to find a way to continue. The four boys all voted not to sell out. I then told them the only way it could continue was to give away the school to a board of trustees on a non-profit eleemosynary basis, and that was agreed upon. I didn't see how it was possible to ask any philanthropists to buy our property at its value, just for the privilege of continuing the school.

We invited a few of our best friends to become the trustees and incorporated them as a non-profit institution. [The Board of Trustees held their first meeting on August 20, 1955, and two family members Howell Webb and Leon Scales, a cousin and former teacher at Webb, were on the board along with four members from the California Educational Aid Foundation (see "Greetings to Alumni, 1947" in chapter 7.)] We then deeded to them the entire school property that was in use, not including 30 to 40 acres adjoining us which was not in use. This we did, and the appraised value amounted to over $1,200,000, leaving us the vacant land, which we proposed to sell at a given sum. The trustees asked me to serve as headmaster for five more years on a salary, which was the first time I had had a bank account of my own. Whatever we had had to pay personally for shoes and doctors and whatnot were charged to me each year in the past. Our board and home were provided by the school. The auditor at the end of the year would write off my account as my salary. It was a kind of good feeling to have a bank account of our own!

During those five years, the trustees raised the money to buy our vacant land as they foresaw the need of it as the school grew. In a way, it was too bad we sold it to them when we did, for now the property around us is bringing $40,000 an acre in subdivisions. We might have realized much more if we had waited, but it has proved a good investment for the corporation.

After my retirement they elected me to the Board of Trustees, and I have spent my time visiting our former patrons and raising money for new buildings. The County of Los Angeles has a very severe building code now, which was not formerly in existence. The buildings that are to be used for children or the aged (and high-school students are called children) are under the strictest regulations that could possibly be. We could burn up their teachers or ordinary citizens, but we cannot burn up paying guests! The result is that where I built a room for a boy in the early stages, the cost was $300 a room. Today, under the new building code and inflation, the room costs $5,000. We couldn't continue on as a proprietary school. Of course inflation is a terrible thing, but it has its good features—if you're on the right side and own the land. I chuckle over the fact that we started here $40,000 in debt and we gave away a million-dollar property and now have something to live on for the rest of our lives, in addition.

When I felt I had to give the school—I couldn't persuade anyone to buy it—it wasn't a business institution, since it had no income, and I couldn't assume that any philanthropist would pay me anything for it. But after I had given it, philanthropists have been very good to us. We had the entire school booked for the following year [1959-60], 40 boys having engaged rooms in a two-story inflammable building, when the fire inspector came out at Easter time [1959] and said we could not put a boy in that building the following year. That was a jolt that looked as though it had killed the school. One of my former students [Frank Gard Jameson] who had been very shrewd in business came out at once and built a dormitory to receive those boys, meeting the building code and being ready, in the rough at least, when the boys came in September. One by one, they have been condemning these buildings, and it has kept us working our heads off to keep ahead of that fire department or the building code and other require- ments that have been put upon us. Thousands of dollars have gone into the ground in the way of sewerage and public utilities, which do not show, but the trustees have been able to raise nearly $2,000,000 in that period, and we do have some lovely new buildings.

We are now putting up a new dormitory at the cost of $250,000, with over $200,000 having already been given. One of my great disappointments came from the condemnation of our swimming pool three years ago. It had been a ranch reservoir in years past, and therefore a makeshift, but it felt pretty good in hot weather! We had chlorinated it by hand every day. We never knew anybody to suffer from it, but the Health Department said, "No more water in that pool," and for three years our boys have had to suffer through a few weeks of heat at the beginning and end of school. Last week, out of a clear sky and unsolicited, came $93,000 to build the new pool, in memory of a graduate [Stephen Sutro '55] who was killed in the Navy. This is to be an Olympic pool, with dressing rooms and showers and grandstands, fences and all that goes with modern pools. We are doing our best to get it ready by September, though I'm afraid we'll be late.

I hope this little account of our history may be of some interest to you. However, I think we have our compensations in the best we turn out, for the occasional disappointments. Only last Sunday I had such an experience.

About 50 miles from here, at the Desert Sun School in Idyllwild, the commencement speaker this year was William Y. Elliott, who has been professor of international law at Harvard the past 38 years and adviser to four different presidents of the United States. I once had the pleasure of teaching that boy at my father's school in Tennessee and, of course, immensely enjoyed hearing him speak and visiting with him. There are many such rewards in the 50 years in which I have taught.

Letter to the Board of Trustees
from letter dated December, 1966. It may not have been sent.
{ }'s set off words that were crossed out.

There is a misunderstanding of the basis on which the Webb family turned over the Webb School of California to a non-profit corporation. I was surprised to find that one of our older trustees did not know the steps involved. Maybe most of the trustees do not remember or never knew. I assumed that my attorneys had given the trustees the facts.

I think it was in 1947 that I had a talk with William W. Clary '35 of O'Melveny & Myers about incorporating the school for its perpetuation after we were gone. I wanted to turn it into a non-profit corporation but did not know how to do it. He admitted that it was complicated and would require time to work out. He asked if I had thought of the problem of inheritance tax if I died holding title. I confessed that I knew nothing about that. At the time he owned a tract of land and a house for retreat behind the school or else had just sold it.

He stated that the school property was worth a million dollars or more on his guess. If I died holding title, the federal government would demand an inheritance tax of half a million or something like that which would be payable within one year. This would force the sale of the property and end the school. He advised that I incorporate the school as a stock company at once, giving equal portions of the stock to myself, wife and four sons. In this way the government would tax my estate on the basis of only one-sixth of appraised value if I died. He further said that this step would help toward converting to a non-profit corporation later. He immediately set up the stock company. I think that the school had no debts at the time and owned 70 odd acres. Up to that time I had never drawn a stated salary from the school and had no personal bank account. The school housed us, fed us, clothed us and paid our doctors' bills. All these personal items were charged to my account. At the end of the year the auditor charged off my personal items as my salary. Many years it was very small, but a few times it was large, especially when there had been sickness.

When the stock company took over, the attorney and auditor set up a salary for my wife and me. I suggested a modest amount, but Ira Frisbee, the auditor, insisted it be much larger as a precedent and in keeping with salaries of headmasters in comparable schools. I hope he remembers this, though I can't quote his exact words. It was in keeping with the salary I had been offered by the trustees of another school if I would come to them. I never mentioned that offer or an offer of another school where I was called. It did not seem fair to speak of either offer and possibly embarrass the schools.

The stock company never paid a dividend in its eight years of existence. All earnings went back into the school, except the salary, and possibly some of that did. We had more students, and for part of that eight years we were netting more money than ever in our history. If we had any debts, and I don't think we did, they were paid off. As many improvements were put in as our profits permitted. We built the Quonset house for shop and storage, four aluminum buildings for classrooms and dormitory rooms, the Guayule house for dormitory rooms. We added rooms to the Alamo and put the tanks on the hill with a 4-inch water line from the water company to the tanks. We finished the chapel, except the tower which was a gift from Mrs. Shirk and Mrs. Paine. They volunteered to do that, unsolicited.

Then inflation began creeping up year by year, and the profit decreased. There was much we sacrificed—no painting of buildings or improvements that did not have to be. The County Building Department got new laws passed, requiring us to put in an expensive electrical system of automatic activators for fire alarms. They began threatening to require automatic sprinklers in every room and warned us that they would soon condemn our old building and swim pool, some of which was done shortly.

I take pride in the fact that I did not borrow money then for improvements since there were no earnings with which to pay back. I did not let our operations get in the red, though the year came when the total earnings above costs were less than $1,000—I think about $500. Our profits were gone, but our real estate was booming to fabulous prices.

An aggressive subdivider called at my office and wanted to buy the school campus. He said he could not use many of our buildings and would wreck most of them and subdivide the land. He said he would give me a big price in cash. I had not planned to sell it, but I asked him how much he would offer. He said he would have to go over it and appraise it before making an offer, but his offer would not be less than $500,000 and maybe quite a bit more. He gave me his card, suggesting that I think it over and call him if I would consider a firm offer after he had made the appraisals.

I never make quick decisions on big problems, and I rolled this one over and over, talking with my wife. We did not want to let our school go under at any price, but before answering this we felt we should consult our four sons, who were married and now teachers. The young people deserved consideration more than we did, for we had lived out our working days. They were our heirs.

When we found the date when Thompson, JR., could come from Wisconsin, we set the date for our family conference. When we sat down, I outlined the problem to them. We could sell the school for a lot of money, maybe a million dollars, a value Mr. Clary had suggested. This would be the end of Webb School of California. I told them that it was a going concern with every place full for several years and fully booked for the next year and a large overflow applying for whom we had no room. I told them that in the inflation it was not a paying business with an earning of only about $500 that year, but no debts. I did not dare borrow money for buildings when there were no earnings with which to pay back. As a privately owed business we could not solicit gifts. I did say that we could raise our prices and probably continue for a few years with what we had.

I told them we could go non-profit and solicit capital gifts and probably carry on as did Harvard, Pomona, Stanford, Andover, etc. But I said to go non-profit we would have to give it away; no one would buy the school at the price it was worth to run a non-profit business. They listened attentively without interruption.

I said, "What do you want to do?" Almost in one voice they said, "Don't destroy the school." It was an emotional experience. My wife and I wept.

Then I told them that we could give the non-profit corporation the entire set of buildings and equipment, everything the school occupied except my house, and we would keep all of the unoccupied land, which was about 30+ acres. The school would then have more land than Scripps College or Claremont Men's College and more land than most schools I knew. We all agreed on that, and that is exactly what we offered to the new corporation.

I wanted Frank Barker for my attorney. He was a friend of long standing and the attorney of my brother, Will, Headmaster of the Bell Buckle school, when he was involved in legal matters. I thought he understood schools of this type. Frank flew out here from Kansas City a number of times {while we drew up papers for incorporation} and worked out every detail for me in my mind and plan.

{When we were satisfied with the arrangements, Frank asked for a California attorney to file the papers as he had no license in California. Then we asked Leon Scales of San Diego. He was a cousin once removed and a former teacher in this school, a much younger man than Barker and a very able attorney.}

Barker and Scales had several long conferences. I supposed that Barker explained everything to Scales, but maybe he did not explain the gift. {I shall find out when Scales reads this.} We made a long list of men and women whom we admired and would like to have on our board. We all sat down together and went over the list one by one to make sure we had chosen wisely. Maybe one was not well enough, another too involved in something else, etc. We had to cross off many dear and admired people. When our list was complete, only one declined. He based it on health and had by doctor's orders resigned from several boards recently.

When our chosen people were legally incorporated, we were ready to sign the deed, free of indebtedness for the land the school stood on, something around 40 acres. We had not offered to sell them our house or the 30+ acres that stood unoccupied. We had not thought of it or planned to do so. It was time to call a surveyor and stake out the land we were keeping and get a legal description of the portion we were giving. Then to my surprise, Barker or Scales came to me and asked what I planned to do with the land I was keeping. I had not offered it to them for sale. They asked for it. I told him that I would sell it when I got my price. Then he said the board thought the school should buy the land for future growth and asked how much I wanted for it. I told him I had discussed the price with my sons and agreed to hold it until I could get $400,000, and [it] would reach that in a few years. I told him that I had set my price to bring in $100,000 to each son. One son recently reminded me of that statement. They have never forgotten.

Later, Barker or Scales or both of them came back with the statement that the board would give me $500,000 for that land, since the original offer on all had been not less than $500,000, but would pay in long-time notes. I told them I wanted $400,000, but that if they made it $500,000 I would give them back $100,000 of the notes in ten years. I put it in my will, which the attorney wrote. I stipulated that the interest would be 4 percent on the notes. There was no argument about that deal. All were happy. I have lived to pay back $94,000.

When the attorneys or maybe the president of the Board of Trustees brought me the $500,000 in notes, he brought a trust deed against the entire campus of 70+ acres. I called attention to the fact that I had sold them only 30+ acres. They replied that it would be difficult and expensive to survey the land and legally describe the specific acreage. They simply threw in the whole piece. I could not object to that. That one thing may have given some of the board the idea that they had bought the school.

In acquiring a standing that would exempt the new corporation from state and federal taxes, it was necessary to fill out lengthy forms and give, among other things, an appraised value of the property. Clifford Sheets of Pomona, a professional appraiser, was employed to make the appraisal. I heard the auditor or attorney tell Sheets that they wanted his minimum appraisal, as low as his conscience would allow. I don't know why, but this caught my attention. I know Sheets said he could appraise only the land, not the buildings and equipment, as he had no former record of sales of school buildings. He said he made appraisals on the basis of what similar property brought on the market.

He set a price on the land at something over $700,000. Then the fire insurance companies set an appraisal on cost to replace the buildings and equipment. The lowest appraisal of the three companies bidding on the insurance was $1,200,000. The actual value of the Webb family gift to the corporation would be hard to estimate from these figures. I did think we had made the corporation a very handsome gift, and we did not offer to sell anything to the corporation. It was their own idea and request to buy the 30+ acres of vacant land. Possibly I asked a big price at that time, for I intended to hold it until it rose to my price. I am led to believe that it reached my price when the president of the board announced at the last meeting that an appraisal made last month put a value of $30,000 per acre on the vacant land the board had bought, or a total of $900,000. I think that is high, but surely in the light of it, the board does not feel $400,000 unreasonable.

At the time we gave the school to the board, every room was occupied. It was not a ghost town. It was worth the replacement value to the board. I obviously would never have sold it for such a price as $500,000.

When we deeded it to the board we gave all the stock in the original corporation, with a fully enrolled school, $40,000 in the bank and no indebtedness except what the board had contracted for in the purchase of our additional vacant land.

I have bought and sometimes sold much real estate, largely in Coachella Valley. I have made quite a bit of money from that. Most of the several hundred acres in Coachella Valley was bought before 1918 when I was farming there, long before this school was founded in 1922. Most of it was bought at prices of $5 to $12 an acre. Some of my earnings on that went into the school, when some pieces were sold, though I still have much left. Most of my inheritance from Father, Mother and Sister Alla went into the school. That was not a large amount. If I had not acquired a comfortable estate on my land deals outside the school property, we could not have considered turning the school over to a non-profit corporation, in what we feel to have been a gift of a sizable amount.

It is distasteful to me to make this statement. I believe in the Scripture, "When thou doest alms, let not thy left hand know what thy right hand doeth." But I do think the Board of Trustees of this school should be entitled to know the exact deal they made. To my surprise they seem not to know it, and thus it became necessary for me to outline the details.

Incorporation and Frank Barker
from letter to Frank Barker, July 17, 1954

Jack and his family are home. He was telling me about a conversation he had with you over my problem of incorporation. He felt that from what you said to him, you had a good many ideas on the matter. What's the chance of my employing you to help us get our school properly incorporated? I suppose I have been stupid, but I seem to have had the impression that I could only use a local man, because he was local. One of my former students [W.W. Clary '35], who is in the firm of O'Melveny & Myers in Los Angeles, has agreed to help me work this out, but he keeps postponing me for the very reason that he is trying to save me money, I know. He wants to take care of it when he is not loaded up on one of the big jobs involving millions. I have the feeling that when he gets ready to get down to business, I ought to have you in on it on a business basis.

Now let's talk about some fun. What are the chances of getting you and Mildred out here within the next four weeks for as much time as you can spare. We have had a wonderful crew working this summer and we have our equipment in top-notch condition. Our enrollment is full. We feel on top of the world this year. A year ago I was at the bottom. Everything was wrong. It has taken a hard fight and continuous pulling, but I feel tremendously encouraged. I was wondering what we could do that would be fun and if you could get the time to come out.

Frank Barker
from letter to the Webb Board of Trustees, which was reprinted in the 1963 Webb School of California Alumni Bulletin, *p. 42*

He was the attorney whom I called in to incorporate this school (in association with Leon Scales), as I had been a fellow trustee with him at the old Webb School in Bell Buckle, Tennessee, and I knew that he understood the background of that school so intimately. . . . I could have had no friend closer than Frank, as we were boyhood friends. . . .

Frank Barker was an old family friend who grew up on a farm in Kentucky, was a classmate of TW's at Webb School in Bell Buckle, and then became a lawyer in Kansas City, Missouri. He figures in "Lamb's Tail Soup" in Chapter 2 of Vol. 2, and he advised my grandfather and his brother Will on legal matters over the years. —TW III

Frank Barker was somebody whom I knew in childhood. We had frequent contacts with the Barkers. In trips back from Princeton, Howell and I would let them know our arrival time, and then they would meet us at the train station in Kansas City for a short visit while the train was there. Howell once dated one of the Barker daughters for a dance at Princeton. Frank Barker, Jr., took me up for a demonstration flight in a torpedo bomber during the war (WWII) when we were both in the New Hebrides in the South Pacific. He went on to be a lawyer like his father and later was a judge. —TW, JR.

Thompson Webb, 1962

Farewell Tribute from Victor Heerman, JR. '42
from the Webb School of California Alumni Bulletin, *1974-76, Vol. 22, p.22*

He [Thompson Webb] taught us not to cheat or be sneaky; he asked that we do our best before we signed our names to a piece of work; he asked that we try to understand those who might differ from the majority, and he was a man who admired integrity and loyalty above all things. Who could place a value today on the worth of living with and being directed in formative years by such a man? Who among us who took his lessons to heart can help but be better men for that experience? He loved us, and he yearned for us, and he wanted for us, and I guess he lived for us. I always liked Mr. Webb, for he was kind and understanding. Later . . . I loved Mr. Webb for what he had told me I would see and feel and be in fear of. This gentle man was still giving me strengths 30 years after I graduated from his school. That, my friend, is an education.

Appendices

Chronology for Thompson Webb

1886	Webb family moved from Culleoka to Bell Buckle, Tennessee
October 24, 1887	Birth, named for Lucy Thompson
1887-1899	Childhood in Bell Buckle, Tennessee
1899 -1907	Attended Webb School in Bell Buckle, Tennessee
1907-1911	English major at the University of North Carolina
1907-1911	Ran Webb Summer School Camp, Walling, Tennessee
1911-1918	Coachella Valley, farming, real estate, worked with brother John Stanford Webb
June 22, 1915	Marriage to Vivian Louise Howell
1915-1918	Married life in Thermal and Los Angeles
March 16, 1917	First child, Thompson JR., born in Los Angeles
Spring, 1918	Crop failure and real estate prices plummet
July 10-Aug. 3, 1918	Worked at the shipyard in San Pedro, California
July 28, 1918	Second child, Howell, born in Los Angeles
August 29, 1918	Moved to Bell Buckle, Tennessee
1918-1922	Teacher/bookkeeper, Webb School in Bell Buckle
1919-1922	Ran Webb Summer School Camp at Walling, Tennessee
March 4, 1920	Third child (Vivian Nancy) born and dies
August 26, 1921	Third son, Bill, born in Long Beach, California
	Interview with Sherman Day Thacher in Berkeley, California
May/June, 1922	Negotiated for school property in Claremont
July, 1922	First visited Webb School in Claremont, California
September 19, 1922	First year of Webb School of California began
March, 1923	Visited by parents Sawney and Emma Webb
Summer, 1923	Camp Robin Hood at Lake Arrowhead, California
September, 1923	Second year of Webb School, discipline and teacher problems
November 4, 1923	Fourth son, Jack, born in Claremont, California
Spring, 1924	Commencement, Leo Chandler and Col. Sutphen offered help
1924-25	Building of Webb family home at Webb School
September, 1924	Third year of school, Parents Association
1924	Accreditation by University of California

May, 1925	Paid back $2,500 loan from his father with interest
December 19, 1926	Father, William Robert "Sawney" Webb died
1928	The Spirit of Webb glider plane and Lt. Deuel
1931	New gymnasium
November, 1936	Bill Webb found peccary skull at Barstow
1937	Thomas Jackson Library, news report of peccary find
1938-1945	Building the Vivian Webb Chapel
1939	Elected honorary member of Phi Beta Kappa, Pomona College
1941	Founding Member, California Association of Independent Secondary Schools
1947	Incorporation of Webb School begun
June 12, 1949	Honorary degree from University of the Pacific
1955	Incorporation of school completed
November 6, 1955	Dedicated the Vivian Webb Chapel and the Kimberly Tower
1959	Original "upper" dorm declared a fire hazard
1961	Dedicated the Price Dining Hall
June 10, 1962	Honorary degrees received from Occidental and Pomona Colleges
June, 1962	Retired as headmaster
June, 1965	Grandson Gordon Webb graduated from Webb
	50th wedding anniversary party
1968	Dedication of the Raymond Alf Museum
May 16, 1970	Rosanna Vivian Webb, first great-grandchild, born
October, 1971	Vivian Howell Webb died
1972	Great granddaughters, Sarah Mariam Webb and Scholle Zismann, born
January 13, 1975	Thompson Webb died

Family Tree

William Robert (Sawney) (1842-1926) and Emma Clary (1846-1937) Webb
    William Robert, JR. (Will) (1874-1960)
        m. Louise Manning (1872-1958)
    Alla (1875-1944)
    John Stanford (1877-1951)
        m. May Bowen (1874-1958)
            Emma (1907-1987)
            Sawney Ben '28 (1910-1971)
        m. Leno Ellen Cooper (1877-1963)
    Adeline (1879-1968)
        m. Josiah Sibley (1877-1963)
            Lois (1914-1988)
            Robert Peyton '35 (1917-1988)
            Josiah, JR. '37 (1919-1966)
    Daniel Clary (1881-1954)
        m. Maude Lindsey (1883-1914)
            Daniel Clary, JR. (1914-1931)
        m. Julia McCulley (1891-1976)
            William Robert III (Bob) (1919-)
            George McCulley (1920-)
            Margaret Johns (1923-)
    Susan (1882-1980)
        m. Edward Thomas Price (1883-1972)
            Edward Thomas, JR. '33 (1915-)
            Emily (1918-2002)
    Emma (1884-1973)
        m. McDugald Keener McLean (1886-1922)
            Susanne (1918-)

Thompson (1887-1975)

    m. Vivian Louise Howell (1894-1971)

        Thompson, JR. '35 (1917-1998)

            m. Diana Stimson (1919-)

                Thompson III (1944-)

                Gordon '65 (1946-)

        Robert Howell '35 (1918-1993)

            m. Betty Docker (1920-)

                Robert Howell, JR. (1952-)

                Betty Ann (Betian) (1954-)

        William Robert IV (Bill) '39 (1921-)

            m. Dorée Fleming (1926-1992)

                Robin Scholle (1946-)

                Nancy Manning (1950-)

                Sally Carruthers (1951-)

                Joanne Cummings (1954-)

        John Lambuth (Jack) '41 (1923-)

            m. Chieko Sakai (1929-)

                Vivian Mieko (1954-1998)

                Kenji John (1958-)

A

B

H-I-J-K

L-M-N-0

P-Q-R

S-T-U-V

W-Z

Author/Editors

Thompson Webb in 1930.

Thompson Webb was born in 1887 in Bell Buckle, Tennessee, as the eighth and final child of William Robert "Sawney" and Emma Clary Webb, where his father was running the Webb School in Bell Buckle. After graduating from the University of North Carolina in 1911, he joined his brother John in the Coachella Valley in California, where he farmed and bought and sold real estate. There he met Vivian Howell and they married in 1915. In 1918 he returned to Tennessee to teach for his father and his brother Will and to run the Webb Summer School Camp. In 1922 he founded the Webb School for Boys in Claremont, California, where he lived until his death in 1975. He served as headmaster from 1922 until his retirement in 1962.

Thompson, JR., Thompson III, and Thompson Webb in 1954.

Thompson Webb, JR., '35 was born in 1917 and was the oldest of Thompson and Vivian Webb's four sons. He graduated from Princeton with his brother Howell in 1939 and, after serving as an officer in the Navy during World War II, became director of the University of Wisconsin Press from 1947 to 1982. Helping to assemble this book was a final project before he died in 1998.

Thompson Webb III, the oldest son of Thompson (JR.) and Diana Stimson Webb, was born in 1944 and grew up in Madison, Wisconsin, before graduating from Swarthmore College in 1966 and getting his Ph.D. in meteorology at the University of Wisconsin in 1971. He is a professor of geology at Brown University, where he teaches a paleontology course that draws on the teachings of Ray Alf from the 1958 Summer Peccary trip.